YOUR FIRST YEAR IN REAL ESTATE

2ND EDITION

Also by Dirk Zeller

Success as a Real Estate Agent for Dummies
Telephone Sales for Dummies
The Champion Real Estate Agent
The Champion Real Estate Team
Successful Time Management for Dummies

For a complete listing of the author's other products
visit www.RealEstateChampions.com.

YOUR FIRST YEAR IN

REAL ESTATE

2ND EDITION

MAKING THE TRANSITION FROM TOTAL NOVICE TO SUCCESSFUL PROFESSIONAL

DIRK ZELLER

CURRENCY
NEW YORK

This book is designed to provide information about investing in and managing real estate. Many of the topics touched on may be controlled by local laws and regulations in your area. Neither the author nor the publisher is engaged in rendering legal, accounting, or other professional services by publishing this book. If any assistance is required, the services of qualified professionals should be sought. The author and publisher are not responsible for any liability, loss, or risk incurred as a result of the use and application of any of the information contained in this book.

Copyright © 2001, 2010 by Three Rivers Press, a division of Penguin Random House, LLC.

Published in the United States by Currency, an imprint of the Crown Publishing Group, a division of Penguin Random House LLC, New York.
crownpublishing.com

CURRENCY and its colophon are trademarks of Penguin Random House LLC.

Originally published in the United States by Prima Publishing, Roseville, California and by Three Rivers Press, an imprint of the Crown Publishing Group, a division of Penguin Random House LLC, New York, in 2001.

Currency books are available at special discounts for bulk purchases for sales promotions or corporate use. Special editions, including personalized covers, excerpts of existing books, or books with corporate logos, can be created in large quantities for special needs. For more information, contact Premium Sales at (212) 572-2232 or e-mail specialmarkets@penguinrandomhouse.com.

Library of Congress Cataloging-in-Publication Data

Zeller, Dirk.
Your first year in real estate : making the transition from total novice to successful professional / Dirk Zeller.—2nd ed.
  p. cm.
Includes index.
1. Real estate business—Vocational guidance. 2. Real estate business. I. Title.
HD1375.Z45 2010
333/33023'73—dc22   2010013696

ISBN 978-0-307-45372-3
Ebook 978-0-307-71765-8

Printed in the United States of America

20 19 18 17 16 15 14

Second Edition

To all our Real Estate Champion coaching clients,

who have implemented many of the techniques, skills, and tools

contained within this book and have transformed their businesses

and lives. I am grateful for the honor of having a front row seat

in your lives. There is no greater joy for me in life than to watch

the results you all are achieving.

CONTENTS

ACKNOWLEDGMENTS

There are so many people who have affected my life that it would be impossible to thank them all. Each of us receives the blessings that people pour into our lives. In my forty-seven years I have been blessed beyond measure.

Certainly, the most important of all is my wife, Joan, without whose constant encouragement and support my real estate career would not have reached the heights that it has. Without her this book you are reading also would not exist. Her advice and wise counsel throughout my real estate career and now, in my speaking, writing, and coaching career, has been truly heaven-sent. She has been instrumental in the building of Real Estate Champions.

To the team at Real Estate Champions. No one could ask for better people to work with. In building a company you need to surround yourself with the best. From the coaches to the administrative staff we have done that.

To Julie Porfirio, the rock at Real Estate Champions. Your endless hours compiling, typing, and creating produced this end result. Without your organizational skills we would not have the global impact for the real estate community that we do.

To my parents, Norm and Becky Zeller. What an honor to be your son. You both have taught me so much. Without your gifts of hard work, passion for learning, persistence, and commitment, I would not be fulfilling my true purpose in life. Thank you for going the extra mile as parents to instill them in me, when it would have been easier not to.

Finally, subsequent to the first edition of this book published in 2001, my life has taken a new turn with the adoption of our 8-year-old son, Wesley, and 4-year-old daughter, Annabelle. You both are such blessings in my life.

INTRODUCTION

The real estate field is one of the most exciting career choices you can consider. Millions of people have considered entering the real estate field, comparing themselves and their abilities to real estate agents they know. Family members and friends tell them, "You should sell real estate!" They often view what Realtors do as easy money. You may be thinking the same thing most people do about Realtors. My first response to those thoughts is that what you perceive from the outside looking in may not be the whole truth about the profession. What many people deem to be easy can often be truly difficult when viewed up close.

According to the National Association of Realtors, the median income for all Realtors is $36,700. The median income for brokers or broker associates is $49,300. This clearly shows that the more educated you are in real estate skills and techniques, the more income that you make. Your goal should be to educate yourself regularly so you can increase your income. The National Association of Realtors is the largest professional association in the field, representing nearly 1.2 million members involved in all aspects of the real estate industry. They are regularly evaluating the profile of their members in demographic, economic, and professional characteristics. As a new agent, you must be prepared to work hard and diligently to achieve success.

My desire is not to paint a bleak picture, just an accurate one. The truth is that with the right steps, desire, and determination, you can earn two, three, or even four times the median income in your first year. I have one absolute belief. That belief is, *If I can do it, so can you.* My journey into real estate started in 1989 when I moved back to Portland, Oregon. I had closed my event promotion business in Denver and was searching for my next career.

I was truly at a crossroads in my professional life. I was twenty-seven years old and had little to show for the six years I had worked after college. The selection of my career was of paramount importance this time.

My desire for a career that enabled me to control the income, the time invested, and, ultimately, the outcome was enormous. I truly wanted the fruits of my labors to be immense. I wanted the reward for my hard work to come to me, not someone else. Maybe you are feeling that way right now.

I was frustrated and discouraged that my last six years of work had not produced more wealth. This was not how I had imagined myself at twenty-seven years old. People often enter real estate sales from similar circumstances. They try many other job options and careers and finally find their way into real estate sales. They blossom in the flexibility of hours. They embrace the opportunity to earn any amount of money they desire. They want to build a business that allows them to continually increase their income by 20 percent, 30 percent, or even 50 percent annually. Those were all the things I wanted as well.

There is nothing more exciting than starting a new venture. For me, the new venture of real estate sales started in December of 1989. I recall that I struggled starting out as most agents do. You, like me, will have that lost feeling many times early in your career, the "Why am I doing this? Is it really worth it?" feeling. Those feelings can be compounded when the income doesn't come as fast as the bills and when there is a lot of month at the end of the money.

One of the challenges in real estate is learning to budget your money. Especially early in one's career there can be a long span of time between commission checks. You have to avoid the temptation to spend it all. To hold some of the money back in savings is a skill that needs to be learned.

For many people it will also be the first time they are responsible for their own taxes. For years we work as an employee and now we are entering the independent contractor world in real estate. We must learn to save a portion of each commission check to pay the taxes on the earnings. I, like most agents, learned that lesson the hard way. My first year in the business I didn't save the money for my taxes. When tax time came around I needed to sell a few houses just to pay the tax bill. Fortunately I had to be taught that lesson only once. There are many agents who replay that song year after year after year.

One of the principles that I have learned in the last twenty-one years since that start in December of 1989 is this: Success comes to those who are willing to persist a little longer. When you have those feelings of frustration and discouragement in your career, you will have to choose to control them or they will eventually control you.

In the end we all have those feelings. It's what actions we take that matter most when we have those feelings. I had them all the time early in my career. I used them to fuel the fire of personal development. If I had not gotten hooked on the books and audiobooks that changed my life, I would not have had the career in real estate sales that I did. You obviously have the same desire that I had early in my career or you would not be reading this book. The quest for personal expansion of knowledge and skill lasts a lifetime. We should never stop learning.

I have a story I like to tell at speaking engagements: It's commencement day at a large university. Two students who are set to graduate later that day are walking through the commons rather excited about the day's activities. One student says to the other, "I am so excited to graduate today. I am so tired of studying and reading that I won't read another book for as long as I live." They both agree and laugh and keep walking. What they don't know is the president of the university is walking behind them and he hears this exchange between the graduating seniors. The university president is disappointed that these two graduates don't understand the value of an education while at his institution. The university and faculty didn't fire up their furnaces of learning while they were there.

In the end these students didn't even understand the word *commencement*. They were going through a commencement exercise later in the day without the true knowledge of what it was about. The word "commencement" means "the beginning." They were at the beginning of their educational lives, not the end. They were at the point when the studying and the books they read from that point forward would have the biggest impact on how their lives turned out. Yet they missed one of the key elements of the university experience, which is to acquire the desire to be a lifelong learner.

My friend Jim Rohn describes it best: "Your formal education will make you a living, your personal education will make you a fortune." Jim is a brilliant man and absolutely right. Once I learned and applied this quote of Jim's, my life was transformed.

At the time I entered real estate sales in late 1989, I didn't need all five fingers of one hand to count the number of books I had read in the six years since I had left Willamette University without graduating. Nor did I need those five fingers to count the number of seminars that I had attended. And sadly, I could also count on one hand what I had in my savings account and checking account. I was to find out later there was a direct correlation between all those numbers.

Since that point I cannot count the number of books that I have read or the number of seminars that I have attended. I don't know how many tape series I own or how many times I have listened to each one. My income and savings have dramatically increased as well. I do not say this to brag but to encourage. I truly believe if I can achieve what I have achieved, you can also. God gave us all tremendous gifts; our job is learning to apply and utilize them to expand our influence and wealth for our families, our communities, and the world.

CHAPTER 1

SELECTING THE RIGHT COMPANY

Welcome to your new career in real estate! You have chosen what is for many people a very challenging and rewarding labor of love: selling real estate. The fact that you are here, reading this book, is a good sign: You are already looking for an edge, advantages, and knowledge that will help push you to the top of your profession. So let's begin.

FIRST THINGS FIRST

It's very easy to get swept away in the emotion and excitement of your new career, to have dollar signs in your eyes without thoroughly researching the facts. Although it is important to dive into your career headfirst, it is also essential to make sure both of your eyes are wide open. You need to research, learn, and prepare for your new profession because, ultimately, the company that you select to first "hang your license" with can make or break your career. As such, you must begin your new career *before* you get your license.

Licensing Training Programs

Many real estate companies offer licensing training programs. These programs will help you prepare for and pass your state and national licensing exams. Some of these firms teach you through classroom programs aimed at meeting the minimum requirements in your state, and often these classroom programs are augmented with tapes, workbooks, and other materials that you can study outside of the classroom.

In addition, many firms offer their own pre-licensing programs at no cost to you; others will charge you a few dollars to attend. There are some that will pay for these programs and even the cost of the state and national exams. These firms usually will deduct these fees from your first commission check. If you are comfortable with a couple of offices, you might consider the one that is willing to invest in your career financially. Seeking out the best firm for you and talking with them will also help you begin networking within the real estate industry.

SELECTING THE RIGHT COMPANY FOR YOU

Choosing a job for yourself is easy, right? Find a company that is hiring, offer your services, agree on money, and it's all done. If it were only that easy.

Truth is, there are scores of questions you need to ask both the firm and yourself. You must discover what the company can do for you, as well as how you will benefit the company. The situation should be mutually beneficial to you and your office. So what should you look for when searching for the best company for you?

WHAT EVERY GOOD REAL ESTATE COMPANY HAS

When you sign on with a company, you become an extension of that organization. Before you ever meet a client, he will already have an opinion of your company, and that opinion will influence what your client thinks of you. Learning how to identify a company with a solid history and positive standing in the community is essential to cultivating business and developing your career. A good real estate company, one that will provide you with the resources to succeed, will have several qualities.

A Solid Reputation Is Essential

The reputation of the company is critical. Remember, you are an extension of the company you work for. Until you are able to build a clientele and a following of your own, you will be relying solely on the company's reputation. A buyer or seller will have a positive or negative impression of your company based on its reputation before you ever work with her. That reputation will be based on the success of the company, such as the market share it has achieved and the number of homes it lists and sells annually. The company's involvement with the community is also important.

> *Until you are able to build a clientele and a following of your own, you will be relying solely on the company's reputation.*

A Passion About Customer Service Is a Must

A company's customer service model and service reputation are also important factors. Real estate sales is a service-oriented business where one is paid for results. To be successful, real estate agents must be customer-focused while carefully monitoring time and revenue invested to complete the job. First, you must be committed to providing outstanding customer service. Second, the company you select to work with must share your passion for customer service and must be committed to helping you achieve the level of customer service required to be successful. How you treat your clients, past and present, has a direct bearing on getting listing contracts from a seller and getting that home sold and closed, which is every agent's desired result. Similarly, your ability to secure your representation of the buyer, find him a home, and close the deal is dependent on your level of customer service.

The company you select to work with must share your passion for customer service and must be committed to helping you achieve the level of customer service required to be successful.

There Is No Second Place

As a real estate agent, you are assuming a big risk by putting in a lot of time, effort, and even money in hopes of achieving a sale. There will be times when you work extremely hard for your client but the home never sells or your client never makes a purchase. Real estate agents get compensated for only the final result. Unlike horse racing, where they pay for Win, Place, and Show—first, second, and third—in real estate you get paid only when the house sells or closes. There is no second place, so you and the company you choose must be results-oriented. And good results are a product of good customer service.

Strong Listing Companies Help a New Agent

Make sure any companies you are considering are strong listing companies. Working for a strong listing company ensures you will have an opportunity to work with a lot of buyers. Most new agents work with more buyers than sellers. Buyers are easier to attract and create relationships with. They are not entrusting their largest asset, their home, to a new agent.

A listing is a contract with a seller to exclusively represent her in selling a home. If an agent acquires a listing, prices the home appropriately, and sells the house, then the agent will get paid. A strong listing office can dramatically help an agent early in her career. When agents and offices have an abundance of listings, they also receive a high volume of ad calls and sign calls. The ad and sign calls lead to buyers and often sellers.

There is an old saying in real estate: "You list, you last." The most successful and productive agents are the agents who focus on listing property, for a regular diet of new listings is the engine that drives the train. To be truly financially successful in real estate sales without having to work all hours of the day and night and on weekends, becoming a strong listing agent is imperative. Aligning with a company that has a large inventory of homes for sale will dramatically help you create success early in your career.

> *The most successful and productive agents are the agents who focus on listing property, for a regular diet of new listings is the engine that drives the train.*

RESEARCHING A COMPANY

Once you have determined that a company has a solid reputation, has an effective customer service model, and is a strong listing company, you must research the company and find out the answers to some important questions. The right answers will help you know whether a company is right for you, while the wrong answers will help steer you away to search for a better match.

Seek Out Market Share Information

First, you should inquire about market statistics. Find out the company's market share, how many listings it takes in a year, how many listings sell, how many fail to sell, and how many sales it actually makes. These are numbers, statistics, and statistics don't lie. This information will give you the bottom line about a company and will reflect on its customer service, position in the market, and the potential for success on your part.

Check with the Local Board of Realtors

You will want to research the company at your local Board of Realtors. The local board may have market share and other statistics for the company you are interviewing. It is critically important that you check with a third-party resource and verify the statistics that a company provides. Authenticate the figures and make sure the numbers all add up.

Who's Number One?

There are many companies in real estate who have claimed in recent years to be number one. Some claim to be the biggest real estate companies, in terms of sales, in the world. They have national advertising campaigns staking claim to being number one. Others claim to be number one in service. No wonder the consumer is confused as to whom to believe and do business with! If the industry can't decide who's number one, how can anyone else? Most likely there are statistics and documentation to back each company's claims—it all depends on how you count the numbers. But the bottom line is: Be sure to validate the information you receive from the companies you interview.

The Multiple Listing Service

Another source for market share and statistics is the multiple listing service. In most marketplaces around the country, real estate companies and agents use a multiple listing service to increase exposure. This allows all agents in the Board of Realtors to access every house and property for sale and allows them to sell it. This service is often a separate entity from the Board of Realtors, and it is an invaluable source of information regarding listings and sales of homes. They will help you interpret the truth on the sales in your local area and who controls the market.

Lots of Agents, Little Production

One word of caution with regard to market share: The number of agents a company has can dramatically affect market share. Many companies have a lot of agents, but each individual agent does little in production. That type of company will not have the personnel who can help you improve your skills much beyond the beginner stage. Make sure you select a company that also allows you to grow and thrive.

Local Business Journals

Lastly, if you live in a major metropolitan area, you may find that the local business journal provides valuable information. Look for special editions that deal with real estate in the marketplace. The journal will often rank brokers in size and scope of services. This is another wonderful resource to ensure that you are obtaining the whole truth and starting your career with the right company.

Take a Drive

Another useful research activity is to drive around the community you want to work in and check out the signs. Whose signs are in front of the houses you would want to represent? How many signs are there?

Take the time to drive to the actual office you are considering. Is it in a location that would be effective for business? For some offices it is difficult to see that they are even there. Look at the office from the buyer's or seller's viewpoint. Would you stop there to inquire about their services? When you walk in the door, does the office have the look and feel of a successful business, or does it look and feel chaotic? Some of your future clients will make their decisions on just such an impression.

For a new agent these questions are critical; when you gain experience and skill, the location and amenities are not as important. At that point you will have clients and the skill to create clients and you can generate new business from any location. For now, the look and feel of your office is what your client's impression will be based on.

Got Advertising?

Be sure to research a company's advertising philosophy. For a new agent, the company's frequency and volume of advertising can help you, as a new agent, generate new clients. There are many companies that do very little advertising and rely on the agents themselves to advertise their properties. These companies have a much higher percentage of experienced agents than new agents. Compare advertising over a two-week period. This will give you a good comparison because some companies do bigger ads less frequently, while others engage in lower-profile advertising more frequently.

Display Ads

Note whether the company does display ads or just classifieds. Display ads usually have the company's banner or heading and they gather in one place all the homes the company is advertising. Classifieds are smaller ads arranged by location of the homes. The display ads will give a more impressive appearance to the consumer than spread-out classified ads. A display ad is more elaborate, since a company will often feature an agent or all their agents. Take the time to look at their ads and see how they promote the agents and the company. Is that the image you want to project? Can you see yourself in the ad with the other agents?

Real Estate Book Publications

Another advertising area to review is the real estate book publications you see at the local grocery store. These publications are very effective in marketing and advertising property. They provide a longer shelf life than local newspaper advertisements and offer pictures of the properties. In most markets there are a couple of different magazines to choose from, of varying quality. In these publications, does your prospective company present the type of image you desire? Are they even present in these advertising mediums? Many companies you will be interviewing may produce their own publication of this nature.

Evaluate the quality, size, and scope of the advertising in these publications. Are there company-sponsored pages with numerous agents on a page, or are there pages for individual agents? When an agent is the only agent on the page, generally the agent has paid for it. You want to make sure that the companies you are considering have space for new agents like yourself to use.

The Company Internet Site

With more and more buyers moving from searching print publications to searching the Internet, the company's Web presence is important as well. According to the National Association of Realtors, over 85 percent of consumers start their search for properties on the Internet. They go there before they venture to newsprint or real estate magazines.

The company you select must have a robust Web site that is highly ranked in key search terms. If you type into Google, for example, the area where you live and add the words "real estate" behind it, the sites that come up in the higher ranks in Web searches are the Web sites that will get the most traffic.

You also want to evaluate whether the company Web site has a method to harvest the leads. Are they offering free reports, Internet data exchange (IDX) listings, or some other strategies to get visitors to leave their names and contact information so a lead can be generated? This is all part of the new lead generation strategy in real estate today.

You Will Be Courted

Most of your research and investigation should be done *before* you ever sit down for an interview with a broker or manager of a company. One of the objectives of brokers is to recruit new agents. Every day they are out "selling" new agents on their company. Most are prepared and have a solid presentation to convince you their company is the best. And if they are truly wise, they will elicit the help of some of their agents to recruit you. Now, who wouldn't get excited about a company that has a great presentation and parades a couple of agents who make, say, $100,000 a year?

Remember, it's very easy to get wrapped up in excitement, emotion, and enthusiasm. A great salesperson will be able to create those emotions in the buyer. As you seek a company, you are in the buyer role. You are going to be buying a company—its training and its reputation. Make sure you are purchasing the right vehicle for your career. The broker or manager's job is to create that excitement, emotion, and enthusiasm while showing you the company has the systems and tools for your success. Always remember: Enthusiasm is to selling what yeast is to bread—it makes the dough rise.

THE INTERVIEW: HOW TO WIN THE COMPANY OVER

After you have done your research on the community; checked out the multiple listing service, the Board of Realtors, and the company's advertising; driven around the neighborhoods; and visited the office, you are ready for the interview! An interview is a chance for you to continue your research into the company, an opportunity for the company to learn how you can benefit it, and the ultimate setting for you to sell your qualities as a potential real estate professional.

What You Need Going into the Interview

The more prepared you are and the better you feel about your appearance and preparation, the smoother the interview will go. Guaranteed. Remember, an interview is an opportunity. Take full advantage of it. Be prepared with a résumé, a sharp appearance, and questions and answers.

Prepare a Killer Résumé

For the interview you must have a résumé. The résumé should be short and to the point; one page is best. The broker or manager is going to weigh your attitude, desire, and appearance much heavier than your experience—she can always teach someone with the right qualities to be a good salesperson. If you are struggling with your résumé, your local public library and bookstores have many books that can help you with that challenge.

Look Good, Feel Good

You have only one opportunity to make a first impression. For an interview, professional attire is a must. Real estate agents pride themselves on being some of the best-dressed professionals in the world. If you go to a real estate seminar or convention, you will think all the attendees make a million dollars a year because they dress like it. Make sure to look the part of a successful person. You want the broker or manager to be able to envision you as a successful real estate agent for his company.

Whether you are a man or a woman, proper dress is a suit. A conservative suit in navy or black is ideal. There have been numerous studies about the power and authority that are conveyed by a well-dressed man or woman in a navy suit and a white shirt. For years, IBM had a saying that you could wear any color suit and shirt you wanted as long as the suit was blue and the shirt was white. They believed in creating a powerful presence. Your appearance *will* play a part in the outcome of your interview. That may not seem fair, but it is reality. Dress for success!

> *Make sure to look the part of a successful person. You want the broker or manager to be able to envision you as a successful real estate agent for his company.*

So You Want to Be a Real Estate Agent

People want to become real estate agents for many reasons, some good, some bad. I will share my reasons with you: I wanted to make a mid–six figure income and achieve financial independence at an early age. I wanted my income to be tied directly to my effort. I did not want a cap on my earning potential. I was clearly motivated by money. What motivates you? Is it money, serving others, helping people, flexible work hours, controlling your destiny? These are all valid reasons for becoming a real estate agent. It's imperative that you know your reasons before you enter the door for the interview!

Prepare Answers to the Broker's Questions

Before your first interview, prepare to answer a number of questions about why you want to become a real estate agent. Many people go into real estate as a last resort or because they lost their job or think they can make a lot of money easily. The broker wants to find out what your reasons are.

There is no one right reason for wanting to become a real estate agent. The key is to figure out why *you* want to be one and prepare to explain to your interviewer why this is a good reason and how it will benefit the company. If your explanation is solid and clearly the result of a positive and aggressive attitude, you have just taken a major step toward getting the job you desire.

In addition, you must prepare for other questions the interviewer may throw your way, including

- Have you ever been in sales? (Even selling Girl Scout cookies is sales.)
- How do you expect to generate business?
- Are you focused on helping people? Why?
- Are you interested in investing in real estate?
- Are you prepared to work hard?
- Do you work better with a team or as an individual out on your own?

These are all questions a good broker will ask if she is looking for your commitment and desire to succeed.

There is one other question you may hear. It's one I use even today on every interview I conduct: "Why should I hire you?" This one question will often turn the strongest people into Jell-O. It is the key question in the sales process, no matter what you are selling. Every prospect or client will be thinking that question as you do your presentation. If your broker asks you this, your answer will reveal whether you have the confidence to be successful. If you have the ability to articulate your skills to others easily and effectively, you will achieve success.

Prepare Your Questions for the Broker

You must also be prepared with your own questions for the broker or manager. You are trying to determine the value of the services the company will provide you in the long run and the level of support and training it will provide for you as a new agent. Here are some of the questions you will want to ask:

What Is Your Training Program for New Agents?
This area is key when comparing companies. Many do not provide the training necessary to set up a new agent for success. Some companies still use the

old-school method: "Here's your desk and here's your phone, go get 'em!" This type of focus will not prepare you for the challenge you are about to face.

However, many companies do provide sales training throughout your career. As a new agent you want as much training as possible, as soon as possible. Make sure to pin down the broker or manager on how often and how soon the training classes take place and where they are held, as well as any costs that are associated with the training.

Often companies will train new agents in contracts and law, but spend very little time in sales skills and time management. In essence, you are going to open your own new business, and the number one reason for failure in new businesses is lack of sales. Whether you are in real estate a year from now or not will depend on your volume of sales, or the lack thereof. The more training you have in sales skills, scripts, dialogues, prospecting, and lead follow-up techniques, the more success you will have. Make sure your new broker has solid training available in the key disciplines of sales.

As a new agent you want as much training as possible, as soon as possible.

How Many New Agents Do You Train Annually?

This will tell you the level of experience the company has with new agents. Be leery of the company that gives you the "no one else but you, so we can give you our full attention" bit. You don't want to be surrounded by "top gun" agents who offer little in assistance. I believe that going through training with others is a positive experience. You will have some comrades and role-play partners to learn from and grow with through the learning curve. Ask about their success rate. How many agents are still there one year later? If they have a high wash-out rate, be careful.

Ask to speak to some newer agents who have gone through the training program. Talk with an agent who has sold real estate for a year. Spend a few minutes with someone who is only six months into the business. You need to get a clear picture of how prepared for battle you will be after you leave the training program.

What Does It Cost Me to Hang My License with You?

Are there any annual or monthly fees that I pay as the agent? Often real estate board fees are charged or multiple listing service fees are assessed monthly. Multiple listing service fees can also be assessed by the properties you place with the service. These are called input fees. Who pays those fees?

In addition, all real estate companies have errors and omission insurance, often referred to as E&O insurance. This insurance protects the agent and company if an error is made in representation or service that causes harm to the buyer or seller. I have seen E&O insurance charged on an annual basis, monthly basis, or even per transaction basis.

Also find out who pays for business cards, real estate signs, letterhead, thank-you cards, postage, lockboxes, and advertisements. These are just some of the costs you will incur to begin your real estate sales career.

Find out who pays for business cards, real estate signs, letterhead, thank-you cards, postage, lockboxes, and advertisements.

How Will You Help Me Generate Business?

Some companies will give you houses to hold open and even run an advertisement for you. Ask if they have floor time. Floor time is the rotation of agents to answer phone calls that come from advertisements and signs. How often will you get floor time? What do you need to do before you are eligible for floor time? These are all key questions. As a new agent, you will be better served by going with a company that gives you floor time. It will give you an opportunity to convert prospects into clients.

Do You Have Regular Office Meetings?

Your goal is to be around agents who are doing well and to learn from them when you can. Find out how often meetings occur and what they entail. Does the company provide training in the office meeting or is it just a general office meeting? You will learn from any such office meetings, but obviously the more geared they are toward teaching and sharing information, the more you will learn.

Do You Have a Formal Company Orientation Process?

This will tell you how organized the company is. Orientation will help you understand who does what in the firm, what procedures you need to follow, and where everything you need is located.

> ## How available are others for questions? You will have a tremendous number of questions early on in your career.

When I Have a Problem or Question Whom Do I Go To?

How available are others for questions? You will have a tremendous number of questions early on in your career. You will need someone who is available to help you make the right choices quickly. Make sure there will often be someone available to help and answer any key questions you may have in a timely fashion.

Where Is the New Agent's Workspace?

There can be vast differences among companies in regard to the workspace they give different agents. Most companies put new agents and lower-producing agents in the "bullpen." The bullpen is a group of cubicles usually at the center of the office. There is less privacy and more interruptions in this work environment. Rarely will a new agent get the private office we all covet. Carefully assess the bullpen area or the area where you may be assigned to sit. Can you work in that environment?

What Computer Software and Hardware Do You Provide for Agents to Use?

One of the mainstays of all agents' business is their database. It's where they keep everyone they know and have done business with and all of their leads for future business. Since this database is so critical to success, many companies provide a computer and database software for their new agents. For you to build a solid long-term business you must be able to use a computer database well. Money does not grow on trees—it grows in databases.

Will You Put an Announcement in the Paper and Pay for Announcement Cards If I Join Your Firm?

It's imperative that you notify everyone you can think of about your new career. Often the company will assist you in this process. You might even ask how soon they usually do that!

What's the Commission Split?

This is the final and biggest question. A commission split is how much you receive of the commission on a sale and how much the company keeps. For a new agent a typical commission split will be around 50 percent for the agent and 50 percent for the broker. Now, that may seem like a lot for the company, but remember that it is doing all the training and providing ongoing support and assistance. It is also, in most cases, providing a desk, a phone, and advertising leads through floor time. The company is making a substantial investment in you. It needs to turn a profit or there will be no company for you to work at!

Make sure to ask if there are any other fees associated with commission. There could be a franchise fee in the range of 5 to 6 percent before the commission split is calculated. You could be paying a transaction fee of $150 to $500 to the company for help with your paperwork. Make sure you get an accurate disclosure of all the costs so you can make the best decision.

The Art of Asking Questions

The last thing to remember is that whoever asks the questions controls the interview or sales presentation. The art of asking questions is the key to success in sales. Many people believe that great salespeople are fast-talking or exceptionally skilled at keeping dialogue going. True master salespersons ask questions to achieve the desired result. They are wonderful at probing for needs, values, and problems and attaching their solution to those needs, values, and problems.

During the interview, you may be fortunate enough to be sitting across from a broker or manager who is a great salesperson. A skilled broker or manager is going to ask you questions to determine if you are the right match for his company. Your job is to turn the tables and ask questions to learn about his company so you can be better informed to make your decision.

This is your first sale and maybe the most important one in your career. Make sure to invest the time in preparation and in evaluating companies before the interview. Practice and plan your questions well and conduct yourself in the interview as a sales professional by dressing the part and controlling the dialogue with thoughtful and relevant questions.

If you have interviews with multiple companies, and we hope you will, ideally they will occur within the span of a couple of days. This way you can keep your questions and impressions fresh in your mind and evaluate the different companies while you still remember them well.

DECISION TIME

After completing the interview process and talking with a few rookie agents in each firm, you are ready to complete your evaluation and make a decision. Always set yourself up to be the one who decides where you are going to work. There are several things you can do to come up with a conclusive decision about a company.

Rank Each Area of Importance

On a scale of 1 to 10, rate the service each company provides new agents in these key areas:

- training
- office environment

- other agents
- broker/manager
- advertising
- reputation
- market share

Weight Your Decision in Favor of Training

Each of these is a key category, with a bit of extra weight on the training area. For a new agent, training can often make the difference between success and failure. I would even go so far as to recommend selecting a company that might have deficiencies in other categories, but is head and shoulders above the others in training. A good training program for new agents involves more than just contracts—it must be focused on prospecting, quality, lead follow-up, the sellers' listing presentation, the buyers' interview, objection handling, and closing techniques. These are the skills of an outstanding salesperson.

Consider Ongoing Training

Be careful to evaluate not only the training a new agent receives, but also the ongoing training the company provides. Are there opportunities for classes, workshops, or even coaching that allow you to continually improve your skills? What form does this training take? Is it in seminars only? Does the company offer workshops where you'll have time to practice and rehearse what you are learning? Is there a role-playing time for new agents and maybe even role-play partners that we work with regularly?

Does the company offer coaching? Very few companies do. Coaching from an experienced professional who has walked the ground you want to travel is invaluable. To have a coach who will hold you accountable for performing the activities that will lead you to success can dramatically shorten and flatten the learning curve. A true coaching program will give you personal attention instead of only a group experience of seminars and workshops. It should be structured and regular in nature, either weekly or twice monthly. It should focus on helping you acquire the sales skills needed to succeed. Your coach should have been a successful agent and have used what she is teaching you. A number of times I have watched agents with passion, desire, commitment, and the right coach to guide them become top agents in the company. Find out more about coaching in chapter 6.

Training and Money

In sales the money you earn is poor if you are simply an average-skilled salesperson. The money you earn improves to average when you are a good salesperson. The income you earn is good when you are a great salesperson. Finally, the money you earn is amazing when you are an outstanding salesperson. The biggest increase in pay is between a great salesperson and an outstanding salesperson. It can mean the difference between earning $100,000 to $200,000 a year for a great salesperson and $500,000 to $1,000,000 a year for an outstanding salesperson. Having coached a lot of agents in the outstanding category, I can tell you that there is a dramatic difference between those outstanding salespeople and the national average income the National Association of Realtors reports for real estate agents, which is $36,700 per year. That's why I say evaluate the training more heavily than the other categories. Your training will determine how high you can go and the income you can achieve in real estate sales.

It's Your Decision

There are many choices in life you have to make. Selecting the right company to start your career ranks only behind whom you marry. If you apply these steps and ask questions, you will select the right company for you and be on your way to a great career in real estate.

CHAPTER 2

GETTING OFF TO THE RIGHT START

You have found the right company and your excitement level is at an all-time high. You are entering a new phase in your life: the phase of self-management, self-discovery, and self-motivation to achieve your goals and dreams. Unlike in most other careers, what happens in your real estate career depends totally on you. You are the one who controls the outcome and your destiny. That first day you feel like Leonardo DiCaprio on the bow of the *Titanic* with the wind in your face, screaming, "I am the king of the world!" You are master of all you can see; however, just as in the movie *Titanic,* there are icebergs out there that can end this wonderful new voyage you are on.

This chapter is focused on getting your new adventure off to that start you desire, from your first day, your first week, your first month on the job. What has happened before you get to this point is not as important as what is going to happen from now on. The first step is to forget your past failures. You are staring at a blank slate—you and only you will decide what you are going to write on the slate. Robert Schuller, the famous minister, said, "If it's to be, it's up to me." That is your new mantra. You have ability and talent, and when you mix them with passion and white-hot desire, miraculous things will happen in your career. You are the determining factor of success.

GET READY FOR A NEW KIND OF EXAM

The first few days of your career will probably be spent in classroom training. When I entered real estate, I had been out of school for many years. I was certainly out of practice in taking notes and organizing thoughts on a lecture for use at a later date. As a new agent, your first few days, and even your first month, are going to be full of cramming for an exam. This exam is different from the one you took to get your license; it's open book and out in the field. It's not necessarily on paper, but it is about action and results. Your ability to learn and practice the material can make or break your first year in the business. The more time you invest outside of the classroom setting, the quicker your first commission check will come.

Seek Help from the Office Staff

Your first day is going to be filled with just learning where everything is in the office: where all the forms are kept, where the supplies are stored. One great resource to connect with is the administrative staff. Seek to create an alliance with the support staff at the office. Set yourself apart from the other agents by treating the staff with true respect. If the administrative staff has experience, they can be a wonderful resource. They are, after all, the eyes and ears of the real estate company. They can help you avoid embarrassing situations and they know the procedures that need to be followed. Many will even pitch in to help when you really need it, even if it's not part of their job. Don't neglect to recognize their value. Reaching out for help is just one step in making your new job a positive experience and successful from day one.

Be There to Pick Up the Keys

Most companies, IBM for example, require your presence at work at a specific time. In your company, You, Inc., time is far more valuable to your success than it would be if you worked for IBM. The job you have at You, Inc., carries with it the keys to financial independence. Make sure you show up to pick up the keys. Those keys to financial independence are given out early, before most agents arrive in the office. Make sure you are there. Most of the other agents thought I was crazy to go to work so early and even made fun of my work schedule, hours, and commitment. They were not laughing anymore when, in my third year, I sold more than 80 properties and became the number one agent in the office. Decide on a time that you will start your workday and don't deviate. A large part of success is showing up regularly.

Start Early

Your first day is when you must begin to set the tone for your career. If there's one secret that all top real estate agents have, it's that they consider their career a real job, with real, regular hours. Because you have control of your time and keep your own schedule, it is very easy to be undisciplined. There were very few mornings in my whole sales career when I was not in the office by seven. I started this habit from day one of my career and it is still with me today.

Believe in Yourself

The best of the best in life believe in themselves. Michael Jordan believed to his core that he was the best. His belief and sheer will to win created his enormous success. I read recently about a survey in which professional golfers were asked, "If you had one putt to win a major championship, whom would you pick to putt it?" Almost all of them chose Jack Nicklaus. Why? Because he was the best at the time and had the ability to *will* the ball into the hole.

You must believe you are the best agent for the job. When your confidence goes up, your competence goes up at the same time. Program your mind through affirmations that you are the best. Each day remind yourself, "I am a great salesperson; I am the best agent someone can hire to do the job; I provide exceptional service to my clients." You must drive your belief deep within yourself. It truly is the secret weapon for all peak performers. Work to improve your belief in yourself. We all came from the same Creator, who didn't create any junk. You have it inside you to be exceptional. The secret edge is belief. As Dr. Norman Vincent Peale states:

Believe in yourself! Have faith in your abilities. Without a humble but reasonable confidence in your own powers, you cannot be successful or happy. . . . Formulate and stamp indelibly on your mind a mental picture of yourself succeeding. Hold the picture tenaciously; never permit it to fade. Your mind will seek to develop the picture.

You must drive your belief deep within yourself. It truly is the secret weapon for all peak performers.

UNDERSTAND THE GAME YOU ARE PLAYING

Peak performers understand the game they are playing and how to score and win. The game of real estate is about skills, knowledge, and time—these are the three things you are really selling. The better you are at controlling them, the more revenue you can generate and the more time you will have for the other areas of your life.

Perseverance + Belief + Desire = Success

When you add belief to the desire that you already possess and sprinkle in perseverance, the results are magical. A friend of mine, Froy Candelairo, who sells homes in the Los Angeles area, is a perfect example that all who persevere and have a desire can have success in real estate. Froy came to the United States many years ago by hanging on to the underside of a train. He and a friend were trying to get to the United States, the land of opportunity, from Mexico. They rode for hours, clinging to the train for their lives. They had no idea where they were and they could not let go for fear of being run over by the train. The miles clicked by and they were getting extremely tired. Finally, Froy's friend could not hang on any longer. He let go and was crushed. Froy was devastated by the loss of his friend, but vowed to hang on. Less than five minutes later the train stopped. Froy had reached his goal. He had made it to the United States.

Let me finish Froy's story. Froy decided to sell real estate. He had to learn English, pass the real estate licensing requirements, and then find a broker. Froy's passion and desire to succeed were unparalleled. He worked diligently to learn and improve his skills. Today, Froy is one of the most successful agents in the country, selling more than four hundred properties a year. The lesson that Froy learned from his immigration experience is that one component of success is being able to hang on a little bit longer than the next guy. Now, if Froy, with all his limitations, could accomplish what he has, you certainly can create a business that will generate the income that you desire.

One of the big challenges for new agents is not turning into seven-day-a-week wonders, where you are on call for clients twenty-four hours a day, seven days a week. It is an agent's ability to control her time, while increasing skills and knowledge, that will prevent her falling into that trap. You must clearly understand the stark reality of the real estate business: Your compensation is a direct result of your performance. You will get paid at the transfer of the property, and anything less is not a commission check.

You must clearly understand the stark reality of the real estate business: Your compensation is a direct result of your performance.

ACQUIRE A WINNING MIND-SET

One of the key characteristics of successful people is a winning mind-set. They have learned to program their minds for success. That's what gives them the edge in competitive situations. This mind-set allows them to hit the winning shot at the buzzer, sink the crucial putt on the last hole to win a tournament, or get the listing signed even when they are up against the best agents in town. The question is, why do some people have it and others don't? How can you ensure that you acquire the winning mind-set? Let me take you through the development of a winning mind-set.

Record and Replay the Tape

Now, you don't have to go so far as to record yourself on tape, but you *do* need to write down and track your victories. We all have a lot of victories daily, weekly, and monthly—we just have a hard time remembering them. If you record them, they can be reviewed during the challenges or rough times. When you lose self-confidence, you can build it back up by reviewing your past triumphs. A lot of our victories come out of very challenging problems or struggles. By taking a look back at your accomplishments and achievements, you will see the direct correlation between the challenges faced and resulting triumphs. The key is to review them regularly. If you do so, they will pay dividends today and tomorrow.

Focus and Stay Positive

Having a successful career in real estate means being able to stay positive and focused on your goals even when all things, people, and conditions are telling you to do otherwise. Make the goal right now to *persevere through the challenges.* Your first year in this business will be your toughest. There will be many times when you will feel like you are working hard with no results in sight. Resolve to continue to move forward to improve your skills, learn from your mistakes, and stay focused on your goals. Don't accept the naysayer's view that it can't be done. Keep your mind-set positive and directed toward success and achieving your objectives. Henry Ford said, "If you think you can or you think you can't, either way, you're right." Ford knew that your belief and mind-set will help produce the results that you desire. Staying positive, every day, is one of the hardest parts of sales for any professional.

Henry Ford said, "If you think you can or you think you can't, either way, you're right."

PICK YOUR COMPANIONS CAREFULLY

Concern yourself with what you think is right, and not with what the other agents think. If I had listened to everyone else, I would not have enjoyed the same success early in my career. Evaluate carefully who you allow to influence your thinking.

Avoid the Coffeepot and Donut Bunch

The coffeepot and donut bunch is in every office. They will be there to teach you how to achieve mediocrity in sales. This group is the easiest to spot, and they are always looking for new recruits. They are more than willing to teach you how to do it and may try to impress you with "I've been in the business X years." All that this means is that they have one year's experience X times over. They have very little to offer a new agent with energy and passion. Flee from that group because they will slowly suck you in and drain your tank.

Steer Clear of Negative Thinkers

It's easy to pick up the wrong ideas and knowledge by hanging around the wrong people. Be extremely selective and careful whom you let into your world. I adopted a rule when I started real estate sales that I still use today: Hang out only with people you can learn from, profit from, or have fun with. Those three types of people help you construct an abundant life. The complainers and lemon-suckers will only pull you down to their level. There is an age-old question: How do you keep a crab from climbing out of a bucket? Answer: You just put in another crab; when one tries to crawl out, the other will pull him back down. Some people in a real estate office are like that. Your objective the first week is to find out who those people are and avoid them as if your family and career depended on it (because they do).

*I adopted a rule when I started
real estate sales that I still use today:
Hang out only with people you can learn
from, profit from, or have fun with.*

Do the Opposite

One rule I learned early in my career that has helped me immensely was the 180 degree rule. The 180 degree rule states that whatever the average agent is doing, do the exact opposite. The average real estate agent makes $36,700 per year, which isn't exactly a smashing success. If you do only what average agents do, you will earn what they earn and achieve what they achieve. Don't think like an average agent; you are better than that.

Invite a Top Agent to Lunch

On your first day find out who are the top agents in the office. You especially want to meet the agents who are most successful in taking listings. These are the agents who have a more stable business year after year. They are the ones you want to hang around, learn from, and profit from.

When you have the opportunity, introduce yourself and ask if you can buy them lunch. You will learn more over that one-hour lunch than you will learn in six months with the coffeepot and donut bunch. Try to schedule a lunch as quickly as possible, preferably that week. If they put you off, keep asking. They'll eventually go. It is hard to resist an eager, hard-charging new agent, and it is actually refreshing to see someone take his career so seriously. If you have more than one "top gun" listing agent in your office, go individually with each one.

Identify People You Want to Be With

Some people fit into all three of my categories: You can learn from them, profit from them, and have fun with them. These are ideal companions, but most people will fit into only one category. Be prepared to enjoy the results of being around people even if they fit into only one category. I have people in my life who are just plain fun to be with. When I spend time with them, we just have fun and laugh. There are other people whom I learn from. This is the group I want to be around all the time. They will lead me to growth, self-improvement, and wealth more than any other group. Your ability to identify this group of people and figure out how to spend more and more time with them is critical to your success.

Share Your Knowledge and Skills

I have added a fourth category of people to hang out with: people I can teach and have an impact on. The greatest joy in my life is to instruct. I love to watch people grow and prosper. The best thing about teaching is that it dramatically improves your skill level in that particular subject. I know more about real estate sales from teaching and coaching for the last handful of years than I learned in my entire sales career. There also is a great joy in the teaching process. Become successful in any field and you will be able to share in that joy. As a new agent, your objective should be to get skilled enough in what you do so you can teach it to someone. I certainly feel blessed for the honor of being able to teach and positively impact people's lives.

Enjoy Other People's Success

I recently had a call with one of my clients. He talked about how his life had changed and how he had listed twelve homes in the last month. He went into detail about the challenges and objectives of each listing appointment and how he overcame them. Then he went on to describe in detail the three buyers who purchased from him in the last week and the five listings that sold that month. After thirty minutes or so, he stopped and realized he had been talking the entire time about how much he had accomplished and how his life had turned around. He was embarrassed to have spent so much time describing the excitement that was going on in his life and had failed to ask how I was doing. He began to apologize for being insensitive. I told him not to be concerned, that I received more enjoyment hearing about how he has reaped the fruits of our work together than from anything else.

There is no greater gift in life than the ability to teach and change someone's life for good. There is no greater honor than to share in the transformation of someone's life. I truly receive no greater joy in life than hearing these stories.

HOW YOUR FIRST DAYS WILL GO

We've covered the mind-set, attitude, and approach you must have as you begin your new career. But what about the actual job? How will you start? Where will you start? How can you keep all of this new information organized? Following are the answers to these questions as well as what your initial responsibilities will be as a first-year real estate agent.

Learn to Use Listing Contracts and Sales Contracts

Both sellers and buyers are making a huge decision, and your job is to help them feel comfortable doing it. You can facilitate this by assuring them that you are the best agent for the job—and that's hard to do with your head buried in a contract.

The first things you will learn are how to prepare a listing contract and a sales contract—two documents that are essential to your success. You will learn these documents inside-out, which gives you the ability to converse and write at the same time and guide your client to the sale on the buyer side or to a representation relationship on the listing side. Your ability to fill out these forms while conversing with the client will enable you to put their minds at ease. In order to accomplish this feat, you must undertsand these agreements intimately. You must know what every line and box and space is meant for and why to check it or not check it. Whether you leave a box blank or check it can mean the difference between the seller keeping the refrigerator or the buyer receiving it in the sale, or whether the seller pays the $5,000 in closing costs or the buyer pays for them. The ability to accurately complete the agreement is critical to your success.

To ensure your success in this area, you must practice. There are many things in life that we must do a certain number of times before we are skilled at them. When you first got on a bike you probably didn't take right off down the street, and more than likely, you fell down a few times. Thus, you were probably allowed to ride only in a controlled environment, like a backyard. And regardless of natural ability, you had to ride the bike many times before perfecting it.

Real estate sales is no different. You have to practice in a controlled environment, without clients. You will make mistakes in the beginning, and it is better to make them in the backyard than in front of prospects or clients. You must practice to be prepared, and you have a choice: Practice on people who can buy or sell (and possibly lose listings, sales, and referrals along the way), or practice on your spouse, children, or other agents in a role-play format to more quickly gain competence. This is true in all areas of the selling process, from paperwork to scripts, dialogues, and presentations.

Mastering Paperwork: Four Easy Steps

1. **Find a partner who is willing to help you, someone who has great knowledge of contracts and agreements.** Your broker or manager would be an excellent choice because she has a vested interest in your completing the paperwork correctly.

2. **Review all the paperwork; study every line of the document.** As you are reviewing the paperwork, write down on a legal pad any questions you have. Review both the listing agreement and the sales agreement used in your area. Often each company, or even each board, has its own agreement. If there is anything you are even remotely unsure about, ask. Ignorance is not an excuse when you are dealing with most people's single largest investment.

3. **Have your partner (your broker or whoever is helping you) assign you homes off of the multiple listing service to list and sell,**

with certain scenarios attached to them. If you are representing the buyer, have your partner assign you a sales price or down payment. You'll need to practice such details as buying personal property, early possession, long closing date, and seller keeping possession for a certain number of days after closing. You may also encounter complications such as wells, septic tanks, and property disputes. There is an endless list, and you need to know all of the possibilities. Familiarize yourself with every one. Then write the contract for this phantom buyer on paper. Have your partner check your language on the agreement. Did you get all the boxes and spaces filled out completely? Did you cross all the *t*'s and dot all the *i*'s?

4. **Review each contract and listing agreement with others.** Don't leave to chance the responsibility to protect your client. It's too important.

This process should be repeated daily for your first month or two in the business. It will give you the confidence to do the job for the client. The more times you have walked through the contracts before you do it live, the easier it will be when the pressure is really on. When you do your first sales agreement with a client, your heart will be pounding out of your chest. You will sweat like you just ran a marathon, but because you practiced well you won't make a mistake. You will still feel uncomfortable, but errors will not be there.

Sales Scripts and Dialogues

Another type of training you must embrace during your first few weeks is that of sales scripts and dialogues. Your commitment to master these will mean the difference between being a big success with a six-figure income or being out of business before the year is out.

Raise the Comfort Level
Many think having a script is manipulating the sale. I think creating a script is part of being completely prepared. Clients who hesitate in a selling situation may be saying that they need a few more facts to make them feel comfortable.

The agent's job is to give clients the data to help them make the decisions that are best for them. Scripting can help the client at the highest level by accurately communicating, in a convincing fashion, the benefits of a particular decision. To be well scripted is to be prepared to help the client evaluate the situation carefully by weighing all sides less emotionally. An agent who is well scripted has a ready response for any given situation. A well-scripted agent has practiced and prepared for the question before it is asked.

Child's Play

At a point in each of our lives we all had tremendous sales skills—and we did not even know it. We intuitively learned and perfected our presentation to the highest level. We persistently pushed forward and never took no for an answer, or at least not without a fight, and we usually wore our opponent down and got the sale. We had it all going for us, we had it all figured out, and then we stopped.

Most of us stopped being great salespeople around ten or eleven years old. Up until that point we were highly skilled salespeople. Have you ever watched children younger than ten at the store? Most are very good salespeople. The highest skilled are the three- to six-year-olds. They know what they want, and they do not take no for an answer. They usually manage to sell their parents on their ideas.

Why are they highly skilled? Because they know their scripts and dialogues. They know what to say to get their parents to do what they want. Agents must also have scripts and dialogues to elicit the desired response from the client. Successful agents need to have scripts for sellers and scripts for buyers. Brokers need scripts for other agents and for staff. The better you define what you are going to say, the more successful you will be in saying it.

Many Professionals Use Scripts

Many professionals in other fields are well scripted. Professional football teams often have the first twenty-five to thirty plays of the game planned. They know exactly which plays they will run. They evaluate how the plays work and continue to use the best ones the following week. Other well-scripted professionals include defense attorneys—many use the same argument this week that worked to get their client acquitted last week; surgeons, who look at X-rays and books to perfect upcoming procedures; and pilots, who take off and land their planes the same way every time, according to script. They have all scripted out what they are going to say and do. As well, real estate agents need to be at that level of professionalism, and you must have expert knowledge of your script.

> *Scripting can help the client at the highest level by accurately communicating, in a convincing fashion, the benefits of a particular decision.*

The Power of Scripts

The following box contains a short list of the scripts agents must use to be skilled at the delivery of the information they need to provide to buyers, sellers, agents, and affiliates. To join those successful agents, you must learn to develop and deliver scripts with effectiveness. If you do, there will be no cap to your income. The different scripts will not change nor will the basic questions, problems, objections, and solutions. Once you learn to effectively cover these areas, you will be unstoppable. There are not many new objections created by buyers and sellers annually. If you have learned all the objections and can deliver your response to the objections well, you will be rewarded. You may need to make modifications and practice them regularly, but you will not have to go through the process of learning forty to fifty new scripts and dialogues. The difference between the amateur and the professional in all things is skill and delivery. Anyone can throw a football, but he cannot throw it like Peyton Manning without dedication and practice. Manning has perfected his skill with long, hard practice.

A Script for Any Occasion

Agents need scripts for many occasions:

- **Prospecting:** past clients, expireds, FSBOs, cold calls, door knocking, apartment renters, and referral clients
- **Buyers:** ad calls, sign calls, the right house, qualifying the buyer, commitment to work with you, open houses, and for all objections
- **Sellers:** listing presentations, qualifying, price reductions, weekly communication, and for all objections
- **Other agents:** getting them to do their job, creating urgency, showing your properties, and negotiating
- **Affiliates:** sending more referrals and taking over more functions

Professional salespeople have perfected their delivery of words. They have practiced how to overcome all the objections. They have practiced how they will list a home. Many of us make new presentations every time we go out. That would be like Manning drawing the game plan in the dirt in the huddle every time. How effective would that be?

Do not be put off by poor salespeople who have poor delivery. Scripts and dialogues are often knocked because of poor delivery. Tremendously skilled salespeople are well scripted; you just cannot tell they are speaking from a script. Constant practice makes the difference.

Computer Training

Another area you must address in your first week on the job is computer training. As a new agent, you will be faced with *multiple listing service computer programs.* These programs allow you to search for properties to show your buyers. They also allow you to determine the value of a home you are hoping to list. There has been more advancement in these programs in the last few years than in the previous ten years. Using the software to leverage your time is essential.

Prospect Matching Programs

One feature that many programs have, but that is not used by many agents, is the *prospect matching* function. That's where you can input the needs and desires of your buyers and the system will notify you when a property that matches your client's needs comes on the market. This feature allows you to provide greater service to your clients with less of your personal time invested. In some boards, this prospect matching feature can automatically e-mail your client about the property and give a virtual tour of the home. We have to be masters of this software for our clients and our time.

Contact Management Software

The software that is most important will be your contact management software, the lifeblood of your business. A good customer relations management (CRM) program will make you money. The better you know and use this tool, the more money you will make. This software will help you keep track of your leads, past clients, sphere, and all your contacts in this business. Your ability to create and keep a solid database will cause your growth to explode. I have a saying that "money doesn't grow on trees; it grows in databases." Some companies have multiagent databases that you can use. Others require you to provide your own. Whichever is the case, you must learn this tool.

There are many contact management programs available especially for real estate agents, such as Top Producer, SharperAgent, ACT!, and Goldmine. Whatever you have available to you, learn it! If you need to purchase one, do so.

This one area seems to trip up too many agents. The most common database in real estate is Outlook. The truth is Outlook falls far short of what you need in your career. Outlook is basically an electronic Rolodex, label maker, and e-mail program. Most agents default to using it because it is free and they have the program. However, Outlook it is not the program you need to grow your business.

A good CRM will be worth the few dollars a month you invest in it because you can automate lead follow-up and past client follow-up with a few key strokes. You will be able to establish plans and launch them so you can keep track of leads, past clients, current clients, pending transactions, and much more. A good CRM, like Top Producer, will have postcards, letters, and other marketing pieces built right into the software. It will allow you to set up a follow-up process and automate your contacts.

I recommend Top Producer because of its longevity of service to real estate agents, tremendous features, Internet remote access, marketing pieces, stability of customer service, and data storage. You can find out all about Top Producer at http://www.topproducer.com/partner/real-estate-champions/8i.

> *Your ability to create and keep a solid database will cause your growth to explode in this business.*

Set Aside Time for Training

Another way to learn is to set aside thirty minutes daily just to work in the software. Plan to spend a certain amount of uninterrupted time learning how to enter prospects, how to create follow-up programs for your leads, and how to keep in touch with your sphere and past clients. There is a large learning curve on the software we must master as real estate agents. The commitment to learn it begins the moment you step into the office for the first time. Remember, the contact management software is the lifeblood of your business. Make sure you are investing the necessary time to master it.

GET ORGANIZED

To create and run a multimillion-dollar sales company takes organization. The ability to organize your paperwork, your leads and prospects, and, most important, your time is essential. If you can learn to control these key areas you will be able to generate a six-figure income.

Take Control of Your Time

The most important of the areas we must control is time because it is the only asset we have where we don't know how much we have. We know what's in our checking or savings account. (For many of us that's not very much, and that's why you are entering real estate.) We treat our money with far more care and reverence than our daily time account. An unknown author describes time this way:

> If you had a bank that credited your account each morning with $86,000—that carried over no balance from day to day—and allowed you to keep no cash in your account . . . and every evening cancelled whatever part of the amount you had failed to use during the day—what would you do? Draw out every cent, of course! Well, you do have such a bank—its name is "time." Every morning it credits you with 86,000 seconds . . . every night it rules off as lost whatever of this you have failed to invest to good purposes. It carries over no balance. . . . It allows no overdrafts. Each day it opens a new account for you. If you fail to use the day's deposit, the loss is yours. There is no going back. There is no drawing against tomorrow. You must live in the present—on today's deposit.

We each have the same set amount daily. None of us has more than twenty-four hours for use that day. Your time needs to be treated as the most precious asset you own. The amount of money we earn is based on our skill and time effectiveness. Poor use of time always equals poor income.

If you want to know the value of a single second, ask the man who lost the Olympic gold medal in the hundred-meter race by less than a second. The winner receives millions in endorsements; the loser gets nothing; we don't even remember his name.

Have you ever called your attorney to ask a question and not received a bill for his time? As real estate agents, we too are selling our time and our knowledge. Those are the assets we sell daily. The better you control your time, the more income you will make. Resolve to let no one take time from you without compensation.

Plan for Tomorrow Today

Let me give you a couple of quick strategies for maximizing your time. First, we need to plan for tomorrow before we leave today. Never start a day before you have it planned out on paper. It is really easy for the time to slip away in real estate sales. There are so many people and activities trying to get your attention that you can arrive at the end of the day having produced little to nothing.

The best remedy is to clearly know your tasks and objectives for the day. Great agents *create* their day and what happens; most agents *react* to their day and what happens. There is a huge difference between creation and reaction. In creation you are in control, while in reaction everyone and everything else is in control. Most people have poor time-planning procedures. If they have not planned well for themselves, I can assure you they have planned nothing for you. You are the only person who can plan for you. Start every day with a plan to wring the most out of the day.

> *Great agents* create *their day and what happens; most agents* react *to their day and what happens.*

Prioritize Your Objectives

Once you have the objectives for the day, prioritize them. Create an order of most important to least important. Then when you begin your day, focus on number one on the list. By giving 100 percent of your attention to number one and working at it until it is complete, you will be able to accomplish much more than the average agent. There is an old adage: "You save ten minutes of execution for every one minute of planning." That's a tremendous return on your investment of time.

Organize Your Prospecting

For a new agent, number one on your list is prospecting. Your diligence and focus on daily prospecting is essential to your success. Eighty percent of all businesses that fail do so because they lack sales. The best way to ensure consistent sales is to prospect daily. We will discuss prospecting in detail in chapter 8. For now, just remember that, for a new agent, prospecting is number one and it must be done daily. Organizing your leads and prospects allows you to know who they are and how often to call. Many agents lose more leads and prospects than they convert. Lack of conversion can be connected to the efficiency of one's organization of leads and prospects.

The best way to ensure consistent sales is to prospect daily.

Create Lead Sheets

Create a lead sheet that has the information and the questions that need to be asked for all prospects and leads. Keep these sheets well organized in a file system based on motivation. Motivation is the gauge of how quickly someone has the desire to do something. The more motivated the client, the more quickly they will buy or sell. The goal for agents should be to prospect regularly to generate the most motivated clients. These motivated clients will list their home at a fair market value rather than overpricing their property. We are not looking for prospects who want to test the market. We are looking for people who want to sell now! We are not looking for people who want to shop for the best deal. We are looking for people who want to buy now! By organizing and controlling your leads you will be able to determine the best leads and focus on them most. Keep your leads organized and in front of you at all times.

Following is an example of a lead sheet that will help you rank your clients and prospects both.

CLIENT/PROSPECT EVALUATION

NAME: _____   PHONE: _____

ADDRESS: _____   E-MAIL: _____

SOURCE: _____   DATE: _____

COMMENTS: _____

_____

CONTACTS (DATES & PURPOSE): _____

_____

MOTIVATION

WHY BUYING/SELLING? _____

WHAT'S WRONG WITH PRESENT SITUATION? _____

HOW STRONGLY MOTIVATED (1–10)? _____

DAYS UNTIL LISTS/BUY: 0–7 _____ 8–30 _____ 31–60 _____ 60–90 _____ 90+ _____

FINANCIAL CAPACITY TO PERFORM

EQUITY: _____ CASH: _____ OTHER: _____

PREQUALIFIED: _____ PREAPPROVED: _____ WHERE: _____

AUTHORITY TO MAKE DECISION

SELF-ONLY: _____ ANYONE ELSE: _____ WHO: _____

PROCESS OF DECIDING WHICH ONE TO BUY OR ACCEPTANCE OF OFFERS

DESCRIBE: _____

_____

WILLINGNESS TO COMPROMISE (1–10): _____

REALISTIC EXPECTATIONS (1–10): _____

WILLINGNESS TO BE COMPETITIVE (BUY OR SELL AT MARKET VALUE) (1–10): _____

REALISTIC EXPECTATIONS (1–10): _____

COMMITMENT TO USE MY SERVICES (1–10): _____

ME IF I FIND WHAT THEY WANT (Y/N): _____

ME IF THEY FIND WHAT THEY WANT (Y/N): _____
ME IF ANYONE FINDS WHAT THEY WANT (Y/N): _____
VERBAL AGREEMENT: _____ WRITTEN AGREEMENT: _____

OVERALL RATING

A   1 _____ 2 _____ 3 _____
B   1 _____ 2 _____ 3 _____
C   1 _____ 2 _____ 3 _____
D   1 _____ 2 _____ 3 _____

A—Will almost certainly take action within 30 days   1—Committed to you
                                                          Committed/almost certainly
                                                          (90%+ odds)

B—Will probably take action within 30–120 days   2—Probably with you
                                                          Probable chance (50–90%
                                                          odds)

C—Will probably take action within 120–360 days   3—Possibly with you
                                                          Possibility (1–49% odds)

Organize Your Paperwork

Lastly, organize your desk area for your paperwork. If you have a file drawer, separate it into listings and sales. Keep the sellers separate from the buyers. Establish a folder for each transaction. Don't lump all your paperwork in one folder. If you list a home for sale and then sell that seller a new home, make sure to create two separate folders.

There are many different types of folders to use. I like best the folders that have space on the outside to put transaction information. If your company does not provide them, find another source that does. Often a title or escrow company will have them available to you free of charge. A company called NEBS sells excellent real estate listing folders in both legal size and standard 8 1/2 x 11 size. You can access NEBS at www.nebs.com or call them at 1-888-823-6327. The more organized you are when it comes to your files, the less time you will need to invest in the administration side of your business.

Organization is critical only because you want to spend the least amount of time servicing and the most amount of time prospecting for new transactions. Most agents spend less than 20 percent of their time in prospecting and lead follow-up. These are the activities that generate the revenue; the more time you spend on them, the more money you make. Take the time to set up your administration right the first time. It will save you in the long run. The next step is to build a strong relationship with your broker or manager.

CHAPTER 3

CREATING A
RELATIONSHIP WITH
YOUR MANAGER

Most brokers and managers do not expect a new agent to walk in the door and light up the sale board. They do expect you to work diligently and daily to find business and improve your skills. When beginning the training process with new agents, the excitement is high and the anticipation is great. Your broker or manager is going to make the investment in you because he believes you have what it takes to succeed. He is willing to invest his time and resources into helping you achieve your dreams. As in any relationship, there will be challenges at times with your broker or manager. There will be times when your performance does not meet the other's expectations. How you talk through it and create specific action plans to improve your performance is essential.

Your Manager Is on Your Side

The relationship you have with your manager can be anything you want it to be. It can be cooperative and mentoring or adversarial and combative. The key is ongoing communication between you and your manager.

I have never met a manager who would not be willing to do whatever it takes for her agent to succeed, provided the agent is willing to put in more effort than the manager.

Many people have the attitude that if the stove would only give them a little heat, then they would put in the wood. Life does not work that way. We have to build the fire before we get the heat.

Zig Ziglar said, "Life is like a cafeteria line: first you pay and then you get to eat." You will be amazed how many people will help you if you start first and keep going.

When you are willing to pay the price, many people will join to help you all along the way. Your manager will be leading the charge.

WHAT YOU BRING TO YOUR TRAINING

Your first year as a new agent is a critical time for you to get from your broker or manager what you need to succeed. Your obligation is to stay focused, excited, energized, and grateful for the opportunity you have been given. If you don't exude those characteristics, your manager will eventually lose interest in training you.

Your career and the quality of your training are entirely up to you; you have the keys to success clearly in your possession. Your manager will help you use the keys better and more quickly. It is up to you to bring them to the office every day. It is up to you to keep these keys shiny and ready to be used at a moment's notice. As a coach and speaker, I will go the extra mile for the people who come to me for help with their keys ready. Most successful brokers feel the same way; they will go all out to help new agents who have a great attitude and positive expectations.

Attitude and expectations—these are the key concepts that lead to success. They affect the successful outcome of your business, your personal relation-

Your career and the quality of your training are entirely up to you; you have the keys to success clearly in your possession.

ships, and many other areas of your life. Although you may have incredible talent and skill, you will fail if you do not master these two concepts. Even if you have limited talent and skill, you will win if you live by these two power words. They will determine your future.

Excel with Attitude

When we hire people at Real Estate Champions, attitude is the first and most important characteristic we look for in a team member. An employee with a great attitude will learn the skills needed to excel.

If you have a positive, forward-looking attitude, you will accomplish great things. How is your attitude? Does it need improvement? Are you positive and upbeat? If you believe that every challenge or obstacle leads to new opportunity, success is all but guaranteed.

If Life Gives You Lemons, Make Lemonade

Thomas Edison was said to have been motivated to create the electric lightbulb because darkness interfered with his ability to conduct further experiments. He wanted to be able to work long into the night. Edison could have moaned about the darkness. That would not have accomplished anything. Instead, he used his positive attitude and solved the problem of darkness. There are thousands of examples in life of how some people took lemons and, with a great attitude, made lemonade.

Build a Positive Attitude

Start building your attitude today. Convince yourself that you are the best agent anyone could hire. You have to be convinced yourself before anyone else will be convinced. The attitude you bring to objections will help you handle them and get the contract signed. The attitude that you take when you have a problem transaction will make the difference between a closing and a deal falling through.

Exhibit Unshakeable Confidence

The second power word is expectation. If you don't expect to win, you will not win. If you go on a listing and expect to take it at your price and commission, you will. If you go expecting a fight on commission and your price, you will receive that also.

Set the positive expectation of success before the appointment with a prospect or client. You also need to set a positive expectation before every phone call you make. Expectation is the gateway to confidence.

The first step to having unshakeable confidence is to believe you are the agent for the job. If your expectation is strong enough people will come around to your way of thinking. You just need to be stronger in will and mental focus than clients, prospects, and other agents are.

I Am a Great Salesperson

To improve your attitude, use affirmations. Affirmations drive positive mental pictures into your subconscious mind.

- I am a great salesperson.
- I am skilled at handling objections and getting the contract signed.
- People do business with me because I am positive, knowledgeable, and professional.
- I will earn _____ (you fill in the blank).

Use these affirmations or create your own to improve your mental attitude daily.

Your expectation will create your reality. You have to expect before you can receive. You need to envision the people and situations that will enable you to create the future you desire. Expectation does not mean you don't have to work. In fact, you will work harder than before to develop the outcome you desire.

The Role of Failure in Your Career

Expectation takes away the fear of failure. Failure is a natural part of success—don't let it paralyze you. You cannot have success without failure. The exhilaration of success would be lost without the frustration of failure. Most people forget the failures over time and remember only the victories. Take Babe Ruth, for example—he hit the most home runs of his time. He also had the most strikeouts. No one remembers that . . . only the home runs . . . the successes.

> *Babe Ruth hit the most home runs of his time. He also had the most strikeouts. No one remembers that . . . only the home runs . . . the successes.*

YOUR MANAGER CAN HELP YOU ACHIEVE SUCCESS

One of the roles of a manager is to help you achieve your dreams. Since she should know the path to success, she should be able to move you toward it more quickly. What your manager does not know is what success is to you, what your dreams are for your new career, and what price you are willing to pay.

Expect to Win

Set your attitude to positive. Look for the opportunities in every situation. Expect to win—every time.

For your manager to hold you accountable for the dreams and goals you have set, you need to share them with her. I can guarantee that there is not a manager alive who possesses the ability of Carnac. Carnac was a character, created by Johnny Carson on *The Tonight Show,* who could read what was in a sealed envelope when he held it next to his head. Your manager needs to know your goals and dreams so a plan can be designed for you to achieve them.

Winning Is an All-Time Thing

Vince Lombardi said:

> Winning is not a sometime thing; it's an all-time thing. You don't have to win once in a while, you don't do things right once in a while, you do them right all the time. Winning is a habit, unfortunately so is losing.

Lombardi had the right attitude and the right expectations. He believed he would win—every time.

SET CLEAR OBJECTIVES

I recently read a statement by Oliver Wendell Holmes. He said, "To reach the port of success, we must sail; sometimes with the wind, and sometimes against it, but we must sail, not drift or lie anchor." To be adrift is to be without specific goals and objectives. We must be clear and focused on where we are heading. This quotation has led me to develop the image of sailing toward a successful life. The first step for a successful sailor is to have a specific port he is trying to reach. We who seek a successful life must also have an objective. The objective must be clear and concise, crystallized, and definite.

Overcome the "Impossible"

Many years ago Henry Ford went to his engineers and told them to build a V-8 engine. They said it could not be done. Ford told them plainly to go do it and report back in ninety days. When the ninety days were up, they again met with Ford. The engineers had spent the whole ninety days dwelling on why a V-8 engine was impossible. They tried to convince Ford it could not be done—a V-8 engine was impossible and could never be created. Ford's attitude and expectation of a V-8 engine were stronger than the engineers' attitude and expectation that it could not be done. We all know who won in the end.

Objectives Versus Goals

Too often, we are very fuzzy about our main objective in life. Our main objective is beyond what we do. It's beyond the income, sales, and money we earn. It's beyond our business and all the challenges that surround it. Too often the objective is monetary. To earn X amount of dollars or sell so many homes, in my perspective, is not the main objective in life. It at best is a goal to be obtained along the way. The desired end is not the money itself. It could be what the money could do for us or the lifestyle it allows us to enjoy.

Your Key Supporters

You have set a specific target and, in order to achieve it, you need other people to hold you accountable. The two most logical people to keep you accountable are your spouse (or significant other) and your manager. Besides you, those two will have the greatest impact on the achievement of your objectives. I can clearly state that I would not have had as successful a real estate sales career without my wife, Joan. She has played an incredible role in my success each and every day. My manager was also a key supporter. He was always supportive, encouraging, and willing to share his wisdom. For either of them to help guide and motivate me, they needed to clearly understand my goals and objectives.

"To reach the port of success, we must sail; sometimes with the wind, and sometimes against it, but we must sail, not drift or lie anchor."—Oliver Wendell Homes

View the Difficulty as an Advantage

One of the hardest tasks in life is to set that clear objective. If it were easy, everyone would do it; everyone would achieve success. But we are often stopped by the difficulty of the task. The difficulty should be viewed as an advantage. Now that's a novel mind-set, isn't it? The more difficult the task, the fewer the people who will master it. The fewer people who have mastery, the lower the level of competition. Few people have mastered success. That's why there is so much opportunity.

Studies have shown that the peak earning years for people are in their fifties and early sixties. For many it takes that long to master success. It takes years of trial and error to get it right. Most people never hit the mark or get it right. If we are progressing, learning, and moving forward, we are successful . . . provided we have a definite aim or objective.

Money Does Not Make a Millionaire

One of my favorite speakers is Jim Rohn. Jim says that it's not the money that makes the millionaire. It is what that person became in order to attract the million dollars. What is truly valuable are the skills, mind-set, discipline, and character the person developed on the way to that objective. The money is fleeting, but the skills of character, mind-set, and discipline last forever.

Make the Most of Favorable Winds

The second key point in the Oliver Wendell Holmes quotation is the concept of "against the wind or with the wind." There will be days when things go smoothly and we are with the wind. We are hot and everything we touch turns to gold. We gain appointments easily. We create trust effectively with our prospects and clients. The market around the country is responding favorably with listings selling within days. A skilled sailor will sail long and hard on those days. She will ensure that she makes the most miles she can by sailing longer, harder, and with more focus and intensity. How often do we let up when we have things rolling and the momentum is with us? When we have favorable wind, do we take a mental break? Do we let up? That's the time to pour it on!

It's human nature to let up or to ease back on the throttle of success. People often neglect what they did to create the momentum in the first place, but you must not. *Carpe diem* . . . seize the day. Seize the opportunity when the conditions are favorable.

Focus on the Mainsail in Heavy Weather

There will also be days, weeks, and maybe longer when the wind is against you, when you feel like you are right in the middle of a squall. A highly skilled sailor realizes that this is a passing storm. He may not know the length and breadth of the storm, but it will pass in time. When the storm hits, you need to understand it will move on. You can weather the challenge.

A good sailor will also go back to basics in a storm. He will take down the spinnaker; he may remove the jib. He focuses all his attention on the most important thing to get him out of the storm—he focuses on the mainsail.

Decide on an objective. Plot the course. Navigate the winds and challenges. Celebrate when you arrive.

What's your mainsail in life? What's the mainsail in your business? Do you focus intently on the mainsail in times of trial or are you concerned about the spinnaker? There will always be peripheral stuff in your life and business, but don't take down the mainsail. Keep working the wind. Use your mainsail . . . weather the storm.

Don't Quit

The last essential point is for you not to stop, never quit. Perseverance leads to success. Champions don't stop when they encounter adversity. Like good sailors they keep focused on the objective and don't let the tides drift them off course. You can learn a lot from a skilled sailor. The skills and challenges are the same in sailing as in real estate. Decide on an objective. Plot the course. Navigate the winds and challenges. Celebrate when you arrive.

CREATE A PLAN AND CHECK YOUR PROGRESS REGULARLY

Once you have set clear objectives, work with your manager to create a plan to achieve them. Decide on the income you desire for the year. Figure out the number of transactions that you need to achieve your set income goal. Ask your manager what she thinks you need to learn to achieve that goal of income. Together, write down the steps so you can check them off as you go.

Commit to a scheduled time to meet with your manager weekly to check your progress. The best results in life come from consistency of activity. To truly be held accountable, you need a regular time with your manager to check your progress. My friend Zig Ziglar describes this as a "checkup from the neck up." To hit the production and income goal you have set, you can't be going in the wrong direction for a month or even a week. Your manager can help keep you on track and focused toward the goals you have set.

Your manager can help keep you on track and focused toward the goals you have set.

GET IN THE GAME EVERY DAY

To create success, what you know is only the first step. A lot of people know a whole lot but don't get very far in life. You will be rewarded based on what you do with what you know. We are scored only on action, on doing what we should and need to do. That means that we must act. We can't sit on the sidelines in observation. We have to get in the game every day and apply what we have learned.

Without reaching out and picking up the phone and making the first lead follow-up call or prospecting call, we are assured failure. It is that one motion of picking up and dialing that first number that separates the winner from the loser. In terms of time, less than two seconds will determine your outcome.

You, Inc.

Your career is up to you. You are the one who will create this multimillion-dollar business. I truly believe everyone in life is self-employed. You are the owner of your own personal service company. It doesn't matter if you are a real estate agent, doctor, attorney, construction worker, or secretary. In the final analysis, you work for your own company: You, Inc.! At this moment, you may be selling your services to any number of other companies, but ultimately you have to view this whole business you are creating as You, Inc.

You are the president of a wonderful new company that is going to take the real estate industry by storm. This company of yours is going to become a whole new powerhouse in the real estate industry. It is you who controls the success and direction of the company. What you do will lead you to the results you seek.

The First Step

Lao-tzu said, "A journey of a thousand miles begins with a single step." John Maxwell said, "Success is a journey not a destination." Combine the two and create "The successful journey begins with a single step." That is what stops most people . . . that first step. That little step separates abundance from failure. Without that first step you are guaranteed not to accomplish your objective.

THE PAIN OF DISCIPLINE VERSUS THE PAIN OF REGRET

Now, I realize that there is some pain involved with lead follow-up and prospecting; however, there is also pain involved if you don't do it. There are two kinds of pain: the pain of discipline (making the lead follow-up and prospecting calls) and the pain of regret. The truth is, we are going to experience one of them—it is impossible not to. You have to choose which you would rather live with. You are the one who ultimately does the choosing.

When we take the step to make the calls, we are experiencing the pain of discipline, the pain of potential rejection, the pain of sacrifice, and the pain of hard work. To avoid the pain of regret you must pursue this course with single-minded purpose. You must decide and commit to the disciplined path. "All glory comes from daring to begin," according to Eugene Ware. If you do not begin, you have selected the pain of regret.

"All glory comes from daring to begin," according to Eugene Ware.

Discipline involves work and commitment. Success is not purchased all at one time, but on the installment plan. We achieve success only through disciplined effort over time. When we make the calls daily to our leads, prospects, past clients, sphere, expireds, and FSBOs, we will achieve success. We will also move far away from the pain of regret. When we create a habit of daily discipline, an almost magical thing happens. One day you will realize that your discipline has turned into desire: the desire to do the calls daily, the wanting to make the calls because of the habit and the results. The road will get easier to stay on.

The pain of discipline will pass and transform into desire. The pain of regret can linger forever.

The pain of discipline we feel now . . . today. We may not feel the pain of regret for hours, days, weeks, months, or years. This will often cause us to make the wrong decision because we would prefer to have no pain now or ever. The pain of discipline will pass and transform into desire. The pain of regret can linger forever. Start today toward discipline and away from regret.

Begin your success journey today with a single step.

Regret

If we don't attack our dreams, we will experience the greatest pain in life, the pain of regret. Sydney Harris wrote, "Regret for the things we did can be tempered by time; it is the regret for the things we did not do that is inconsolable." There will be regret for not doing what we know we should do; regret for not achieving our goals and dreams; regret for not crafting a grand lifestyle for our family and ourselves; regret for not living up to our potential. At what point does potential turn into regret? There is that one moment in time. It's different for each one of us. Are you nearing that point?

DO WHAT NEEDS TO BE DONE DAILY

What happens in You, Inc., can be defined by what needs to happen daily. The most successful people in life are skilled at doing just that, never neglecting to do what needs to be done now. Neglect is one of the key reasons for failure.

True success comes from accomplishing daily the activities that will lead you to your ultimate goals in life. Failing to accomplish the daily disciplines will lead you down the path of lost opportunities and lost income.

If we were zapped today for neglecting daily disciplines rather than in the future, our daily disciplines would change. We need to associate pain today with not doing our daily disciplines in the real estate business. We have to experience the neglect as more painful than the activity.

Pay Later

If the penalty for not accomplishing your daily activities or disciplines were assessed today, you would look at neglecting those activities differently. The truth is that the penalty for neglect resides more in the future than in today. The person who eats fried foods does not pay the penalty at thirty-five; he pays at fifty-five. The person who fails to save 10 percent of his income for retirement is not penalized at forty, but at sixty. The prospecting we fail to do today does not hurt our income today, but 90 to 120 days from now.

THREE DISCIPLINES FOR SUCCESS IN REAL ESTATE SALES

Three disciplines must be practiced daily in real estate for success: fueling growth, attending to administration, and working on your business.

The more of your day you spend in growth, the more income you will make.

The Power of Commitment to Growth

I have a client named Rich Purvis who lives in Midland, Michigan. Rich is one of the nicest guys you will ever meet. He came to us in March of 2000, frustrated about his career. He had been a part-time agent for a handful of years, but had recently gone full-time after twenty-five years as a firefighter. He had a solid first year, doing about nineteen transactions. We started coaching Rich to help him zero in on his activities and his prospecting.

Rich was focused on making his ten contacts a day to his sphere and past clients. I can count on one hand how many times he failed to meet his daily contact goals over the past nine months. Those ten contacts took him roughly an hour to do. By year-end, Rich had almost tripled his income and more than doubled his number of closings.

If you had the opportunity to talk to Rich, he would humbly say that he was not the most skilled agent when he started making the ten contacts a day. He just made a commitment to the growth area of his business daily. As of this writing, Rich is on track to double his business again this year. How many agents or companies do you know that will more than double their business two years in a row?

Make the decision to spend time daily in the growth area of your business. Your broker will respect and applaud your efforts. Rich's broker is a huge fan because of Rich's discipline. You will achieve the same relationship and respect from your broker by focusing on growth daily.

Fueling Growth

Growth is the part of the business that brings in the revenue. The more of your day you spend in growth, the more income you will make. Most agents focus little time each day on growth activities. They work on growth activities at the last minute, when they are running short on funds. That is too late. To have a steady business income you need a steady approach to growth.

Growth occurs in the prospecting that you do daily. It is in the listing appointments that you have for the day. It is the lead follow-ups that you are doing on the people who want to buy or sell. It is the meeting with your lender to work on your competitive advantage in the marketplace.

Growth is the indispensable part of any business. Without growth a business will fail. I know a lot of agents who are highly skilled in growth and poorly skilled in administration and working on their business who earn large amounts of money. I know of very few successful agents who are not highly skilled at growth. You can have huge deficiencies in administration and working on your business but still win the game. You cannot be deficient in growth and win. At Real Estate Champions our focus is to help our clients achieve a high level of skill in all three areas, but growth is the engine that powers the train—you must first pay attention to growth.

Growth demands a minimum of three hours daily: prospecting, appointments, lead follow-up, and meeting with affiliates. Prospecting should be 65 percent of your growth time daily. If the prospecting does not happen, the other growth areas will wither. Remember, the higher the number of hours spent on growth, the higher your income and profit.

Administrative Activities

These are the activities that complete the income stream:

1. Processing the listing so agents can find it in the multiple listing service,
2. Processing the sold property through escrow,
3. Communicating with your clients on a regular basis, and
4. Directing your staff and monitoring their progress.

Attending to Administration

You will need one to two hours daily for administration. If you create a good system, your time spent in this area will be reduced. In the ideal system administration gets done well, but the agent spends little of his personal time on it.

You Own Your Business

We are all really owners of our own little real estate business. We are the ones who bring in the business and make the system go. The more time we plan, read, strategize, practice, role-play, and implement our ideas, the more ownership we gain. Becoming the owner of your real estate business happens only through diligent work on your business. Instead of being the employee who works to draw a salary and pay the bills, why not become the one who orchestrates the company? Be the one who has something of value to sell when she wants to try something else or retire.

Working on Your Business

This is the time most people neglect. Working on your business really separates success and growth from just running faster on the treadmill of life. Long-term financial success lies in this section of your day. The ability to earn more profit is also located here.

Schedule Your Routine Activities

What do you think your business would look like in 90 days or even 6 months if you were to implement this daily routine?

>   Growth: 3 hours
>   Administration: 1 to 2 hours
>   Business: 1 hour

Schedule these activities into your daily routine. You will be amazed at the results you will achieve, even in 1 week.

Working on your business is taking a step back from the daily rat race and looking at your growth and administration areas for ways to improve them. Look at your productivity and profitability, then evaluate your progress. You cannot make meaningful change without evaluation as an owner rather than as an employee on a treadmill. Working on your business is essential to moving to the next level of production, decreasing time worked without reducing income, and finding where to cut expenses by 10 percent. Working on your business will help you create economies of scale in administration and new ways to produce growth and income in your business. Plan to spend one hour a day on this.

Do not allow distractions to overtake you and your new daily focus. Do not neglect to do the things that will lead you to success. Do them daily without fail. Being disciplined is a struggle for every person in life, but it's a lot easier to do a small amount daily and establish a disciplined habit. The level of our discipline can often dictate the level of our success.

> *Being disciplined is a struggle for every person in life, but it's a lot easier to do a small amount daily and establish a disciplined habit.*

CUSTOMER SERVICE

Brokers are especially sensitive to customer service. They view poor customer service by any agent as affecting the whole company and the other agents in the company. In the end, they are right. Your ability to create satisfied customers is crucial to the business of You, Inc., as well as the company you work for.

What Does Customer Service Mean to Your Clients?

The first step to providing great customer service is to find out what it means to the customers you are working with now. On the listing appointment ask the sellers these questions:

Because I desire to provide the highest level of customer service, what
*   are your specific expectations of me?*
What are your expectations regarding my communication with you?
What other services can I provide for you?

When you go through their answers you will develop a very clear picture of their definition of customer service. This knowledge will enable you to exceed their expectations and provide exceptional service.

Great Customer Service Is What the Client Thinks It Is

Giving great customer service is difficult because each person you are dealing with has his own definition of what great customer service entails. In his book *Selling* Mark McCormack describes great customer service this way: "You can be doing the best job in the world for your client but if there's something missing, if the client is unhappy, then all your opinions about your performance are worthless. Great service is a matter of perception. Great service is what the client thinks it is."

Schedule Contacts Regularly

The second step is to create the procedures that will enable you to provide exceptional customer service. Most consumers equate consistency of communication with customer service. If you agreed to call clients once a week to update them, then do it every week without fail. Schedule the calls in your contact manager software. This reminder will ensure that you make the call. If you agreed to do a written report monthly, block out a few hours once a month to complete all the written reports to your clients. The more automated you become, the more consistently you will be able to provide exceptional service every time.

Meet Your Clients' Customer Service Expectations

Don't leave to chance your ability to create clients for life. You may get busy and drop the ball mentally. It's easy to overlook your commitments when your life and business are in chaos. Systematize your mailing, phone contacts, and correspondence. It's the only way to ensure the result you and your clients are looking to achieve. Make sure you clearly know the standard they have for customer service. All clients desire to have that standard met. If you can't meet it, refer them to someone who can before you enter into the relationship. Then move on and find other clients.

Lack of communication is the largest complaint consumers have against Realtors. Resolve today to start to communicate with your clients weekly or every two weeks. Even if you have nothing to report, you need to check in. Your clients will appreciate that you came through on your commitment to contact them. They will respect you for your integrity of purpose. The most efficient way to do that is through your contact manager software (SharperAgent, ACT!, Top Producer, Goldmine, for example). The contact with your clients must be preprogrammed. Note all additional needs of your clients so you can ensure their timely completion.

Learning to focus is one of the most valuable skills you can acquire.

THE FOUR RULES OF REAL ESTATE

There are four rules of real estate. If you apply them each moment of each day, you will have success. You will also build a wonderful relationship with your manager. Your ability to focus on these four rules will make or break your relationship with your manager and your career.

1. **Be there.** There is an old saying, "Wherever you go . . . there you are." Now that's a cute little saying, but the truth is most of us have to struggle to live it. How many times have we gone to work or spent time with our family and we weren't really there? We were certainly there in physical body, but were we mentally there? Were we really in the moment as we needed to be?

   "Be there" has two meanings for us as real estate agents. First, be physically there:

   • Show up on time. Being on time to a listing appointment can often mean the difference between getting the listing and not getting the listing.
   • Prepare well before you go on an appointment.
   • Treat your real estate career like a real job. Show up at work every day at the same time. My day started at 7 a.m. during my sales career. It was very rare for me not to be in the office at that time.

It's Only a Small Detail . . .

It is usually a small detail that separates success from failure. Just ask the United States women's soccer team or better yet, ask China. One penalty kick made the difference between first and second place at the World Cup. The difference between the number one PGA tour player, Tiger Woods, and number 150 is about one stroke per eighteen holes and over $9 million in earnings. Focus mentally on the moment you are in.

---

2. **Focus mentally.** Be in the moment with intense concentration. The better you focus mentally, the more results you will get for your time invested. If you need to be listening to the client, focus on what the client is saying. If you are formulating your answer or response, you are not listening to the client. Learning to focus is one of the most valuable skills you can acquire. Focus always comes before success.

Pay attention to what is happening around you; pay attention to the details of success.

Be a Hall of Famer

Lawrence Taylor had a great thought that he shared at his induction into the National Football League Hall of Fame. He said, "A Hall of Famer is not someone who never falls down. A Hall of Famer is someone who continues to pick himself up and gets back into the game after he has fallen down."

3. **Tell the truth.** In every situation tell the truth. Agents often have to tell people something they don't want to hear. For example, their home is worth $150,000, but they want $165,000. What do you do? Many agents will take the listing at $165,000 and deal with the $15,000 price reduction later. My belief is that it is better to tell the truth. You may not get the listing, but at least you will know you were honest. Too many of us hedge or shade the truth. Understand there will be a time of reckoning. It may not be now, but it will come. It may be when the market slows and you have a bunch of listings that will not sell.

4. **Accept the results and move on.** We need to accept the results we get. Work to understand them and the reasons why, and then move on to any necessary changes. If you are worried about the lost deal, you won't be able to focus on the one that is currently in front of you.

ACCEPT THE CHALLENGE

It's easy to lie on the ground in the mud when the challenges come at you. There will be times when you feel like lying there—when the buyer you have been working with makes a deal with someone else, when you lose a listing you thought you had, when the deal you have been working for weeks on keeping together finally falls apart despite all your efforts.

Your manager will want to clone you if you apply the ability to be there in all situations, to focus mentally in the moment you are in right now. He will have incredible respect for your telling the truth in all situations and your philosophy to accept the results and move on. You manager has enough people who are blaming others for their lack of success. You commitment to acceptance and improvement will have him firmly behind your success.

CHAPTER 4

BUILDING RELATIONSHIPS WITH COWORKERS

A real estate sales career is an incredibly unique business. It takes a special person to achieve a high level of success in this industry. Successful real estate agents have to wear many hats to be successful. They need the evaluation skills of an analyst, the consulting skills of a psychiatrist, the knowledge of legal contracts of an attorney, and the patience of a saint. Most successful agents also have very high ego strength.

Because of these special skills and the close proximity in which agents work and compete, the relationship with your coworkers is unlike any other in the business world. Gaining and maintaining the competitive edge will create revenue for you. Your ability to understand the game of real estate and put your best competitive foot forward will advance your career quickly.

The structure of the relationship between you and your broker as well as the other agents in the office can sometimes lead to difficulties. In this chapter we discuss the nature of your employment and how that affects competitiveness and cooperation. We also look into strategic partners and how to manage your relationship with them.

THE INDEPENDENT CONTRACTOR

The first unique element of the real estate business is your employment status. As a real estate agent, you are an independent contractor. That means that the federal government does not recognize you as an employee. The broker and the company you represent do not actually employ you. You are an independent contractor for the real estate company. For many people entering real estate, this is the first time they have not had an employer.

The broker saves a significant amount of money annually due to this type of employment status. You, as the agent, will have to pay for your own insurance and your own self-employment taxes. Self-employment tax status means that you pay the employer portion of the taxes as well. That amounts to 7.5 percent of the total income you generate. Your broker will give you a 1099 form at the end of the year instead of a W-2. You alone are responsible for saving the money for your taxes.

Real estate agents need the evaluation skills of an analyst, the consulting skills of a psychiatrist, the knowledge of legal contracts of an attorney, and the patience of a saint.

COMPETITION FOR COMMISSION DOLLARS

Independent contractor status can lead to the wrong kind of competition between agents. A lack of cooperation can occur because sometimes you and another agent in your office could be in competition for the same client. This means you are competing for the same commission dollars. I have witnessed arguments firsthand between agents over clients and commission dollars. Agents can get very emotional about their clients and their income since we are all operating without the safety net of a base salary. There is no security regarding the income you make. Essentially, every day you are unemployed and you have to go out and find a job. There is also no bonus program from the company—the only bonus program is the one that you create daily for yourself. It's you and the phone and your clients and prospects. The pressure is on to perform.

Competition from Outside Your Office

Although there is competition among the agents inside the office for the commission dollar, the greatest competition comes from the agents in other companies. Most successful managers and companies control the negative competition inside their office, but outside the office there is no control. You will run up against some agents who are very cutthroat. They will even do unethical things to try to obtain a client.

Cooperation Among Agents

We walk on a razor's edge as salespeople because it really takes all of us to be successful. You might have heard the term *co-op broker*. This is short for cooperating broker. Over 90 percent of the transactions in real estate are done through co-op brokers. We have to compete with each other, but we also have to work with each other. I would not have had the success in my career if not for the other agents in my marketplace helping to sell my listings by showing them to their buyers.

Be Your Client's Advocate

The ultimate goal is to develop cooperation out of a very competitive environment. To achieve a high level of success in real estate, you have to play competitively, play cooperatively, and still be on your client's side. There are times when you must be your client's advocate above all else. You may have to ruffle the feathers of the other agents and brokers to protect and represent your client properly. You have to be willing to take the negative heat for the benefit of your client.

DEFUSING CONFRONTATION

In moments of confrontation or impasse, here is an effective question for any agent, especially a new one:

If you were in my position, what would you do?

This type of question defuses the confrontation quickly. The agent may give you an insight that you had not yet considered. We can get so focused on our point of view that we never consider another person's. It may also force the other agent to view the conflict from your perspective.

The best agents have the objectivity to stand away from a problem transaction and see all the pieces. They don't allow the emotions of all the parties to affect their advice and counsel. They have the ability to view the whole picture as well as each piece of the puzzle that makes up a transaction. Being able to work in that competitive environment without getting emotionally attached is essential. That marks the skill of a tremendous agent. That is also what the clients hire an agent to do.

> *Being able to work in that competitive environment without getting emotionally attached is essential.*

Stand Your Ground

Too often, agents err by getting too cooperative with others at their own expense. This can cause you to become a pushover for the other agents in the office. Others will lose respect for you over time if you fail to hold your ground. Other agents in the marketplace can often bully a new agent. Don't become intimidated by another agent.

There Is No Second Place

Setting your focus and mind-set for winning the listing or closing the sale is paramount in your early career. When I started in real estate sales in 1989, my mentality was the same as when I played sports. I was a professional racquetball player for a handful of years in my twenties. I started playing and competing in racquetball tournaments in grade school. My attitude at a racquetball tournament was always "There is no second place."

My focus was the first-place trophy. Anything short of that one mark was failure. I felt the same pain if I lost in the first round of a tournament or if I lost in the finals. To me there was no difference. There was only one trophy and that trophy was first. I was so focused on winning the whole tournament that I was not satisfied with anything else.

That mind-set and focus really helped me to achieve in real estate sales. I programmed those thoughts and attitudes into my mind early in my real estate career. I realized early on that in selling real estate "There is no second place."

The Importance of Preparation

Personal preparation before each competitive moment is essential. Take the time to prepare before each listing presentation, property showing, offer presentation, or negotiating moment. The time you invest analyzing the value of the home you are going to list or sell creates credibility and confidence in you. Too many agents do not do the preparation necessary to understand the properties and to know the market condition. You can never have too much information.

A final word on preparation for a client is this: Don't announce to the world that you are a new agent. The client you are representing doesn't need to know that fact. Furthermore, the other agents you are in competition with do not deserve that information. If you prepare well, they will never know you are in the first year of real estate.

WINNING IS THE ONLY THING

In the game of real estate sales you either get paid or you don't. Selling real estate is like that tough teacher you had in junior high who would not give out partial credit on your exam. She would give you credit only when you got it exactly right. Being a real estate agent is exactly like that. You get compensated only for the whole job—after that deal closes and title changes hands. That's the only place and time you get paid.

The Dead Deal

In coaching sessions, we often hear agents lament about all the work they do just to have the deal fall apart at the eleventh hour. We hear stories every week of how hard someone has worked and then, in one moment, the deal is dead. There are many moments in a real estate transaction when you could finish in second place. The seller might call you after you present a great listing presentation and say, "Susie, we really appreciate your coming out to share how to sell our home with us. We see you are extremely professional. We also think you would do a great job, *but* we have decided to go with someone else." At that moment the fact that you placed second to another agent gives you no comfort. It also provides zero income to you and your family. When you finish in second place enough times it will cause you to close a little harder.

Play to Win

What can you do to make sure you walk out of the listing appointment with the contract signed? Try using more probing questions in your appointments. Focus on handling every step completely and to the best of your ability. As a salesperson you have one moment to make the sale. Are you going to seize that moment? Are you going to push for the tape to win the gold? Now is the time to go for the winning shot!

There is always a critical moment in each selling situation. The question is "Are you going to recognize it and take advantage of the opportunity?" That moment, and what you do in that moment, will separate first place from second place. Seize that moment. Play to win.

BECOME INVOLVED IN THE NATIONAL ASSOCIATION OF REALTORS

The National Association of Realtors (NAR) is one of the most active lobbying groups in the country. A fantastic way to create connections in the real estate community is to become active in your local board. The board is always fighting for your rights as a real estate agent. It lobbies for the rights of the consumer as well. By becoming involved, you will learn a tremendous amount about the career you have selected. You will become more recognized in the real estate community. By gaining recognition, you will improve your impact when dealing with cooperating agents in a transaction. Being recognized as a leader on your board or being a Million Dollar Club member has its advantages. It gives you extra exposure to the public, your clients, and to the other agents on the board.

A fantastic way to create connections in the real estate community is to become active in your local board.

STRATEGIC PARTNERS

There are other key coworkers in a real estate agent's career—what I call "strategic partners." There are many professionals who provide services and generate revenue from a real estate transaction. The most common are mortgage originators, attorneys, home inspectors, repair people, and in many states, title companies and escrow companies.

Make Beautiful Music

Just as all members of a quality symphony orchestra perform with precision, you and your mortgage partner need to have that same precision. In a quality orchestra, violins flow with the brass section. The percussion section needs to be aware of its volume and not drown out the other instruments of the orchestra. The conductor will direct and guide the symphony so the desired result will be achieved. If one instrument in the orchestra is flat, the music does not have the same sound or lasting impact on the listener; one instrument can ruin the whole sound instantly. You, the real estate agent, need to take the role of the master conductor if you want to ensure the quality of your product. If one part of the transaction goes flat for your clients, you can lose future referrals from these clients. For many clients, it takes only one sour note to turn them off. Protect your business against that one bad note.

The Mortgage Originator

The most important individual to your career is the mortgage originator. Having your mortgage originator as a key strategic partner can dramatically improve your early real estate career. By being interdependent, the two of you can provide outstanding service.

Being able to work in harmony is essential. Mortgage originators and real estate agents need to work in concert to achieve the beautiful music of satisfied customers. There is nothing more pleasing than a phone call from a satisfied client, except perhaps a referral from a satisfied client. If you desire to create the symphonic music of referrals from your clients, you need to have the synchronized efforts of your mortgage partner.

Here are the five steps to protect your client when working with a mortgage originator:

1. **Select your mortgage partner well.** In every marketplace you will be able to form a partnership with many different mortgage originators. Make sure the partner you are pursuing can add true value to you and your staff. I recommend selecting one mortgage partner and sending business to that individual exclusively. You need to define clearly the criteria under which you will do business. I have seen enormous conflicts between real estate agents and mortgage partners because of differences in business philosophy.

I recommend selecting one mortgage partner and sending business to that individual exclusively.

You both need to understand clearly the philosophy of each other's business. Ask your partner the following questions:

How often do you both expect to be updated and in what form?
To whom do the updates go—to the agent or to the staff?
What happens in a crisis situation and whom do I call?
What does the mortgage originator have authority to handle on his own?

There is nothing worse for a real estate partner than to be blasted by a client without being warned by the mortgage partner. If you operate your business at a waltz tempo and your mortgage partner is dancing to a polka, that spells trouble. You and your mortgage partner need to be reading from the same sheet of music.

2. **Understand how mortgage partners run their business.** Some mortgage originators move from one crisis to the next. If the mortgage originator practices this type of crisis management, it will affect your business. You will get clients who expect crisis management to be the norm. Their emotional ups and downs will be greater and more pronounced.

The crisis mode will also affect the quality of the clients mortgage originators refer to you. You cannot allow people who are constantly in crisis mode to enter your business with regularity. Ultimately you will lose control of your business. The value your mortgage partners place on their time will also reflect on you. If they are not prudent with their time, they certainly won't be with yours and they won't teach clients the value of your time. Do you want clients who do not understand your value?

BUILDING RELATIONSHIPS WITH COWORKERS

Don't Be Like Lucy and Ethel

Many mortgage originators have haphazard systems. The process is not well defined from the moment a lead is generated until the close. Many mortgage originators have conveyer belt systems that look like an episode of the *I Love Lucy* show. Remember the episode in which Lucy and Ethel are working in a candy factory trying to box chocolates? The conveyer belt speeds up, and Lucy and Ethel can't keep up with the increased production. At first the chocolates drop off the belt. Then the women begin to eat the chocolates to try to keep up. Many mortgage originators run their businesses much like this episode. Poorly organized mortgage originators eat your current income and your past clients. They are eating your future income. They are eating your referral base. As hard as you work to generate clients you can ill afford to lose them at the end of the transaction. If your mortgage partners do not have a solid system, I guarantee they are eating your past clients and future business.

How well does your mortgage originator qualify prospects? You can work only with mortgage originators who control their clients. Any person you allow to become a mortgage partner will have some control over your business because of the clients she refers to you and the systems she has in place to run her business. Make sure your mortgage partner has the ability to control her clients because if she cannot control her clients, neither will you.

Remember, mortgage originators sometimes make the first impression, and therefore they can set the tone for the transaction.

Be Part of a Team

The goal is to create strategic partnerships with your affiliates and to help them increase their business, income, and market share. They must also share the same desire for you. The old days, where the agent was the uncompensated and unappreciated sales staff for the lender, title, and escrow industry, are over. We all need to raise our level of service to each other a notch or two. We all have to play together in harmony to achieve longtime clients and profitability. It is in all our best interests to work as a team so that we all can win.

3. **Expect your mortgage partner to send you some business.** You need to set a standard for the business the mortgage originator sends your way. This standard can be set by the number of transactions or in revenue dollars or both. The days of a mortgage partner saying, "Send me the deal and I will close it," are gone. As agents, we should require our partners to participate in the creation of our success. Your mortgage partner should be committed to helping you achieve your goals. He should account for some of the revenue generated in your business.

4. **Make sure your mortgage partner's conveyer belt is solid.** Your business is intertwined with your mortgage partner's. If they have weak systems, your clients will know it. Weak systems also cause more strain emotionally for agents, lenders, and clients. If your partners do not have a solid system, or conveyer belt, for their business, you will be adversely affected. You will either need to help them yourself or find someone to help them construct and manage their system properly.

5. **Make sure your partner is committed to improvement and change.** We all need to be changing and growing. The competition will leave us behind if we don't. Your partner must be working to stay on the cutting edge of the mortgage business. If your partner is not willing to change and grow, search for a new partner. The changes in our industry will only accelerate as we move forward. We have seen tremendous growth in technology in the last three to four years. Your partner needs to embrace the technology revolution.

Working daily on your education will cause you to stay ahead of your competition and enable you to enjoy life at a higher level.

Create a Mastermind Alliance

You need to have what Napoleon Hill used to call a "mastermind alliance." According to Hill, a mastermind alliance is a "coordination of knowledge and effort, in a spirit of harmony, between two or more people, for the attainment of a definite purpose." Having at least one other person whom you can labor with and problem-solve with is essential. You can create a frenzy of ideas and excitement by working in concert with another like-minded person whose desire is mutually beneficial. Everyone needs a few good mastermind alliances. I have a few such partners. I have learned a tremendous amount from my mastermind alliances. We all have a strong focus to improve ourselves daily. When we get together we all know we will learn. Your partner needs to be committed to being a lifelong learner.

You and your partners must commit to being lifelong learners. Time dedicated to self-education has to be a scheduled daily activity. Your formal education will allow you to make a living. Your personal or self-education will position you to make a fortune. Becoming highly self-educated will allow you to craft a lifestyle of your dreams. Working daily on your education will cause you to stay ahead of your competition and enable you to enjoy life at a higher level.

Your mortgage partners need to have the same commitment to educating themselves. If they do not, you will leave them behind.

ORCHESTRATE YOUR CLOSINGS

The true goal is to make beautiful music for your clients by putting a smooth, professional, and unemotional closing together. Success starts with the proper selection of the instruments and the players. You must be sure everyone is reading from the same set of sheet music. Of course, you need to make sure your partner is as committed to practicing as you are. Lastly, remember you are the conductor. Ultimately you are responsible for how the music is played. You know what the music should sound like. Do not compromise. If you do, you will have a hard time getting the concert hall filled in the future. Finally, we are all looking for an encore. The encore makes the growth in your career easier. The goal is to create clients who are so happy that they send you referrals.

BUILD RESPECT AND RECOGNITION

Building a bridge to the other agents in your office and the co-op agents in your marketplace takes time. You will not get recognized overnight. It will take you a number of years to earn the respect and recognition that you desire. Consistently attend events put on by the board and work cooperatively with other agents. Don't be affected by the negative talk of other agents. Stick to building the key relationships that will impact your business and life.

CHOOSE THE COMPANY YOU KEEP

Successful people spend time with only four groups of people:

> people they can learn from
> people they can have fun with
> people they can make money with
> people they can teach

Spend your time only with people from these four groups and you will be on your way to the top.

CHAPTER 5

DEVELOPING RELATIONSHIPS WITH CLIENTS

One of the most difficult challenges for you as a new agent is to create a client relationship with prospects, convincing them that you are the answer to their problems. You don't yet possess the confidence or skill to convert the best prospects all the time. In this chapter we take a look at the different types of clients you will encounter and consider the importance of good communication in nurturing the client-agent relationship.

The way to end up with wonderful clients and satisfied clients is to select them correctly in the first place.

SELECT THE RIGHT CLIENTS

The most important element in creating a solid client relationship is selecting the right client in the first place. I believe that selecting the right client leads to greater success. Too often we work with people who don't have enough desire or motivation for us to do business with them. As a new agent, you are tempted to work with any warm body that is on the phone. (Many agents' idea of a lead is a human being who creates condensation on a piece of glass held close to his mouth.) However, the way to end up with wonderful clients and satisfied clients is to select them correctly in the first place.

Know When to Walk Away

The path to failure is trying to please everyone with whom you come in contact. When I was in sales, my belief was that I was not put on this earth to help everyone buy and sell. I could not help everyone who showed up. By excluding people, I was able to define and develop better, more loyal clients.

Many of the people we meet are unreasonable and should not be anyone's clients. They become a burden on any agent's time and attention. Our job is to recognize the low probability of their ever becoming quality clients and to take the necessary action of declining to work with them. What a great feeling to be courageous enough to walk away from someone who would otherwise cause my staff and me great frustration. Few agents ever experience the joy of doing business on their own terms, because they compromise their philosophy and belief system for dollars.

THE FOUR TYPES OF CLIENTS

Here are four different categories of clients with whom you will find yourself working on a regular basis:

Terrific Clients

Most salespeople are just looking for the sale. A professional salesperson is always on the lookout for terrific clients. Terrific clients

- respect people who are highly skilled at their profession
- listen to advice and guidance that is presented well and that has supporting documentation

- open up about their goals and desires for real estate and their expectation for service

---

The Magical Sixth Sense of Truth

As a new agent one disadvantage you have is that you have not yet developed the magical sixth sense of truth. Your sixth sense of truth is activated when prospects are not being honest with you, when they don't fully disclose their "hang-ups" in selling their home. They hesitate when you ask them if they are working with another agent. You sense that they have not disclosed the extent of their financial picture and find out later there was a bankruptcy two years ago.

You will always know where terrific clients stand; they don't play "hide the ball." You are not the enemy. You and the terrific clients will be on the same team, working toward a common goal. They also will be fantastic referral sources for your business.

No-Clue Clients

No-clue clients live in a dream world. It is difficult to get them to look at the facts and figures that might upset the fantasy world in which they live. These clients really don't want to know the truth that their homes are worth 15 percent less than they think. Each one believes that she will land the one buyer who will pay dramatically above fair market value. Unless the no-clue client has an extremely high motivation, such as a job transfer, divorce, or new children, you will have no sale. If the bottom line is that they *have to* move, you may be able to bring them to reality. In that case, the no-clue client could eventually make progress toward becoming the terrific client.

Information-Only Clients

These people just want information and expertise from you. They have no intention of creating a relationship of trust; you are there only to provide

Unless the no-clue client has an extremely high motivation, such as a job transfer, divorce, or new children, you will have no sale.

your knowledge. The information-only client truly believes this approach is justified. He also believes that if you are foolish enough to give your knowledge for free, that's your problem. These clients will take your knowledge and either use it to buy or sell on their own or give it to a friend or family member who doesn't have your skill level and put the business into that person's hands.

Information-only clients will rarely answer direct questions. They are evasive and will challenge your knowledge, beliefs, advice, fees, and services. Ultimately, these challenges will become their justification for not working with you. Sometimes they get offended at your questions. Their belief is that the expertise they can get out of you is useful, but their way is better.

Distrust-Everyone Clients

These clients believe

- everyone is out to get them
- everyone is trying to reach into their back pockets
- every question you ask comes with its own hidden agenda
- what you are really looking for is the weak point that will allow you to destroy them

Even when, with a lot of care and attention, you manage to win these people over, if you or your team makes one honest error, these clients will be gone. This occurs because they believe that all their negative experiences are just part of a big conspiracy against them.

THE LAW OF ATTRACTION

The Law of Attraction states that we will attract what we are looking for or we will attract what we become. "Like will attract like." I used this law in making decisions regularly with regard to clients. It kept me out of many potential problem-client situations.

Stop the Flow of Problem Clients

Clients who are disrespectful and uncooperative will refer people like themselves to you. I believe people socialize with people like themselves. This type of person stretches your patience and puts a damper on your passion for this career. Do you honestly want more of this type of client? Stop the flow of problem clients. Resolve right now to turn down all clients who demand high effort and energy to maintain.

Work Only with Terrific Clients

Selecting and excluding people at the outset is the best way to ensure good client relations. Many problems with clients are caused not by external events or by deficiencies in our interpersonal skills but by the perceptions and expectations of the clients themselves. Some people just don't make good clients.

Create a strong interview process so that you can quickly and efficiently remove the problem prospects before they get inside your inner circle. The price you pay for letting them inside is wasted time, wasted energy, emotional drain, and certainly loss of revenue for you. Focus on working only with terrific clients. You'll be amazed at the increased income and job satisfaction you will enjoy.

High-Maintenance Clients

Problem clients remind me of the scene in the great Billy Crystal–Meg Ryan movie *When Harry Met Sally.* They are at dinner and Billy says to Meg, "You are the worst type of woman. You are a high-maintenance woman who actually thinks she is low maintenance." Many of your clients, if not screened properly, will be like Meg Ryan's character in the movie. They will be high maintenance when they think they are low maintenance.

"BEING THERE"

There is one myth we need to address about clients and prospects and our service as real estate agents. For thirty years we have been taught that as real estate agents we must be there for our clients. I hear that all the time from agents across North America, "I want to be there for my clients." What does "be there" mean? Does "be there" mean we are available twenty-four hours a day, seven days a week? Does it mean that we miss soccer games, tee-ball games, or piano recitals? For many agents that is exactly what it means.

Many of us equate access with service. We have been trained for years that access is the primary vehicle of customer service. We feel we need to be there for our clients. We grant them access to our lives whenever they want it. They can, and will, take over our business, and our lives, if we let them.

SEPARATE ACCESS FROM CUSTOMER SERVICE

I want to share with you a new concept: *Access has nothing to do with customer service.* There are many professionals we do business with who are less than accessible. A skilled doctor cannot be contacted via phone and certainly will not respond within minutes. A skilled doctor is busy with other patients and will get back to the caller during the course of the day. A professional attorney may be in court, in conference, or taking a deposition. When we need to contact them, we don't expect them to return our call immediately. I would certainly question the ability of either of these two professionals if either got back to me right away. Why is it that being phone-available is like a badge of honor for a real estate agent?

Pushing the Wheelbarrow

Ben Franklin said, "If you want a job done right, ask a busy man to do it." Mr. Franklin understood the perception of industrious diligence. He also understood human nature. When Ben Franklin was a young printer he was seen daily on Market Street at noon pushing a wheelbarrow stacked with reams of paper. After becoming successful he confessed that the paper was not in the wheelbarrow because it needed to go somewhere; it was there to promote Ben as a busy man. He created a public perception of value through his daily wheelbarrow walk!

If we choose to meet with clients at all hours of the day and night, they begin to wonder if we have any other clients. We are not promoting being a busy real estate agent. We are promoting that we are not busy or skillful. In order to clearly separate access from customer service, here are a few steps:

Strategy 1: Set Boundaries

Your clients will respect you if you set specific boundaries. Set boundaries on your time away from selling real estate—your personal time. Take out the days off, the family activities, the time with your spouse, and the time for you. Do that before the week begins. The most effective way to lay out boundaries is to execute a set schedule. A set schedule allows you to make each week exactly the same as the week before.

Create specific boundaries by taking your home phone number off your business card. Professionals in other disciplines seldom give out their home number. Turn your cell phone and pager off at specific times each evening.

Strategy 2: Treat Everything as an Appointment

Once you have set boundaries, establish the goal of treating everything as an appointment. Quality time with your family is the most important appointment you have. Don't infringe on this important time. Don't break your personal appointments such as exercising, reading, and relaxing.

You also have appointments in your workday. You have appointments to prospect and to follow up on leads. These time slots will have a tendency to get pushed out of the way by clients. If you allow that to happen, you will see a drop in business within ninety days, when you have no closings. It's easy to let other things take precedence over those prospecting and lead follow-up appointments, but you must overcome the urge to take care of clients in those times.

Strategy 3: Set Specific Times to Return Calls

Many of the calls we get are just not that critical. Clients are trying to give us information they deem as urgent. These calls are rarely emergencies and seldom must be handled right now. Most calls can wait a few hours to address. Set specific times when you return calls, say, once in the late morning and again toward the end of the day. Let people know that you are in appointments and you will be returning calls at specific times.

> *Set specific times when you return calls, say, once in the late morning and again toward the end of the day.*

PROVIDE VALUE FOR YOUR CLIENT

Now that we have examined a few myths about customers and customer service, we need to look at what to do to provide value for your prospects and clients. Value is created by establishing and maintaining good communication with your buyer or seller and by developing good questioning skills.

Limit Instant Access

You need to separate the concept of access from customer service. Customer service is about getting the job done well. Although your client would prefer total immediate access, they will, in the final analysis, remember your professionalism. Become respected like your doctor, dentist, or attorney. Limit the instant access you grant to people. Don't be fooled by the old access model of total customer service for real estate. To stay competitive with all the changes in the real estate industry, you need to raise the bar on service and professionalism. Access is not in either of these categories.

EFFECTIVE COMMUNICATION

One of the key elements of keeping a good prospect or client is effective and consistent communication.

Most of your clients could accept a few reasons for the home not selling. What is unforgivable is silence . . . on your part. Most listing agents become embarrassed or disappointed that the listing has not sold after several weeks so they stop all regular contact with their client. They are afraid of confrontation or a few tough questions, so they have no conversation at all. When a home is on the market for a long time, the worst remedy is no communication.

When to Communicate with Sellers

Sellers you represent should be called weekly. Select a set time each week when you will call all your sellers. Our time was Friday afternoon between 2:30 and 3:30 p.m. This way sellers know exactly when you are going to call. If they are not home, leave an encouraging and informative message.

What You Don't Know Can't Convince You

The value of good communication cannot be stressed enough. We might have to convince the seller she is overpriced and that a price reduction should be considered. But, if we just show up one day after no contact for thirty days and talk price reduction, we will rarely achieve a lowered price. The reason homes don't sell for months on end is always the price; an adjusted price will usually fix whatever ails the transaction. If we don't communicate this basic fact of real estate to the seller, she will have no reason to understand the importance of a price reduction.

The key is to update sellers on the activity of their property. Here is what to share with them:

1. **Market activity for the week:** Indicate the number of homes that went pending in their area at their price range. This will help you in achieving price reductions later on.

2. **Your office activity and your activity:** This confirms that they made the right selection of agent and company. It also shows there is activity in the marketplace.

3. **Specific efforts you made to get their home sold:**

   - Did you show it?
   - What ads ran for the property?
   - What type of prospecting and how much prospecting did you do to generate new clients?
   - Did you do a broker open house and how many people came?
   - Was there any interest in showing it by other agents?
   - How many buyer calls did you receive on the property?

4. **The marketing plan for next week:** Most sellers want to know what to expect from you.

"They pounded a sign in the yard and I never heard from them again."

As a specialist for years in selling expired listings, I got an earful at most listing presentations about the communication from the previous agent. Expired listings are properties that were listed with another agent or broker. Property listings are signed for a specific term and when that term is complete and the property isn't sold, the listings are deemed expired. Lack of communication was the biggest complaint from the seller whose listing had expired. It wasn't that the home did not sell; it was the quality and quantity of the communication. I heard hundreds of times, "They pounded a sign in the yard and I never heard from them again."

5. **The feedback from the showings:** One of the reasons we did updates to our sellers toward the end of the week was that it allowed us
a couple of days to collect feedback from the agents who showed the
property. There is an element of excitement for the seller when he
comes home and a business card is sitting on the kitchen table. This
business card from another agent alerts you that a showing was completed. The seller immediately wants to know if the prospective buyer
liked the home.

   We always tried to get feedback from other agents to share with
our seller. This also enabled us to have a few extra sets of eyes with
regard to the property's condition and price. We used the other agents'
evaluations to help us retrieve future price reductions if required.

By contacting your sellers weekly, you increase the level of respect and trust
they have for you. You will avoid the biggest frustration for your sellers—lack
of communication.

When to Communicate with Buyers

Buyer clients have communication needs as well. Regular contact with a highly
motivated buyer builds trust. A buyer who is looking to purchase now needs a
lot of communication, care, and attention. There is no such thing as too much
communication for this type of buyer. You can't call them frequently enough.
When a buyer is extremely anxious to purchase a home, call her every day. Call
her just to say, "I have looked at the hot sheet of new homes on the market today twice. There are no new properties that meet your criteria. Let's hope that
tomorrow there will be something new. Thanks for the opportunity to serve
you. Have a great day."

This approach repeated day after day will let your buyers know that nothing
will get by you. Demonstrate that you are an expert and a professional and they
will come to know that they hired the right person to represent them. You will not
receive that call from the buyer to tell you she found another house over the weekend at an open house and purchased it from the agent who was holding it. That is
one of the most gut-wrenching calls an agent can receive. All that time, effort, and

energy you invested to earn a commission has vaporized. Constant and consistent communication is the best insurance policy against that painful experience.

A buyer who is looking to purchase now needs a lot of communication, care, and attention. There is no such thing as too much communication for this type of buyer.

Communicate During the Closing Process

Your communication doesn't stop after you sell a house, whether it was your listing or not. Once you accomplish that goal you must still communicate with the client weekly through the closing process. To help you develop a long-term client relationship, your communication should be ongoing and helpful.

During this period there are inspections, repairs, and appraisals of the home for value, and often title challenges or even loan problems. Our job is to communicate fully with all parties in every transaction that we represent. In addition, we have a responsibility to communicate with the other parties who facilitate the transaction, such as the other agent, title company representative, loan officer, attorneys, appraisers, home inspectors, and repair contractors.

Happy Clients Generate Referrals

The goal for anyone in a sales profession is to generate referrals from their clients. Those referrals are the evidence that the job was done professionally. They also provide an excellent source of revenue to your business long term. Remember that it costs ten times as much to find a new client than to retain the client with whom you have already done business. Communication is a huge factor in retention.

Communicate After Closing

Most agents rarely call their clients after the transaction closes. The National Association of Realtors did a study recently. They interviewed home buyers and sellers and found out 80 percent of the consumers never went back to their original agent for one reason . . . the agent never called them again. Now isn't that fascinating? As a new agent who is going to be a professional and call your clients regularly, you have a tremendous opportunity. You can retain your clients and acquire the clients of many other agents because those agents are not going to be doing what you will do.

Communicate After Transfer of Title

Let me outline a plan that will connect you with your clients for life. The mainstay of the plan is personal contact with the client. This plan starts right after the close and transfer of title.

1. You call your client one day after the closing and thank her for the opportunity to serve her. Ask if there is anything she needs from you.
2. Call her the fifth day after closing and see how the move went. Did she live through the process? How is she settling in? Did she find anything not quite right with the home that she needs your assistance to solve? Thank her again for the opportunity to serve her. Then ask her for referrals. Here is a great script:

   > Betty, I am sure all your friends and coworkers are every excited about your move into your new home. In your conversations has anyone mentioned wanting to make a move like you have just done? Please keep me in mind when they do. My business is built on referrals from great clients like you.

3. Repeat this process about two weeks after the close and thirty days after the property closes. By continuing to communicate after closing, you are adding value. Great salespeople are always adding more value

than they receive in income from a sales transaction. In the client's mind the sale was made weeks ago and your compensation happened then. He is amazed that after you've been paid you'd call to see how he is doing. The more you follow up after the close, the more likely the chance that the client will separate you as a person from the commission you were paid.

Express Your Concern

Imagine how you would feel if that salesperson who sold you the new car called you in a week to see if you were enjoying it! You would feel totally different about that salesperson. You would say, "He got paid for the sale, but he is still calling to check on me. He is really concerned about me. He is more focused on my satisfaction than the money." Your clients will feel the same way about you when you call after the close.

Don't Forget to Keep in Touch with Past Clients

A great salesperson is never done providing service and value to his customers. You want to continue this process of follow-up at least twice a year for the rest of your career. Don't make the mistake that many agents make early in their career and not call your past clients. I meet agents daily who are five, ten, even twenty years in the business who are not doing this simple past client follow-up. They have to go out and find new clients daily because they did not care for their past clients. It's like the rancher who continues to bring cattle into the barn but never checks to close the back door of the barn. He will always have to bring in more cattle to feed his family. Don't make the error that most agents make. Start to follow up and build that solid relationship with your past clients today.

The basic precept for a terrific past client relationship is consistency of communication. You will need to communicate regularly with your past clients and sphere of influence. Your "sphere of influence" is all the people that you know. At a minimum you should send them something every sixty days. That something could be a newsletter informing them of real estate activity, sales, and trends. The newsletter could be delivered via snail mail or electronically.

There are numerous low-cost newsletters that can be quickly edited to reflect your tastes and style. I think the *Realty Times* has a low-cost version that is quite good as a basic newsletter.

You then need to establish a frequent calling pattern to contact your sphere—which, of course, includes past clients. In the end, the personal contact, either face-to-face or phone-to-phone, will yield the best results in terms of client retention and client referrals. Too many agents fail the personal contact rules and rely solely on e-mail or snail mail to generate repeat and referral business. Don't make their mistake!

DEVELOP YOUR QUESTIONING SKILLS

The last essential skill in developing strong relationships with your clients is the ability to ask probing questions. The best way to build trust and be recognized as the expert is to ask questions. Highly skilled salespeople understand the power of questions.

The questions you ask lead to or away from the sale. For too long we have been led to believe that highly successful salespeople are fast-talking motormouths who can talk someone into buying. "Gary is such a great talker he could sell a refrigerator to an Eskimo." A great salesperson, however, will question the client or prospect completely and realize that an Eskimo has no need to purchase that refrigerator—a space heater might be something she really needs.

The best way to build trust and be recognized as the expert is to ask questions.

As a future top gun agent, your ability to question your prospects and clients will enable you to help them achieve their objectives. You will not be able to help them achieve their goals if you don't know what those goals are.

Some key questions that are often overlooked by agents are

> Why are you moving?
> What are you trying to accomplish by moving?
> Where are you hoping to move to?
> How soon do you want to be in your new home?
> Describe for me the home you want to live in?
> Ultimately, what will a move into the home you described do for
> your family?

The last question is significant because in the answer you will find the feeling, emotion, or value your clients attach to the move. You may discover the driving passion underlying why they are making a decision to move. With an understanding of that feeling, you will be able to help your clients meet their objective.

GO FOR FIRST PLACE

Building strong relationships with clients and prospects will increase the speed at which you reach the top in real estate sales. Having the mind-set to play for first place, never settling for second, will help you avoid many of the frustrations in working on 100 percent commission.

CHAPTER 6

FINDING MENTORS

According to *Webster's* dictionary, a mentor is a "guide or trusted counselor or teacher." You can have mentors for different areas of your life. You could have a mentor for your health, for your business, or for your spiritual life.

Mentors help you define your philosophy of life, develop your skills, and lay out a plan for you. An effective mentor should be an outstanding role model whose lead and guidance you are honored to follow. She should be someone you envision being like in the future. A true mentor is there to come alongside you and show you the ropes, helping you formulate your goals and assisting you in your plan to achieve those goals. She is also there to correct you when you have taken a wrong turn and to map out for you a more effective approach.

An effective mentor should be an outstanding role model whose lead and guidance you are honored to follow.

AVOID CHOOSING A MENTOR ON THE BASIS OF "THE SHOW"

One of the most challenging steps for a new agent to take is the selection of the right mentor. Too often you can be lured into believing a particular person would be a quality mentor and later discover, with great disappointment, it was a mistake. As a new agent, you can easily be influenced by someone who appears to be an expert or "top gun" agent. We see the agents who drive expensive cars and live in big houses and conclude that we want to be just like them. In many cases you would feel differently if you knew the whole truth. Some of these agents are paying an incredible price to live "the show" and often spend too much time at work, investing very little in their family or spouse. They may be in debt up to their eyeballs to keep "the show" going. As they often say in Texas, "Big hat, no cattle." There can be a lot of show with little substance behind it.

THE MYTH OF SALES VOLUME

As agents, we become caught up in the myth of sales volume. Belief in this myth causes some of the greatest damage in this industry. Do not be fooled by the sales volume myth. More agents have gone down in flames chasing their sales volume than from any other myth in real estate.

We glorify the agents with high sales volume and promote and encourage other agents to be more like them. We award agents and offices based on sales volume, with little regard to the other factors that make up success in careers and lives. New agents look on in reverence, thinking the person who has the most production in sales volume is the example to follow. I would like to take an objective look at the true value of sales volume and point out some other factors to keep in mind when evaluating your business and other agents when considering a mentor. These are also questions you will need to answer about your own business someday.

We need to see beyond "the show" to the real truth. I believe that ultimately character counts far more then the plaques and awards. When we strip everything away, it is not about the plaque. We don't want to end up saying, "I ran the race, I got the T-shirt, what's next?" Let's take a look at six important questions. I believe you will come away with a different perspective on sales volume.

Consider These Questions When Selecting a Mentor

1. Is the better salesperson the one with more sales volume or the one with more sale units sold and closed?

2. When does profitability enter into the picture and does it have any importance?

3. Should the amount of time actually worked be considered when evaluating an agent's ability?

4. What is the true quality of life for the agent, in terms of health, time worked, time off, stress, and so on?

5. How does the quality of service delivered to clients factor in?

6. Is she taking steps to achieve financial independence based on her own definition of success?

IS THE BETTER SALESPERSON THE ONE WITH THE HIGHER SALES VOLUME OR THE ONE WITH MORE SALE UNITS SOLD AND CLOSED?

Clearly they both possess merit for what they do. However, we know historically that the one with the highest sales volume is traditionally placed on a pedestal, while the one with the most units sold is placed only halfway up.

In some cases, sales volume can reflect the value of the market, not the value of the agent. For example, one agent's average price range is $100,000, so his average commission check is $3,000. This agent closes sixty-five deals a year and earns a gross commission of $195,000. Across town there is another agent with an average price of homes sold of $300,000 and an average commission check amounting to $9,000. This agent closes twenty-five transactions a year and earns a gross commission of $225,000. Who has more options in his business and just may be a better salesperson?

I think there are strengths to both. The agent who does sixty-five deals only needs to raise his sales price because he already demonstrated that he is able to achieve sixty-five closed sales per year. He understands the process and if he has set up his business properly he only needs to apply his philosophy of business in a higher sales price range to earn more income. He also did almost three times as many transactions.

Usually the agent with the higher average commission receives all the rewards from peers, brokers, owners, and the company. The second agent is held in high esteem because he was the high producer in the office. This agent has a good business but sold only two homes per month (by most sales standards this is not earth-shattering). This agent needs to learn how to close more transactions to increase his business. Which one really has a business that is poised to go to the next level?

WHEN DOES PROFITABILITY ENTER INTO THE PICTURE AND DOES IT HAVE ANY IMPORTANCE?

In my career of selling real estate, coaching, and speaking, I have met many agents who are making a very high gross income but have little net income.

Every New Idea Must Pay for Itself

Some agents invest all their income back into their business in the form of gimmicks, marketing, gifts, mailings, advertising, and overpaying staff. They make decisions based on the idea that if they get one more transaction per month it will pay for this new gimmick. The unfortunate thing is that they evaluate many parts of their business this same way. Suddenly they need nearly all they make monthly just to cover these gimmicks. Every new idea must pay for itself as well as generate a satisfactory profit. I expected at least a tenfold return for any investment. If I spent $1,000 on a new idea, I planned to receive $10,000 in return from it.

The Real Cost of a Promotional Idea

Most agents do not factor their time, or the staff's time, into the cost of a new idea. That is a legitimate cost that must be included. For example, the cost to mail something is not just the cost of the stamp. It's the cost of the letterhead, envelope, stamp, label, staff time to prepare it, and your time to oversee the process. That's the overall cost and you should demand a tenfold return.

You must evaluate each program so that you remain profitable. We all work too hard to earn wages without profits. The best mentors understand the profit formula in real estate. They clearly watch and evaluate the cost of their business. This mentor will be of great value to your career.

> *The best mentors understand the profit formula in real estate. They clearly watch and evaluate the cost of their business.*

Profits Go Farther Than Wages

Many agents have bought themselves a job and never make a profit. A wise man once said, "Profits are better than wages." Profits are the dollars you have left after you pay your wages and all your bills. Profits, when invested, beget more profits, creating financial independence. Wages merely cover the monthly bills.

Agents need to view the whole picture: the gross and the net. To find the best measure of your profitability after all the hype of sales volume, gross commission earned, and all the other ego-stroking we do, look at line 32 on your federal tax return. That is where you come face-to-face with reality—what you truly made for all your efforts last year. Do not kid yourself! Too often agents talk about what they grossed in income. You will hear the term GCI, or gross commission income. That term means only what you brought in, not what you net—get to live on, invest, and spend. Don't get faked out so easily! What you are taxed on is what you really made. What you really made is after your expenses.

SHOULD THE AMOUNT OF TIME ACTUALLY WORKED BE CONSIDERED WHEN EVALUATING AN AGENT'S ABILITY?

I know many agents who work six to seven days a week in order to generate their income. If they factored in the actual time worked versus what they earned, they would feel sick, because their actual per-hour wage is so disappointing. In fact, if you asked them if they would do what they do for that hourly wage, they would say, "No."

If you want a dose of reality, divide your hours worked into line 32 on your federal income tax form. That is what you truly made per hour. That is what you would earn if you were an employee. For some agents, this exercise is too scary to even imagine. But you may want to ask yourself this tough question: Do you want to make that again this year?

Work Less, Do More

We all can do more in less time. In my fourth year of real estate sales, I switched to a four-day workweek, Monday through Thursday. My production increased more than 30 percent each successive year. I reduced my time working by at least one full day while showing increases in after-tax earnings. My skills improved exponentially, and my focus and concentration intensified. I also reclaimed my life for my family and myself. I was able to spend three days a week with my family. I also increased my time investment in personal development, which leads me to the next question.

WHAT IS THE TRUE QUALITY OF LIFE FOR THE AGENT IN TERMS OF HEALTH, TIME WORKED, TIME OFF, STRESS, AND SO ON?

You cannot be a seven-days-a-week wonder forever. At some point you need to reclaim your life. You have to control your clients and the other agents. My philosophy is that earning large sums of money is the easiest area of your life to improve. However, working to improve your spiritual, mental, physical, and family areas is far more challenging.

Give Your Time Off the Same Value as Your Work Time

When you schedule your time off and place the same value on it as you do on your work time, you will have the opportunity to reclaim your life. Your productivity will increase dramatically during your work time. The value of my time with my family is worth more than my work time. If you have that philosophy, you will focus on your family when away from work and focus on work when at work. While many agents are at work, they think they should be at home. When they are at home, they are mentally reviewing their work rather than focusing on their spouse and children. Wherever you are, be there!

> ## *The value of my time with my family is worth more than my work time.*

HOW DOES QUALITY OF SERVICE DELIVERED TO CLIENTS FACTOR IN?

To create a sustainable business you need to take care of your clients. The agent who continually works with new clients and rarely gets referrals or repeat business is lacking in service. Although we all need to spend some of our day finding new clients, realize that long-term success comes from repeat and referral business from clients who are already sold on our service. Are you doing the job you were hired to do? Do you provide the best service you can in your present marketplace?

The Product You Are Selling Is Yourself

Part of providing better customer service is improving your product. The product you are selling is first and foremost yourself. If you are not spending significant amounts of time improving yourself, your competitors will eventually pass you. Jim Rohn reminds us that you need to work as hard on yourself as you do on your job. Following this advice will lead you to both personal and professional greatness. If you are not investing at least half an hour a day in personal development, you will be left behind.

Spend Time Investing in Yourself

When I entered real estate sales in 1989, I started in a very successful office where all the agents were veterans of ten years and more. Most of the agents were not spending time in personal development of their own lives. This resulted in my being the top agent in the office by my third year in the business. In another short period of time I was in the top ten in a four-state region of over 1,400 agents.

I share this not to brag, but to encourage. If you spend the time to invest in yourself you will achieve the same results. Your personal education will have as much to do with your future success as anything else you do. My biggest challenge in life is getting the hours that I need daily in personal development to stay ahead of my coaches, my clients, and the real estate community. Your mentor also has to be focused on personal growth.

Great mentors will always be spending time in personal development. They will allot time weekly to improving themselves. This type of a mentor will be able to help you long term. A mentor who does not want to improve will be of little value after a few years and in that situation the master will, in the near future, become the student.

ARE YOU TAKING STEPS TO ACHIEVE FINANCIAL INDEPENDENCE BASED ON YOUR OWN DEFINITION OF SUCCESS?

Everyone has her own definition of what constitutes financial independence. Take the time to clearly define yours. Plan how you are going to get from where you are today to where you want to be. Your mentor can help you with your plan, but make sure your mentor has a plan as well. Unfortunately, too many people fail to plan their future.

Include Savings in Your Plan

Often the agents with the highest gross commission save and invest little or no money. They believe there is always tomorrow, and if they could just earn more they could then save more, but they have no plan for how they will do that. We often spend to make up for shortcomings in our unbalanced lives. We need to create a plan that includes savings so we can achieve financial independence.

Develop the discipline to save right now, today. Saving does not get easier when the numbers get bigger. Instead, the want list gets longer because you think you deserve what you want and can afford it. Only you control the destiny of your money. You must create that savings plan today.

Financial Independence Is a Measure of Success

Our goal in life should be to be financially independent. We should all have the desire to amass enough assets to retire comfortably by living off the income or interest they generate. When we get the financial issue out of the way, we can really begin to live life to the fullest.

Financial independence is the true measure of success in the real estate business. In fact, it is the measure of success in any business. Why should we as real estate agents be any different?

Most people don't know how to achieve financial independence because they don't have the key to one important secret. But before I reveal this secret I will tell you that in my travels as an international speaker in sales and real estate, I have given presentations before audiences on five continents in the last few years. I have met hundreds of thousands of real estate agents. And out of those hundreds of thousands of agents, every one started their real estate career with the goal of financial independence. It is that important.

Now, the secret to achieving financial independence is having a clear definition of *what it means to you*. Too frequently we have a general definition but not a specific one. Everyone knows the dictionary's definition of "financial independence": the ability to live off our net assets. But few people stop to think about its significance. The real definition of financial independence boils down to a number. It is at its core an amount of money—the amount of money that will allow you to choose your own lifestyle and live happily and comfortably with that choice. The real question is what's your number and are you working toward it?

SELECTING THE RIGHT MENTOR

The ideal mentor possesses many different qualities. If you cannot find one person who has them all, select several mentors who, combined, possess all the guidance you need.

Look for a person who is several levels above your present situation. The biggest producer in the company, for example, may be exciting, but could be a very poor choice. Often, these individuals have been at the top so long they have forgotten how they did it. The game of real estate sales may have changed since they where climbing the ladder. On the other hand, if you identify a person just a few levels above you, you are more apt to find a more relevant and helpful mentor. You also want to select someone who is growing, not stagnant. If you determine that he is not growing, you will have to change mentors in the near future.

You want to select someone who is growing, not stagnant.

QUESTIONS TO ASK A MENTOR

When you approach people about being your mentor, ask them some key questions:

1. **What are the essential skills to achieve peak performance in real estate sales?** This question will assess prospective mentors' knowledge of real estate sales. The key word is *skills*. Many agents you ask will not mention true skills such as prospecting, knowing your

scripts, effective lead follow-up techniques, managing the revenue, and controlling expenses. You will hear answers as superficial as: You have to like being around people or You have to be available for your clients to service them. These are not skills, they are feelings, and you can't build replication and increased revenue in your business based on feelings.

2. **What are some of the obstacles I am going to face?** These obstacles need to be identified and defined in order for you to be prepared to face them. A good follow-up question here would be "What could I specifically learn about obstacles from your experience in real estate sales?"

3. **What resources are available that will better ensure my growth and success?** Your prospective mentor should be able to tell you about specific classes, tapes, books, scripts, and coaching.

4. **What expertise did you have from your past that helped you develop the skill to excel?**

5. **How did you decide to enter real estate?** At this point they might share with you a little of their personal history and philosophy regarding real estate sales. This will allow you to gauge the depth of their success in life.

6. **What are your goals and how do you plan to achieve them?** The answer will tell you how big a thinker they are right now. You always want to hang out with big thinkers because they make you think bigger. Don't spend your time with people who only want to make enough money to buy a new piece of furniture. They may be ahead of you today, but very shortly they will be behind you.

Be the Lead Dog

There is an old saying: "The only dog in a dog sled team that gets to see the world is the lead dog." The others behind the lead dog all have the same view: the others' behinds. You were created to take the lead so you can control your income. Because you are going to have the same view for a while, make sure at least you are moving forward.

7. **How can I help you achieve your goals?** When you ask this question you may get a blank stare because most potential mentors have probably never been asked such a question. Remain silent and wait for their answer. You have to ask this because you will learn more while helping them than you will on your own. The more experience and opportunities you have, the more quickly you will learn and grow.

8. **Can I share my goals with you?** In order to share your goals, you first need to have some. We are going to teach you in depth how to create solid, compelling goals. Good follow-up questions are

What do you think of my goals?
Would you help me achieve them?

These questions will give you feedback about your goals. They will cause the mentor candidates to evaluate their own level of involvement. You will learn right away if they are the right person for you. I would be cautious about those individuals who want to think about it for a week. They either have the desire to do it or they don't. They either have a passion to invest in others or they do not.

HOW TO ASK SOMEONE TO BE YOUR MENTOR

Once you have defined and identified a mentor, what is the next step? At this point I would encourage an indirect approach. You don't go up to someone who you have decided would be a great mentor and say, "Here I am." Share with the potential mentor how valuable his advice has been and how much you have already learned. People appreciate hearing that their counsel helped you better define your goals and objectives.

A True Mentor Sees What You Can Become

I speak, write, coach, and create tools like tapes, CDs, and videos not for the money, but for the joy and satisfaction of learning how the lives of others are being changed and improved. A true mentor does it for the satisfaction of seeing another achieve her full potential in life. A truly skilled, caring mentor does not look at you the way you are now. He looks at you the way you will be. I see my coaching clients the way they will be or could be. I see them with their business and life in order. My job as a coach or mentor is to draw for them the exciting picture of what their life will be like in the future. Then I can help them craft the plan and the steps to achieve and fulfill that vision.

WHAT MENTORS REQUIRE OF YOU

Many mentors may test you at the very beginning of the relationship. Once someone approached me about mentoring him, but I was not sure if he would be the type of person I could teach to be successful in real estate. In order to test him, I asked him to read two specific books and call me in a week. I thought that would be the end of him. I told him in no uncertain terms that a week meant seven days, not eight, not ten, but seven. He called me back in a week. He had read the books and asked, "Now, what's next?" Then I had him practice a couple of scripts that he would role-play with me in five days. He came back in five days and had them down pat. I gave him instructions to listen to two tape series in five days and report back to me. He did what he was told and had some of the concepts down from the tapes. This process went on for almost a month. He did everything I asked him to do in the time frame required. At the end of a month he became my mentee. He earned my respect by doing each thing that I asked.

Mentors Look for a Strong Desire to Succeed

Most mentors will expect you to have a strong desire to advance to the top and make the effort to get there. They may send you away with assignments as I did to see if you have the passion to excel. The mentee has to bring a high level of passion into the relationship. That is the value a mentee brings in. The mentee just discussed ignited a fire in me that burned for some time. He helped me improve my skills along the way. Knowing a skill and being able to teach it are two different things. The benefit for the mentor is a rekindling of the passion for the business and an extra boost from someone young or new in the business.

THE VALUE OF COACHING

Coaching is another form of mentoring. Coaching for peak performers has been around for years. For many decades the most successful athletes have been coached to win the big event. Tiger Woods would not be the golfer he is today without his golf coaches. Michael Jordan, John Elway, and Michael Johnson have all had coaches. The leaders of some of the most successful companies in the business world have coaches. Behind each great milestone or accomplishment stand two people—the one who executes the task or carries out the game plan and the one who helps to create the game plan and teaches the executor to improve his skills. Maybe it is time to evaluate and consider the benefits of a coach.

A good coach has five basic traits. When these traits are used to help you move forward in your life, the results are amazing. A coach can help you increase your production and enjoyment in life and help you craft a life of long-term success.

The Ability to Listen

The first trait of a great coach is the ability to listen and help you clarify your goals and vision in all areas of your life. Earl Nightingale, the famous speaker, stated that we are goal-seeking organisms. Our purpose is to set and achieve goals in life. The difficulty for most people is not in trying to achieve their goals, but in setting them in the first place. We can accomplish anything in life provided we truly decide to do it.

The Belief That Goals Must Have Deadlines

The second trait of a successful coach is the understanding that all goals must have deadlines. Deadlines get one's juices and thoughts flowing to create the desired result. Have you ever planned to go away for vacation and two days before you are to leave you go into a flurry of activity in your business? It is because of the deadline that the activity increases and things begin to happen. How would you like to have that kind of production level ongoing? Determine effective deadlines for all areas of your business.

Deadlines get one's juices and thoughts flowing to create the desired result.

The Ability to Create a Game Plan and Execute It

A great coach will take the goals and vision you set for yourself and teach you to achieve them. She will help you create the step-by-step game plan to reach that envisioned future. Even the big projects that seem like mountains can be broken down into bite-size pieces, which are called daily disciplines. A great coach will also show clients the consequences of not following through on their goals and commitments.

The Ability to Motivate and Inspire

The coach will provide ongoing motivation and inspiration during the storms of life. We will experience many storms in this world; we cannot avoid them. Because we cannot avoid them, we must prepare for them. It is not the storm that causes the problem; it is how we react to the storm. A great coach will help you brace for the storm that otherwise might overwhelm you. Coaching provides the motivation and inspiration to overcome life's storms.

Feed Yourself Bite-Size Pieces

I had a client in 1998 who wanted to earn more than $250,000 for the year, when the year before he had earned only $130,000. We worked diligently to break down into bite-size pieces what he needed to accomplish in order to achieve his goal. Once the bite-size pieces were determined, we were able to set the daily disciplines for him to undertake. Because he had to focus just on his daily disciplines, the task was not paralyzing. When he got behind in achieving his goal, it was always caused by his not doing his daily disciplines. As his coach I helped him create the game plan and targeted him to execute it daily. He achieved and broke his goal by earning more than $265,000 for 1998, which was more than a 100 percent increase in his business. Coaching really works in real estate sales as in other fields.

The Habit of Accountability

Lastly, a great coach provides accountability and is available for you. A great coach will help you evaluate your progress against your goals and vision. He will hold you to the standard that you have set for yourself.

THE BENEFITS OF COACHING

The truth is that everyone needs a coach. Hiring a coach is making an investment in you. The benefits of coaching produce years of dividends. Where would Michael Jordan be without his coaches? Great coaches enable their clients to increase their abundance more rapidly without experiencing the many mistakes and pitfalls of being on their own. We all have had coaches and teachers throughout our lives. The most successful people never outgrow mentors. They work with coaches to achieve peak performance. Do not neglect to make the investment in yourself for you and your family.

Since I started the first edition of this book in 2001, I am even more convinced of the merits of coaching, especially for new agents. The learning curve is so steep when you are a new agent. There is so much to learn, retain, and master. A new agent typically won't be able to afford the more intimate one-on-one coaching that more advanced agents gravitate toward for help and guidance.

In the last few years, there has been a technology explosion in the training and coaching industry. Delivery vehicles such as WebEx and GoToMeeting provide powerful coaching and training experience targeted to new agents who can't afford expensive alternatives. Because of this technology, a new agent can get personal coaching for less than they invested in their real estate license.

I encourage you to go to our Web site at www.realestatechampions.com, where you will find many coaching programs designed for novice agents.

CHAPTER 7

MEETING CHALLENGES

Most people enter the real estate sales profession without a clear understanding of how to run a business. New agents enter the field from different backgrounds. The readers of this book may be former homemakers, flight attendants, students, salespeople, or restaurant workers: a true melting pot of professions. But most new agents have never dealt with the issues of running a business; they usually are just beginning or have just finished their classroom training to receive their real estate license.

THE PROFIT FACTOR

As I have said for years to my audiences and my coaching clients, training has nothing to do with running a profitable business. I have always considered myself a businessperson who happened to sell real estate.

The purpose of a business is to create and keep customers. When I ask at a seminar, "What is the purpose of a business?" most people answer, "To turn a profit or to make money." Eighty percent of businesses fail because they lack customers or, put another way, ample sales volume. The objective, then, is to service your customers well so you keep them for life. Profit is the natural result of a well-run business. Profit will happen if we create and keep customers and watch expenses. The greatest challenge is to learn to understand and to run your business. This challenge is not unique to real estate.

Even a Dentist Must Know How to Run a Business

My father, Norm, was a dentist for thirty years, and he taught me a great deal about how to run a business. A large degree of his success was attributed to two factors: He knew how to run his practice and how to live within his means. I asked him recently what he recalls as the hardest part of starting his dental practice. He didn't hesitate in saying, "Learning to understand and to run my business." Just as in your real estate school training, he was not taught in dental school how to run a business. They taught him the skill of being a dentist—tooth extractions, gold crowns, cleaning, fillings, and drilling. They never taught him the billing part of the business, the part where you collect your money. They also never taught him the value of time.

TIME AND PROFIT

The biggest obstacle to success in any profession is getting paid for your time. Real estate school education will not teach you how to be successful. It will not teach you how to run a business. The school will not teach techniques for mastering time. Ultimately, your time is your most precious resource. It is far more valuable than money. Time is ever ticking and advancing. Time is the true asset of life.

The real difficulty is not the lack of time; it is what we do with the time that we have. It is how we control our daily allotment of twenty-four hours. Actually, we really only have sixteen hours to use because we need eight for sleep and rest. It's what we do in those remaining sixteen hours during each day that results in success or creates failure. Because we can never stockpile, accumulate, or turn back time, we have to control the passing of it.

So it comes down to being a matter of learning to do what is most important first each day. When at work we must do what generates the most revenue in the shortest time.

When I am on the road speaking, I see agents daily who earn more money only because they spend more time on their business. Now, anyone can earn more money if she invests more time. Even a ditchdigger can do that by working overtime. But successful people prefer to increase the return on the time they invest.

Mastery of Time Gives Us More Options

Ultimately, it all boils down to what you are worth per hour. This number is critical to know during your entire sales career. You must check this number with regularity to ensure its improvement. By raising your hourly rate, you gain more choices in life. If you were earning $25 an hour selling real estate and you controlled your time better and improved your skills so that just six months later you were earning $50 an hour, you would have options you didn't have before. You could now work fewer hours and make the same amount of money. You could now spend more time with your family. You could also choose to work the same amount of hours, but double your pay. This would allow a better lifestyle, more investments, more savings, and better schools for your children. The combinations and possibilities are endless. You have now created options for yourself and your family. The key to growth and abundance in real estate sales is mastery of time.

The key to growth and abundance in real estate sales is mastery of time.

We Are Selling Our Time

As a real estate agent, there are only two things you are selling. Neither of these assets is houses. You are selling your time first and foremost. Your time is the commodity that's for sale. If it takes you fifty hours to find the buyer for a home, you will not get paid the same for your time as you would if it took you only twenty-five hours for the same task. Because the price for our service from agent to agent is fairly constant, time is the asset we are selling.

We Are Selling Our Knowledge

The other asset we are selling is our knowledge. We control our knowledge by controlling our time. As a new agent, you are going to be selling time more than knowledge because your knowledge has less value today than it will in the future. However, many agents have not increased their knowledge in twenty years, so they still have to sell their time. The only way to increase knowledge is to invest time in reading, studying, attending seminars, practicing scripts and dialogues, viewing videotapes, and actually working with buyers and sellers. You must have time to be able to increase the value of your knowledge.

HOW TO FIGURE YOUR VALUE

The more I coach and train agents, the more I realize the biggest battle they have is on the battlefield of time. Maximizing the dollars we earn per hour separates the extremely successful agents from those who are frustrated. Many agents across the country are merely trading more time for more money. They are simply spending more and more time with people other than their family. However, if you know your hourly rate you can change that. Here is how to figure out your value: To figure out what you make per hour, take your gross commission (that's before company split) and divide it by the number of hours worked. To find hours worked, take the number of hours you work in a day, multiply by the days you work a week and the number of weeks you work per year, then divide that into your gross commission.

Task Analysis

We are all squeezed for time. We all feel there are not enough hours in the day. We all feel the tug between our family and our business and the battle for abundance in both areas. If you truly want to find a few hours daily, try task analysis.

First, find out what it is you actually do each day. Take an old appointment book page and make a few copies. Then every fifteen to thirty minutes, write down what you are doing. Do this for two weeks. This process will enable you to know with certainty where you are investing your time.

What Is Worth $50 an Hour?

If you know your value per hour, you will be able to evaluate what you do on the basis of whether or not it really pays you that amount per hour. Let's say you make $50 an hour. There are only certain activities in selling real estate that will pay you that $50 per hour. The rule is if you would not pay someone $50 to do something, neither will anyone else. This means that you will not be earning your $50 an hour doing those activities. For example, making flyers, inputting listings into the multiple listing service, putting together bulk mail, and typing letters are all activities that I would not pay anyone $50 an hour to do. But these have to be done. The question is, are you the person to do them or can you spend less time doing them?

You will be amazed at the allocation of your time. Most agents who have completed this task find ten to twenty hours a week that can be better spent. That's anywhere from 25 to 50 percent increased efficiency when fully implemented! To know what that really means to you in dollars, multiply your gross commission by 25 percent. That is what you can earn in addition this year without more expenses, without the latest marketing gimmicks. The best part is that you are in total control of that number. The market, your broker, buyers, and sellers have no effect on your ability to increase your income by the amount you wrote down.

Work diligently on the task analysis process. Really track your activities and the time invested in each. At the end of each week add up the time spent in each activity. Ask yourself these questions:

1. Am I getting paid _____ per hour for each activity?
2. How can I reduce the time I am spending in each activity that pays less than _____ per hour?
3. Do I really need to do this activity?
4. Can I get someone else to do this activity?

You Control Your Own Time

Knowing what you are worth per hour and how you are investing your work time are the first two steps to time mastery. Once you have started down the road to time mastery, you are moving toward sales mastery and finally life mastery. Make the commitment today to yourself and your family to do this exercise. The harsh reality of life is we do not know how long we have to enjoy it. We can make up lost revenue, but we cannot make up lost time. Know that your time is the most valuable resource you have. Start the process to reclaim more of it today.

> ## *We can make up lost revenue, but we cannot make up lost time. Know that your time is the most valuable resource you have.*

We have the ultimate control of our own time. We are the owners of our time and it is our responsibility to control our time. It rests on no one else.

CLIENTS' VIEW OF A REAL ESTATE AGENT

One challenge of being a real estate agent is that clients don't regard us as professionals, and sometimes even we ourselves don't. If we were playing baseball, we would have three strikes against us before we even got up to bat.

Strike One: Unreasonable Requests from Clients

The general public has little or no respect for us largely because they do not understand what we really do. Most people think that if they call or page us we should return their call within minutes and be ready to drop everything to show them a home or meet with them. They think we should show them our listings at any time of the day or night, even if they have no serious intentions of buying—it may be out of their price range or perhaps they have not met with a lender yet. For example, once I received a call from someone because his agent was out of town and he wanted me to show him a home. This person wanted me to leave my family for one or two hours on the weekend so he could see the home. This potential buyer was never going to buy the home *through me* even if he decided to buy! The odds of his actually purchasing this particular home were maybe 10 to 15 percent. Why would I want to break away from my family for one of my listings to sell at that rate? I would not make such a poor decision.

My belief is that I am not obligated to fulfill any such unreasonable requests. I am not obligated to take time away from my family to show potential buyers a house because they want to see it right now. If most people called their doctor and wanted to see her right now, they could not. Why should real estate agents be treated any differently than doctors? If the prospect on the other end of the phone has no respect for your time, he will not have respect for the other aspects of your service either. He also will not have respect for you as a person. If a prospect has little respect for you, his attitude will not change when he becomes a client.

Respect Your Billable Hours

How many times have you called an attorney to ask a few quick questions and you are billed for 15 to 30 minutes of time? You will receive a statement almost every time. Rarely do attorneys not start the meter when they pick up the phone. They do because the caller is buying their knowledge and their time. Why should we as agents be different? I know I provide as much value as an attorney, do you?

You must earn a level of respect for your time on the first call, whether you call the prospect or the prospect calls you. You must set the tone that your time is valuable, and if you are going to give the prospect some of your time, expect to be paid—by turning him into a client.

Strike Two: Twenty-Four-Hour Access

We help perpetuate the problem by not controlling access. Too many agents are available twenty-four hours a day, seven days per week. There is no other profession whose members are on call 24/7, yet we seem proud that we are there for our clients at all times. Our clients do not work a schedule like that in their job. Take back your family time. Inform your clients of your days and evenings off and stick to your schedule. Do you really want to do business with someone who does not want you to have days off or family time? It is solely up to you to set a clear standard.

Strike Three: Haphazard Work Habits

We are independent contractors. We get to do what we want when we want to do it. I have observed some of the work habits of my colleagues. It is not a mystery to me why many of them do not make any money, and some of these agents have sold real estate for ten to twenty years. If you want to make any money, you must treat yourself and your career with respect. Show up at the office at the same time every day. Complete your workday at the end of the day. Do not regularly take a two-hour lunch break. Treat this career like a real job or a real career. Your clients are counting on you to do so. If you have that philosophy, you cannot help being successful. I have never seen an agent who came in early and put in a full day's work who was not successful. Remember that no one is going to help you develop the time management disciplines you need but you yourself. Your broker or manager will not be able to magically give you that ability.

There are some specific techniques that will help you achieve more in less time. There are also sales skills that will enable you to produce at a higher level. We will be sharing those in chapter 8. First, we need to reduce the strike count, so you are able to see more pitches to hit. Your second goal is to be a better hitter, whether you are trying to hit for an average and do a lot of transactions or are looking to hit the long ball out of the park with big deals.

Compressing time is the ability to accomplish more in less time. If you analyze the highest producers in business, you will observe they all have this skill.

COMPRESSING TIME

One of the skills top achievers have is the ability to compress time. Compressing time is the ability to accomplish more in less time. If you analyze the highest producers in business, you will observe they all have this skill.

Plan for Tomorrow

Plan your work for tomorrow before you leave today. If you spend a few minutes planning your day on paper the day before, your subconscious mind will kick in, working on your challenges of the next day while you sleep. Your mind will be working like a rotisserie, turning the challenges and your time for tomorrow all night while you rest. When you get up, you will be ready to attack the day.

Focus Your Day

Before you start your workday make sure to ask these key questions:

1. What is the highest payoff activity I can do?
2. What activity, if done with excellence, can make the biggest difference?
3. What can I do well that no one else can do?
4. Why am I on the payroll?

Do What You Do Best

These questions must be asked each day before you begin. The most successful people don't try to be a jack-of-all-trades. They are the people who specialize in performing activities that no one else can do. They perform these actions with excellence. If you do that you will be highly sought after.

Know the Difference Between Urgent and Important

Successful people understand the trap of *urgent* versus *important*. As real estate agents we are faced with that challenge every day. We get interrupted constantly by phone calls that are urgent, not important. We have to make quick judgments on unexpected calls from other agents, sellers, buyers, title companies, and escrow people. The consequences of selecting the urgent, not important, can easily cause us to lose productivity.

Often urgent matters are not important in the long run. Here is a good rule to use when evaluating urgent versus important: Important things are usually self-directed or self-generated. These are things you can do to move your business and life forward—important things, which will have the greatest impact on you and your family: prospecting, lead follow-up calls, the appointments that you have scheduled for buyers and sellers.

> ### *"Those who make the worst use of their time are the first to complain of its brevity."*
> ### —Jean De La Bruyere

The urgent matters are the phone calls from other agents, lenders, and title companies, all emotionally charged. Too often, we select the urgent over the important because someone else's emotional state influences us. When you feel yourself being swayed by someone's emotional state, take a few steps back to analyze the situation. Often people want their urgent problems to be assumed by you. Someone else causes urgent activities. By setting boundaries as to when you will be dealing with urgent activities, you will be able to accomplish much more in your allotted time.

Look for the Limiting Steps

To compress your time you must recognize the limiting steps. For every achievement or accomplishment there is a limiting step along the way. The sooner you overcome the limiting steps, the more you can accomplish. These limiting steps can create a barrier to your plans for each day. If you want to be successful, you must identify the limiting step quickly. You must focus with laser intensity on removing it.

For instance, the limiting step in prospecting might be being prepared. Often we don't have all the people we are going to call organized to begin prospecting. We then spend time in preparation when we should be on the phone. All during preparation our minds send us mental images of how hard this is going to be. By the time we get ready, we have psyched ourselves out of doing the prospecting. The preparation is the "limiting" step. The solution is to prepare today, before leaving work, for your prospecting tomorrow. That way you just walk in and do it.

If you are trying to make a flyer for a property you have listed, the limiting step could be just finding the time to drive out and take a picture of the property. Plan a time to do it, or see if you can get someone else to take the picture. Can you pay a staff person in the office a few dollars to drive out on his lunch hour to help you? Define the limiting steps in everything you do.

Define Your Time and Values

Successful people have clarity of purpose and clarity of value. They know the direction to travel and what they stand for. They have decided what is important to them. They have determined their priorities and they take action based on that order of priorities. They have also clearly defined their values, for both business and life. They are determined that their values don't conflict with work. By applying these simple steps for action and clarity you can compress your work time. You will also be able to double your effectiveness when you are at work.

Successful people have clarity of purpose and clarity of value. They know the direction to travel and what they stand for.

CULTIVATE YOUR KNOWLEDGE ASSET

Now that we understand the value of our time and how to control it, we need to learn to increase the other asset we are selling, which is knowledge. The challenge facing all agents is acquisition of knowledge. New agents in particular must seek every opportunity to improve their knowledge and skill in real estate sales. Investing some of your time in studying and learning will yield fruit.

Enroll in the Audio University

In my early career in real estate sales I spent a minimum of two hours a day practicing scripts and dialogues that related to my listing presentations and objection handling. I am a huge believer in the audio university—listening to audiobooks in your car whenever and wherever you drive. Your capacity to learn while you drive is enormous. I would spend hours daily listening to Zig Ziglar, Jim Rohn, Brian Tracy, Earl Nightingale, and many others. They helped mold and shape my thinking, my skill, and my desire.

I took to heart Jim Rohn's great thought that your formal education will make you a living but your personal education will make you a fortune. I want to say Jim is exactly right. I did not finish college or receive outstanding grades in high school. But I did invest large quantities of time starting in my mid-twenties into my personal education. I can honestly say that I would not be writing this book today without those years of study. I would not have the honor to speak in front of large audiences without that personal investment. I would not get to work with some of the top agents in the country, agents who are selling 30 and 40 million dollars' worth of real estate a year.

The Importance of Books

The average person reads less than three books after he leaves his formal schooling. That's truly a pitiful statistic for our society. No wonder the average income for a person in the United States is far less than $40,000 per year.

A study conducted on homes valued at $300,000 or greater found that eight out of ten of these homes contained one thing that homes worth less than $300,000 did not have—these homes contained a library. The questions you have to ask yourself are: Did the owners just suddenly decide to get a library or did they start it years ago? Did they start that library in the corner of a small, nearly empty apartment ten, fifteen, even twenty years ago? Did the owners buy, collect, and read good books to improve their skills, expand their thinking, define their character, and impact their life? For me that was the case. My library started in that little studio apartment. Then it moved to a one-bedroom apartment and then to a little 800-square-foot house where my wife, Joan, and I lived when we started my real estate career. When we moved into a home on a golf course, our library moved and grew with us. Then a second library was created in a vacation home where we spent three days a week.

My path to success can be yours. I believe God gave gifts for success to all of us to use. You have the seeds of greatness inside you ready to be watered and germinated and grown. The water and fertilizer are books, seminars, and audiobooks and the investment you make in yourself. With that focus your success is assured.

ARE YOU BURNING BRIGHT OR BURNING OUT?

Many people are heading fast toward burnout or just recovering from burnout. Burnout is a real happening for many real estate agents. We get calls from agents daily who are struggling with this dilemma. Burnout occurs when reality and our expectations don't align over time. Burnout can also trigger anger. The anger grows from the feeling that life is not working out the way we had thought it would. We feel powerless to make the changes needed, or we don't know the changes that we need to implement.

There are seven key factors that can cause one to experience burnout.

Burnout occurs when reality and our expectations don't align over time.

Key Factor 1: We Fail to Pace Ourselves

We all have an optimum pace we need for work and life. Often we exceed that pace. We can exceed our pace for only a short period of time. When we fail to slow down and reestablish our normal pace, trouble sets in. Are you pacing yourself? What is the pace at which you are most effective at work and at home?

Key Factor 2: We Try to Do It All Ourselves

We often take on the whole world single-handedly—it's me against the world. Are you delegating all you can to others? Are your affiliates, lenders, title officers, escrow people, and home inspectors doing all they can to help you succeed? Are there services you could have your broker provide and compensate her for performing them?

Key Factor 3: We Accept Everyone Else's Problems

Too often we accept problems that are out of our control—for example, the client who "needs" a certain price for his home, the other agent's emotional or financial problems, or repair costs the seller didn't anticipate.

Key Factor 4: We Major in Minor Things

It's really easy to get worked up by the little stuff. The skill is allocating the right amount of energy and time for the size of the challenge. A good rule to follow is, if it deals with the health of you or your family or if it deals with the quality of life and relationships between you and your family, then it's big stuff. Everything else is minor—it's small stuff.

A good rule to follow is, if it deals with the health of you or your family or if it deals with the quality of life and relationships between you and your family, then it's big stuff.

Key Factor 5: We Have Unrealistic Expectations

We live in a world filled with instant everything. We have been trained by society to want it all yesterday with no effort on our part. A recent study showed that 80 percent of the late-night infomercials deal with instant weight loss or instant financial success. There are few occurrences of instant success in life. Most people have toiled for years perfecting their abilities. Measurable progress in reasonable time is the barometer by which we need to gauge our results.

Key Factor 6: We Poorly Prioritize the Important Aspects of Life

We are often so busy living we don't have time to create an abundant life. What is the most important area of your life? What area has more value than all others? Do your time, energy, and passion reflect the priority you need to have in that area? If you cannot answer these questions with confidence, what changes should you make to your priorities? I regard this point as being one of the biggest challenges for real estate agents. We often neglect our family for income opportunities.

> *We are often so busy living we don't have time to create an abundant life.*

Key Factor 7: We Are in Poor Physical Condition

Without a strong body, our energy and mental focus escape us. When we are in a regular exercise routine, we can relieve some of the stress that causes burnout. Prepare for the day by setting aside time for exercise in the morning or perhaps schedule a midday break. Some of us may elect to work out as an end-of-the-day stress reliever before we go home to our families.

DON'T LOSE TOUCH WITH YOURSELF

One of the major steps in avoiding burnout is to know yourself. We can often burn out if we lose touch with ourselves. There are three skills in knowing oneself. They are to know

- your behavioral or DISC style
- your purpose
- your passion

These three areas make you an original. There is no one else like you.

Know Your Behavioral or DISC Style

DISC is a system for evaluating behavioral style. DISC stands for Dominant, Influencing, Steady, or Compliant.

Dominant: If you have a high Dominant score, you are competitive, quick to make a decision, and very results oriented.

Influencing: If you have a high Influence score, you are people oriented, warm, caring, active, in charge, and trusting of others.

Steady: If you have a high Steady score, you are nonconfrontational, stable, and want to get along with all people.

Compliant: If you have a high score in Compliant, you are systematic, accurate, numbers and data oriented, and believe facts are facts.

These styles determine your communication patterns and how you process information. The style you are affects formality, pace of speech, and body language. Knowing your style will drastically improve your effectiveness in relationship with your spouse, children, and business associates. It will also enable you to be a more effective salesperson. You will see the blind spots in your skills and abilities more clearly. Lao-tzu, the Chinese philosopher, said, "He who knows others is learned. He who knows himself is wise."

If you have never taken a DISC assessment, you can go to our Web site at www.realestatechampions.com/freedisc and take a free assessment.

Understand Your Purpose

My belief is that we all have a purpose to fulfill while we are here. The question is, What is yours? What is the ultimate outcome that you are trying to create in your life?

Mary Kay Ash, founder of Mary Kay Cosmetics, describes her purpose this way: to provide unlimited opportunity to women. The interesting thing is that her purpose has nothing to do with the sale of cosmetics. Purpose adds stability to life when you hit turbulent waters or when you have more opportunities than time to take advantage of them. At this point you have to be careful to select the opportunities that align with your purpose.

Know Your Passion

What causes you to get excited? What are you willing to stay up day and night for? What would you rather do than anything else in life? When you are tired, what gets you charged back up? Passion helps keep you on track. Passion also snaps you back on track when you get off track. Day-to-day pressure and wear and tear can overwhelm us when we don't have passion.

Burnout is a reality we all can face again and again if we are not vigilant in watching the seven key factors. We must take action in each of these areas. Invest the time to know yourself, define your purpose, and tap in to your passion. Life is meant to be spent in abundance. Are you moving toward abundance or burnout?

Create a Long-Term Vision

Another hurdle in building a successful real estate sales career is creating long-term vision for your business. Too often we are just working day by day and moment by moment. The most successful individuals are those who have a long-term vision of what their business and life will look like in five to ten years.

Have a Plan on Paper

Build a vision for your business to ensure continued growth in your real estate sales. We have to have a clear objective and a defined plan to achieve our goals. Having your plan in print on paper allows you to remain consistent and true to your objectives and goals. Too often, when agents are not certain of their goals, objectives, and values, their prospects and clients will cause them to move into the gray area of their business. This gray area doesn't necessarily mean they are participating in unethical transactions, but it does mean they are adjusting their personal or core values to earn a commission check.

Know Your Core Ideology

Truly great individuals understand the difference between what should never change and what could be open for change, between what is sacred and what is not. Change is inevitable in every business. The real estate sales business is not exempt from having change forced upon it regularly. What should never change is your core ideology: that which defines your character. Your core ideology will transcend the market, technological advances, changes in brochures, and the latest magic marketing gimmick. Defining who you are and what you stand for in your business will enable you to attain the success you desire.

Your core ideology consists of two main areas:

> core values
> core purpose

Know Your Core Values

Core values are essential to guide your business and your career. Core values are what you stand for even when no one is looking. They are what you believe in so strongly that your children are taught them. Small companies grow up to be large companies because of their adherence to their core values.

Let me share a few examples. There is a tremendous retail company in the Pacific Northwest called Nordstrom's. Nordstrom's started in 1901 as a shoe store in downtown Seattle, Washington. It started as a small business just as your real estate business is now. Nordstrom's has a core value that sets them apart:

> Service to the customer above all else.

Nordstrom's employees are world famous for their service. They will go to great lengths to ensure customer satisfaction. Their core value of service was created decades before customer service was fashionable.

Another example is Disney. Disney's core values include creativity, dreams, and imagination. Their values produce the Fantasy Island that we get to experience. The Disney company makes fantasy seem to be reality. Walt Disney said, "If you can dream it, you can do it."

Even my company, Real Estate Champions, has core values. One of ours is the exceptional execution of the fundamentals.

Our Core Values

I believe that mastery of the fundamentals in your business leads to success. Without the mastery of fundamentals, it's only a matter of time before the house of cards falls. That's why our focus at Real Estate Champions is to help you acquire the mastery of knowledge and time management in your business. The key fundamentals in your real estate career are sales skills, time management skills, business skills, and leadership skills. I believe all other skills are secondary to these. People avoid the fundamentals because they are hard. To master the fundamentals takes work. It takes willingness to practice, learn, and put it on the line daily to achieve success. We as a company will always stand for excellence in the fundamentals. It will always be what we teach because it is a core value for our company.

Know Your Core Purpose

The second key area is core purpose. Simply stated it's why you are in real estate. Have you ever thought of why you decided to enter real estate? Why did you pick this career over all the others that are available? The desire to make a lot of money is not enough of a core purpose to sustain you as a real estate agent. To be sure, lack of money can motivate us to do certain things. But once we have solved the immediate money problem, we will be forced to reevaluate why we are doing what we do. At that time reevaluation could be harder because we have raised our standard of living. We think we can survive only on the higher income level. We then paint ourselves into a corner with fewer options. A true core purpose identifies why you are in real estate and captures the soul of your business. The core purpose describes your income or commission volume and even the customers you are going to serve.

A true core purpose is a long statement and should not be confused with the goals you have set. Goals can be achieved but a purpose cannot. You are going to achieve your goals, cross them off, then set new ones. A purpose is a direction that you are going to work toward your whole career. The core purpose itself does not change, but it causes change. It causes change over time in goals, status, proceeds, and service that you provide. Let me share with you a few examples:

Walmart's core purpose is to give ordinary folks the chance to buy the same things as rich people. Walmart's focus is on consumers and their access to goods and services. They have built an empire on value to the consumer.

Mary Kay Ash's focus is not on men. It is not even on cosmetics. The purpose is providing unlimited opportunity to one segment of society . . . women. Mary Kay realized how hard it was to achieve success as a women in her era. She wanted to help others succeed at her level. She didn't want them to have to struggle to the top as she had.

A true core purpose identifies why you are in real estate and captures the soul of your business. The core purpose describes your income or commission volume and even the customers you are going to serve.

UNDERSTAND HOW TO MAKE A PROFIT

The last major challenge is to be profitable in your business. Profit is a natural result of a well-run business. A business whose only reason for existence is money will not stand the test of time. The real focus for the business is to create and keep customers, and the profit we desire is an actual outcome of that.

Keep an Eye on Your P&L Statement

The primary tool for business is a regular profit and loss statement. Most businesses refer to this as a P&L. Having a regular P&L allows you to understand and control your expenses. The only way to properly control expenses is to know them and watch them. It's easy to expand your spending when you start to make money. Agents are famous for throwing money at anything and everything as they are trying to acquire more business.

Define Your Core Values and Purpose

Defining your core values and core purpose will enable you to set your course in your career for years to come. They will help you remain true to your principles when money gets tight. They will ultimately attract the people you are looking for in your business.

Watch Your Expenses and Increased Service

If what you are spending money on doesn't increase the service you provide to the client, you have to question the expense. Ask yourself:

> Will it help the house sell more quickly?
> Will it provide the seller with a competitive advantage over other sellers?
> Will it increase the quality of the communication?

A yes answer is needed for the expenditure to be made.

The other question to ask is Does the expense increase net profit? This is the second reason to spend money in your business. You are making an investment for a future retirement. That return could be in dollars or in time saved by you. I once spent $3,000 on a prelisting package video that covered selling qualifications and marketing plans and how important pricing is to the sale. It allowed me to cut my listing presentation from about sixty to thirty minutes. When you go on twenty listing appointments a month like I did at the time, you can pay for such a video in time saved in just a month. That was a very good return on the investment I made.

Be Cautious About the Latest Gimmick

Be cautious of agents who try to convince you of the latest and greatest gadget or gimmick. They are everywhere and they always target new agents. These agents are really trying to help. For the most part, the systems or ideas they recommend were recently mentioned at some seminar. Even if they are using the techniques themselves, they usually don't know the return on profit but just thought it was a good deal at one time.

Be sure to evaluate your spending well. For years, I have watched agents become successful in real estate only to find out they are making the same net profit at $250,000 as they were making at $75,000. It is easy to fall into the trap of spending as a real estate agent. Your insurance policy for not going broke is your P&L.

Act Like a Business Owner

When someone is giving you advice, always ask how it will take your business to the next level and get some cost information.

Ask them these questions.

1. How much does this service cost?
2. How much time do you or your staff have to invest in it?

3. How many transactions has this generated in the last year?

4. How many transactions did this generate in the last thirty days?

5. What is your actual investment in the project?

6. What's the commission dollar you have earned in the last year and in the last ninety days?

7. What was the biggest challenge you encountered while implementing this idea?

A business owner would ask all these questions of a salesperson before she bought the program or product.

The biggest challenge is for us to become business owners, to take control as the CEOs of our own multimillion-dollar sales company. Running your real estate business as a business is a must for wealth, independence, and peace of mind. Review the material in this chapter regularly.

CHAPTER 8

MASTERING YOUR SALES SKILLS, PART I: PROSPECTING, EXPIRED LISTINGS, AND FOR SALE BY OWNERS

The X factor in your career will be the execution of your sales skills. Without exceptional sales skills you will have to continue to trade large amounts of time for your income. Good sales skills separate the most successful people and successful companies from all the others. This happens in every job, career, and profession. The most financially successful doctors, dentists, accountants, and attorneys may not be the most technically proficient, but these people have the best sales skills. In this chapter we will take an in-depth look at the sales skills you will need to develop in your first year as a real estate agent.

THE IBM MODEL

When I was in high school and college in the late seventies and early eighties, one of the companies everyone wanted to work for was IBM. IBM prided itself on delivering the best training in the world to its salespeople. In that era if you had IBM or "Big Blue" on your résumé you were employed for life. You were one of the most sought after salespersons in the world.

In the middle nineties IBM went through a gradual transformation. They slowly demolished their wonderful sales training. Upper management was filled with accountants, engineers, and "slide rule" types. These people banded together to do away with the salespeople. They believed salespeople were beneath them. Slowly "Big Blue" was dying. Their stock took a nosedive. There were rumblings of IBM being sold, acquired, and closed. Finally, someone realized what the engineers and accountants didn't understand: Products and services are sold not bought. The IBM theory at that time was "Build it better and it will sell itself." Sadly, their thinking failed for lack of sales. They restarted the sales training and now they are back on top.

Products and services are sold not bought.

SALESMANSHIP IS A PART OF LIFE

I share this example because many of you are thinking that you don't want to be a salesperson. The truth is that you already are one right now. Earl Nightingale said many years ago, "We are all paid in life based on our ability to sell." Mr. Nightingale was exactly right. From the receptionist who wants a raise and has to sell it to her boss, to the spouse who wants an increase in the discretionary spending in the household budget, to the attorney who is trying to attract new clients, to your junior high schooler who is trying to convince you to increase her allowance—we are all going to be successful in life based on our ability to sell. Your effectiveness as a parent is based on your ability to sell your children on your rules and your values. For example, when you are in conflict with your children because they want to stay up later, you will usually first try to sell them on the idea of going to bed before you whip out the authority tones. Selling is a natural part of life. Developing sales skills helps you in all areas of life.

Earl Nightingale said many years ago, "We are all paid in life based on our ability to sell."

> ### The Greatest Sale I Ever Made
>
> The greatest sale I ever made was not a house or piece of property, nor was it a seminar or training program. The greatest sale I made was over twenty years ago convincing a woman named Joan that this ex-professional racquetball player could become something special off the court and that she should decide to spend the rest of her life with me. As long as I live, it will be the greatest sale I've made. I can tell you it wasn't the most eloquently worded presentation, but it did have passion and enthusiasm behind it. Joan was ready to buy, but some of your clients will not be. That means your words and presentation need to be a ten.

SALESPEOPLE ARE THE HIGHEST PAID PROFESSIONALS

At the end of the day whoever has the best sales skills wins the game. Therefore, your sales skills must be developed. I don't believe in natural-born salespeople. You can rise to the top of the amateur level if you are gifted. But if you develop your gift, you can rise to the ranks of a professional. Salespeople are the highest paid professionals in the world. Careers in sales have produced more millionaires and multimillionaires than any other profession. You have the opportunity to earn an income that most people only dream about and few people achieve.

The Secret Ingredient: Practice

Why aren't most real estate agents in this highest paid category? Let me share with you the missing component: practice. Most agents don't practice their craft. They don't practice the words that will lead a client from sitting on the fence to a committed client relationship. If you practice using your sales skills, it will not matter what the market is doing or where interest rates are. All those outside factors will have little or no effect on your income. You can become bulletproof in your business. The name of the game is practice and most agents rarely practice. Most true professionals practice long and hard. An NFL team, for example, practices forty-five to fifty times more than they play in an actual game. What would happen to our sales careers if we did even one-tenth the amount of practice these professional athletes do weekly? I have seen the results when agents adopt this challenge. Their income skyrockets. They double, triple, and even quadruple their income in less than a year. To become a sales master you have to practice your craft.

YOUR KEY SALES SKILLS

The key skills we need to practice are prospecting, lead follow-up, qualifying, listing presentations, buyer interviews, objection handling, and closing techniques. These are the tools of a "top gun" agent. None of these other skills can be used unless you prospect and generate leads.

PROSPECTING

Prospecting is essential; it's the engine that drives the train. *Webster's* defines *prospecting* as "seeking a potential buyer or customer; seeking with the vision of success." The real estate agent version for most agents is "the most unimaginable pain—worse than being boiled in oil."

We have to clearly understand that prospecting is part of the job we have selected. Many people will tell you that there is a prospect-free system to selling real estate. Sadly, they are just plain wrong. The only place where *success* comes before *work* is in the dictionary.

Your Sphere of Influence

There are many people you can prospect. Start with your sphere of influence. Your sphere of influence is all the people you know and your family knows. When you really think about it, you probably know 200 to 250 people. How about the people you went to school with, the people you know at church, the parents of your children's soccer friends, or even the people you see at your athletic club. All these are in your sphere and they all want you to succeed in your new career.

Collect information such as name, address, phone numbers (work and home), and e-mail address. Then call these people and announce that you are in business. Ask them if they know of anyone who is thinking of buying or selling real estate. Often the initial answer is no. Ask them if they would call you right away if they hear of anyone and, lastly, don't assume they will remember.

The Seven Secrets of Prospecting

For many salespeople, prospecting is the most difficult activity they do. They dread the thought of picking up the phone to make a living. However, long-term success in sales is built through solid prospecting. In order to be successful and profitable, salespeople need to apply these seven secrets of prospecting daily.

Long-term success in sales is built through solid prospecting.

1. **The first call is always the most difficult.** I prospected solidly for over eight years in real estate. I never got over the difficulty of making the first call. Getting yourself to make the first call is the highest hurdle. The only solution is to just do it. After you make the first call, you realize it was not as difficult as you imagined. The person on the other end of the line was not as difficult as your imagination had made him out to be. In many cases calling begins to get fun after a few calls. The problem is most people just never break through the initial barrier.

After you make the first call, you realize it was not as difficult as you imagined.

2. **Establish a routine.** To be successful, you should have a scheduled time for prospecting daily when that is the only activity that you are doing. Treat prospecting as an appointment. Do not allow anything to

interfere with your prospecting. We often allow distractions to creep into our prospecting time. The salesperson who has a set daily routine of making prospecting calls at a specific time and adheres to his schedule without distraction is guaranteed to succeed. This person will not only succeed but he will be a "top gun" agent, the best of the best.

3. **Develop "Big Mo"—Momentum.** At first prospecting will be very difficult. Your skills will not be developed to the level of an expert. Once you start the process, do not stop. Momentum is critical to prospecting. Once you get going, your skills will improve to generate more leads and to set more appointments. Do not break your momentum.

   Another agent in the real estate office where I worked once issued me a challenge. The challenge was who could list more homes in a month. I knew I would win since I had momentum and he did not. He had not been consistently prospecting previously, so he had no momentum. I must say that he did have the best month he had ever had. But that was because he was finally consistently prospecting and had been following up on the leads he was generating. At the end of the month, my team had taken eighteen listings and he had taken six. Do not bet against "Big Mo."

Get Off to a Great Start

I always prospected early in the morning because that was when I had the most energy. It also got me off to a great start, which would carry me through the rest of the day. If I had a good, disciplined day of prospecting, then I felt I had a successful day regardless of the number of leads, number of appointments set, or anything else that happened.

4. **The best time to prospect is when you have the most energy.** The best time to schedule prospecting calls is when you have the most en-

ergy and when you actually will call. There have been tremendous arguments over this point by agents and trainers. Set a time to prospect and call at that time. Do not worry about things you cannot control, such as someone being home or not. Focus on your skill level, avoid distractions, and prospect. These factors you can control.

5. **Focus on the goal or objective.** Set a specific goal of what you want to happen on each call. Know what you want that prospect to do. It is hard to achieve success in prospecting without a clearly defined objective.

The first objective is to set a qualified appointment with the prospect. If you are unable to accomplish that objective, then the next best objective is to get an agreed-upon action by the prospect within a specific time frame. For example, the prospect is going to be interviewing agents next week. You and the prospect agree to speak on Thursday about getting the appointment scheduled for next week. The last objective is to generate a lead that will buy or sell in the future. This objective depends on your definition of what a lead is for a buyer or a seller.

6. **Believe in the power of scripts.** Highly successful salespeople use scripts. To effectively prospect, it is crucial to know what to say before you start to prospect. Scripts provide a guide and a logical sequence of questions to follow. They allow you to focus on the response of the prospect rather than fumble around trying to find the words.

The only way to move to the highest form of communication is to know what you are going to say to the prospect. The words you say account for only 7 percent of the communication. If you know the words, you can begin to focus on your tonality and body language. Tonality accounts for 38 percent of all communication and body language accounts for 55 percent. Your body language plays a huge role in conveying energy via the phone. If you are sitting and slumped over, it's hard to generate enthusiasm and energy about anything. If you are standing up and have a little movement in your body when you prospect, you will convey passion, confidence, and conviction through your communication. On the other hand, if you are focusing and stumbling through the 7 percent of the words, you will be ineffective in prospecting. We have all heard unskilled telemarketers stumble through their scripts and dialogues. Develop, learn, and practice your scripts so you can effectively communicate and reach your prospect through your tonality and body.

7. **It is a numbers game.** Prospecting is truly a numbers game for two reasons. The first is the more prospecting you do, the less rejection bothers you. The best way to deal with rejection is to get as much as you can as soon as you can to reduce its effect on you. Most people you call are very nice and pleasant. They may not need your services at this time, which is fine. Rejection is rarely as bad as you imagine. The only way to find this out is to make more calls.

The second reason is you can replicate your business via numbers. Prospecting will allow you to plan your income and results. If you track your prospecting efforts, you will find you have ratios in your business. I would make fifteen expired listing contacts and get a listing signed. If I wanted to list a property a day, I needed to make fifteen expired contacts daily, which would then create the desired income for my family.

What is your desired income? How many prospecting contacts do you need to make to achieve it? A contact is a prospecting call that results in talking to one of the decision makers in the household. As you get more skilled, the number of contacts needed will decrease. When I first began prospecting, I needed to contact over one hundred people to get a listing. Start tracking your numbers so you can play the game. To play the game well is to know and understand it.

A contact is a prospecting call that results in talking to one of the decision makers in the household.

Know the Game

Michael Jordan was the best basketball player of all time not only because of his abilities, but also because cerebrally he knew the game better than any other player. His physical skills were not at their highest levels late in his career, but his mental skills were beyond comparison. Develop your verbal and mental skills.

Develop the Habit of Prospecting

Prospecting is truly an integral part of success in any sales profession. Do not be fooled by the prospecting-free system to success. Apply the seven secrets of prospecting success. Develop the habit of daily prospecting and you will become one of the "top gun" agents in the world.

We can all learn to prospect more effectively. Make sure you find the place and the time. Don't dwell on past failures; just put them behind you. Be determined to fight for your time and fight for your focus. Create and follow a great plan of action. Be faithful to yourself and to your clients and family, and finish what you start. You will find success knocking at your door in a short period of time.

Getting Started with Prospecting

Before you pick up the phone for the first time today, you need to pause and look at the larger picture for the day, week, and month. The greater the clarity of purpose in what your production goals are, the higher the likelihood of your achieving them. What's more, an agent will get in trouble if she doesn't hit the sales numbers that cover her basic needs for the month. A long-term plan—at least a monthly plan—is a must. Every agent should ask him/herself:

- How much money in commission do I need this month to fund my lifestyle?
- How much money in commission is my goal for the month?
- How many sales do I need to make to achieve the commission goal?
- How many appointments or sales presentations do I need to achieve the number of sales to reach the goal?

- How many contacts do I need to achieve the required number of appointments?
- How many dials do I need to reach the contact goal?
- What must I do this week to reach the contact goal?
- What must I do this week to achieve, at a minimum, one-quarter of my overall goals for this month?
- Who are my most probable targets for achieving sales or making sales appointments this week?
- Do I have enough of them to achieve my goals?

Sales success is created first through refinement of your objectives, and then by taking action on those objectives in a consistent, disciplined manner. Knowing what you want and the steps to get there and acting on them leads to success.

Each morning a salesperson must have a game plan for the day. It's not enough to walk in the door, put your stuff away, grab a cup of coffee, switch on your computer, put your headset on, and make the first dial. The first key is to plan each and every call . . . no exceptions. This is the most important step in the sales process.

Why are you calling this person?

- Is it to book an appointment?
- Is it to confirm that information was received and reviewed?
- Are you making a presentation on the call?
- If so, what type of presentation is it? what is it for? what are you selling? will the close happen on the call?
- What's the goal for the call?

Ask yourself what you want to see happen before the end of the call. Let me give you a warning, however. When you ask this question, you want to be optimistic but also realistic. We want to be positive and forward thinking but not delusional. To expect to pique interest, secure information from the decision makers, receive permission to send information, qualify their needs, and book an appointment to make a listing or buyer presentation to the decision maker next week is optimistic.

There should be a primary objective for each call that you make to a prospect. That primary objective needs to be tangible. A tangible objective would be to book an appointment, create a lead with full contact information, or ask all of your qualifying questions to a prospect.

You should also have a secondary objective to fall back on. Don't hang up the phone without getting at least the secondary objective accomplished if possible. A secondary objective would be sending out information to a prospect who truly wants it and has committed to reviewing it, or securing information about the current desires, goals, and expectations concerning homeownership.

Coming to Grips with the Do Not Call Act

In January of 2003 the Telemarketing Sales Rules (TSR) were amended to include a Do Not Call Registry. The Do Not Call list went into effect on October 1, 2003. For the real estate salespeople who prospect using the telephone, the rules changed on that day.

There has been legislation on the books for years to regulate telemarketing, but in January 2003 the Federal Trade Commission amended the Telemarketing Sales Rules to prohibit telemarketers from calling consumers who have put their phone numbers on the National Do Not Call Registry. In effect, the legislation has had a two-part impact: It eliminated unrestricted contact with a huge pool of potential clients, and it created additional work and expense to determine exactly who those people are who can't be contacted.

According to the FTC, "The Do Not Call provisions of the TSR cover any plan, program or campaign to sell goods or services through interstate/intrastate phone calls." In short, telemarketing is defined as calls that solicit the sales of goods and services. We as real estate agents fall within the confines of the Do Not Call regulations.

Exempted from this definition are calls from political organizations, charities, telephone surveyors, or companies with which a consumer has an existing business relationship.

As real estate agents using the phone to access a group of targeted prospects, such as expireds, we must deal effectively with the Do Not Call list. There are over 150 million people registered on that list. To access further information or to receive a copy of the Do Not Call list, go to www.telemarketing.donotcall .gov. You will be required to update your Do Not Call list every ninety days if you are going to call consumers directly.

There are a number of exceptions to the Do Not Call act on the books. There are organizational exceptions to the rules. Charitable organizations do not need to comply with the Do Not Call act. They can call anyone from whom they acquire a phone number. Amazingly enough, the politicians who passed the law also excluded themselves from the law . . . imagine that! Political organizations are also exempt from the Do Not Call act.

There is also an inquiry provision. If someone makes a call about your company, services, or even to ask for directions to get to your office, that's considered an inquiry. Because they initiated the contact, you have ninety days to follow up with them over the phone to secure a sale.

If a prospect hits your Web site and leaves contact information, that also would legally be considered an inquiry. You won't be able to contact them after the ninety days unless you have gotten written permission to do so, or they make another inquiry. You can continue to contact anyone beyond the ninety days or eighteen months provided they give you written permission to do so.

Leveraging What You Can Do

The truth is, some of the most fertile and productive population segments to call for prospecting purposes will be the people who are on the Do Not Call list. These people will be receiving fewer calls, but they are still receiving calls. With so many exceptions and provisions, if you prepare and have an effective strategic plan, you can approach untold consumers over the phone and still be in compliance with the law.

A key step in dealing with the Do Not Call act is to document everything you do. You must document each call, correspondence, and what was talked about. The more effective you are at documenting your conversations with a prospect or client, the longer you can extend your established business relationship provision. If anyone, even someone who has previously signed something to allow you to call them or someone you sold a product to as little as thirty days ago, asks you not to call again or tells you to put them on your in-house Do Not Call list, you have to comply with their wishes. If you don't, you will be risking being hit with the $11,000 fine from the FCC, which is the governing body that enforces the Do Not Call list.

Using the Survey Method

Another exclusion in the law are surveys. You can approach a consumer on the Do Not Call list and still be within the law through the use of surveys. This technique will work provided you are using it to screen the prospect to go to the door for a face-to-face visit. You can't ask for an appointment. That would be turning a survey call into a sales call. The real purpose of using a survey technique is to identify potential leads.

As a real estate agent working expireds, you could survey home buying and home selling trends, why this home failed to sell, neighborhood activity, longevity in homes, services consumers want from a Realtor. The survey technique will allow you to talk with someone carefully to determine the quality of the prospect.

Once you determine that they are a quality prospect, you will need to market to them through direct mail or e-mail to attempt to create an inquiry on their part, and then you will have ninety days, once they inquire, to follow up with them on the phone. The best option is a personal visit. Using a survey to identify a prospect, then going to their door to meet and greet, drop off information, and ask for permission to follow up with them is a very effective strategy to create sales. I have coached numerous agents working with expireds in the last few years who have employed the survey method and techniques with tremendous sales results.

Using Technology to Create Inquiries

These techniques work to create inbound lead calls via Web site, call capture technology, and direct mail. Using a Web site or call capture technology to create inbound sales calls from the expired or sales inquiries can help you avoid all the management headaches of the Do Not Call list. Another tried and true option is direct mail. All of these techniques work to create inbound lead calls.

You should offer free reports, streaming audio files, free newsletters, and other items of value on your Web site. By offering these items you can create prospect inquiries and harvest leads that can be followed up on for ninety days, as well as drive a segment of expireds to your Web site. If you manage to secure work numbers from the expired prospects, you are now exempt from the Do Not Call act; you can follow up indefinitely. Implementing marketing strategies of direct mail, podcasts, blogs, and other informational sites that direct prospects to hear more information through a call capture system enables you to track the effectiveness of your marketing, while harvesting Do Not Call act exempt leads.

Overcoming Call Reluctance

Everyone who sets out to prospect faces call reluctance—Do Not Call list notwithstanding. This is a natural feeling for any salesperson. I don't buy it when agents tell me they don't get call reluctance.

We are all faced with call reluctance at one time or another in our sales careers. We all know that we need to prospect and make calls daily to generate new business. Knowing and doing can be two entirely different things. The fear of calling can be a career-ender for many salespeople.

Let's take a look at what most agents do when call reluctance hits. Most agents take the worst possible action . . . they avoid initiating the calls. Are you avoiding the calls when call reluctance hits? The problem with that plan is that avoiding something out of fear only teaches you to fear it more.

Call avoidance only makes the challenge larger and harder. Your call avoidance intensifies your anxiety, which leads to greater reluctance and greater avoidance. We have all lived this pattern, leading us further down the slippery slope of call reluctance. How do you break this pattern of destruction? Here are five strategies to overcome call reluctance:

Strategy 1: Take Stock of Yourself and Your Skills

Most people who are chronic call-reluctance sufferers are their own worst enemies. They are experts in all their own faults and shortcomings. They see only their weaknesses, never their strengths. To be successful at prospecting over the phone, we have to have a clear sense of what we can provide to the prospect. Until we have a clear understanding of our own value, we will never achieve comfort in prospecting.

Evaluate what you have to offer the prospect. Take inventory of your skills and abilities. Know your track record of results or your company's track record of results. Review your list of satisfied clients and the reasons that they're satisfied.

To be successful at prospecting over the phone, we have to have a clear sense of what we can provide to the prospect.

1. List the things you can do for the prospects.
2. List the qualities that make you the person they should buy from or list with.
3. List the specific benefits of your services.

Always have these lists ready by the phone so you can review them before you begin to call. You will also be able to use them during your call to convince the prospect to work with you.

Many of us are intimidated because we view making a call to a prospect or even a cold opportunity as an unwanted interruption. By using this list, you can change your mind-set to see that you are giving the prospect a valuable opportunity to be served by you.

Strategy 2: Set Realistic, Achievable Daily Goals

We can easily get ahead of ourselves. By setting a daily goal that is realistic, we can create momentum. People who are challenged by call reluctance often believe that they need to make twenty, fifty, or even a hundred calls a day to make a difference. Because they can't do that, they avoid making even one. Start with a small number you can commit to daily. We have seen agents double their businesses in a year by making five to ten contacts a day. A little goes a long way. Prospecting is like Brylcreem: A little dab'll do ya. It just has to be used every day.

Set manageable goals for each week, and then break them down into a goal for each day. If you are struggling to hit the daily goal, break it down to each part of the day, or even each hour, if necessary.

Set manageable goals for each week, and then break them down into a goal for each day.

Strategy 3: Control Negative Self-Talk

We all have an internal voice. Sometimes that voice is our biggest fan and cheerleader. Other times it feels like that little voice is chaining us to a cement block and pushing us into a deep river. That internal voice can encourage us; it can criticize and chastise us as well.

Reward Yourself

Make it into a game. How many calls can I make before lunch or before my next appointment at 10:00? Make the target achievable. You want to have a feeling of accomplishment. When you achieve the goal, reward yourself. We call if celebrating the victory. Part of being effective in calling is learning to reward yourself along the way. The mouse wouldn't work as hard to get to the end of the maze if the cheese weren't there. The reality is that we are no different. You have to create small rewards along the way.

For those of you who are regularly challenged by call reluctance, this negative self-talk can be particularly aggressive. It can become almost paralyzing when you are preparing for a sales call. When you are going to pick up the phone, the negative self-talk turns up the volume and intensity.

"She is going to reject you."

"Why would he use you instead of these other agents?"

"Maybe there is another way to do this."

"I should really be handling a problem transaction."

"I need to do more research before I make this call."

Meet the challenge of the negative self-talk head-on. If you do, the voice will get quieter, and after a few dials it will go away completely.

If you are really struggling, write down what the negative self-talk is saying. By having the words down on paper, you can refute what is being said in your mind. The only way to repel the voice is to create the responses that defuse the arguments. It's the difference between your thoughts controlling you and you controlling your thoughts. You must take charge of this challenge.

Strategy 4: Visualize the Perfect Call

We often begin each call by envisioning rejection. We begin each call with the thought, "I hope they're not home." Do you visualize them hanging up in disgust, or is there a voice telling you they will be happy to hear from you? We often have a horrible movie playing in our head. Those negative images make the calls more difficult to execute.

We can create the outcome before we ever pick up the phone. Those negative visions create self-fulfilling prophecies and we get caught going through the motions without achieving the results we desire. There are two key reasons we end up short of the outcome we planned for:

1. **The negative visions generate stress and the mental stress blocks performance.** We are preoccupied with the stress. We are waiting for the other shoe to drop so we can be right.

2. **The negative visions are a rehearsal.** The more you run the negative through mentally, the greater the probability of reproducing it in reality. You will create the outcome you visualize.

We must visualize ourselves talking on the phone with confidence. We must have a "bring it on" attitude. We must visualize ourselves handling the objections efficiently and effectively, and we must visualize ourselves setting an appointment.

Strategy 5: Use the "Ten-Minute Strategy"

It's really easy when you are in call reluctance to envision hours of calling and toiling on the phone. You believe that you are going to have to bear hours of rejection to generate one measly lead. Then you figure you might as well give yourself the day off and you can make it up tomorrow.

Resolve before you give up for the day to make calls for ten minutes. Any of us can make calls for just ten minutes! When you have completed ten minutes or a certain number of contacts, such as two or three, you can quit guilt-free. You have "bought" your freedom for the day. You have taken a big step toward breaking through call reluctance. Do the ten-minute drill and know you are progressing out of call reluctance.

Call Reluctance Is Real

You will discover that the hardest part is behind you. You can tap in to the momentum you have just created. I guarantee that the next dial will be easier and not feel intimidating. You have started to control the negative self-talk. You can choose to continue on. This is the best commitment you could make and keep for yourself.

Call reluctance is real for every salesperson. There is no one who doesn't suffer from some form of call reluctance. If some claim they don't ever have it, just realize they must have deeper psychological problems to deal with. Apply the five strategies today, and work to overcome call reluctance.

Referrals Can Come from Unexpected Places

I had a coaching client recently who was one of the best agents in his market. He had been selling real estate for more than ten years and had never gotten a referral from his mother. I asked him if he ever prospected her and asked her to send him a referral. He said, "No, I didn't think I would have to remind my mother that I am in real estate sales." My response was for him to call her and ask for referrals. Two weeks later he called me and said she had given him two referrals in the last two weeks. It wasn't merely a coincidence—it was because he asked. "Ask and you will receive" is true. Prospecting is the process of asking.

Expireds are a great option. They have already raised their hands and announced to the world that they want to sell.

A vast majority of agents never call these people to apply for the job of selling their home. In my market, there were more than seven thousand active licensed agents. I would say less than one hundred agents worked the expired market with regularity rather than trying to find people who wanted to buy and sell in a larger untested group.

Expireds are a great option. They have already raised their hands and announced to the world that they want to sell. Your only job is to call them and ask for an appointment. It is very difficult to convince anyone today to do business with you over the phone. Your objective is to set up an appointment with all the decision makers present to make a presentation in person.

Expired Listings

Expired listings are another excellent source of prospecting opportunities. These are listings that were with another agent who failed to sell the home. For most of these people the need to sell is still urgent. Most of them have not selected another agent to represent them.

Call Consistently

Your objective is to call consistently until they list or die! Too often we stop short of the mark. You need to call until you are certain they will never list their home. Often the expired will give you the "reflex no" because of the volume of calls they are receiving from others. The "reflex no" is a no that is given without thought. Let me give you an example: You go into a department store and the clerk asks if she can help you. Your immediate response is "No, I'm just looking." That is a "reflex no." Even though you go to the store to buy something, you have learned to give that response to disengage the salesperson. The expired will often give you a "reflex no" and hope you will never call back. They will often tell you they will never put their home on the market again and next week you see it has been listed.

Phone call consistency is essential for success in the expireds.

Phone call consistency is essential for success in the expireds. Calling the new expireds every other day for a week or every day for a week is essential. Don't assume they will remember you, because they won't. I have called people back even after talking with them for ten minutes about their home and they don't know me from all the other calls they have received. One element of skillful prospecting is to be there at the right time. The only way to ensure that is to call often and ask for the appointment.

How to Make Six Figures Prospecting Expired Listings

Prospecting expired listings can be the core of anyone's business in the real estate field. You can create a system that will give you repeatable results for your effort. Let's look at these three characteristics of prospecting expired listings.

1. **They are easy to find.** The expired listings come up every day. You will always have a handful that you can work on. Expired listings provide a steady stream of new leads of people to contact for listing appointments. There are usually a few very heavy days in each month. Set your schedule to take advantage of these days. The end of the month is usually one of the heaviest times for expired listings; up to 25 percent of the expired listings for the month may come up on a heavy day.

2. **They want to sell.** Unlike many other types of clients, the people whose house listing has expired had their property on the market at one time. They had a plan laid out to sell and move. Their plan did not work out and in most cases they wish it had. There will be some expireds that were listed by people who are now tired of the process, but the majority of them still want to sell.

3. **The bulk of them are looking for an agent.** If the expireds still have the desire to sell, as most do, they may be ready to consider changing agents. They are looking for someone who can solve their problem. Most do not know why their home did not sell, but they are frustrated with their previous agent and sometimes with all agents. They will rarely return to their previous agent.

The Truth About Expireds

Now, I don't mean to toot my own horn, but I would characterize myself as an expert on expireds. Expireds made close to 50 percent of my annual units and revenue during my sales career. When I really understood the process of prospecting, lead follow-up, qualifying the presentation, presenting, objection handling, and closing, I would list between 75 and 85 expired properties a year. Almost all of them would sell within the initial listing period; very few would re-expire with me.

I started working expireds on my first day in real estate sales and I worked them on my final day in real estate sales some eight and a half years later. Over the years I tweaked, adjusted, overhauled, and amended my marketing pieces, scripts, dialogues, systems, strategies, and tactics looking for the edge over the competition to increase my market share in expireds.

I made thousands of mistakes on phone calls, marketing pieces, presentations, qualifying . . . you name it I probably made it, and that is one of the reasons that I am an expert on expireds today. It isn't because I made the least amount of mistakes; it is because I probably make the most mistakes.

My personal view is that working expired listings is an all-or-nothing game. You can't proceed in a half-hearted, here today gone tomorrow fashion. Either you work expired listings—every day and on a consistent basis—or you don't.

You can't try to work expireds for a few days when you find yourself low on listings, and then quit for a few weeks only to return to the effort again later. There's no such thing as a kind of expired agent. If you want to capitalize by converting expired listings, be ready to make working expired listings your way of business life.

As a new agent, my work life revolved around expireds. I learned that in any given month most listing expirations occurred over the course of a few days, and that is still the case today. Up to a third of all the listings that expire occur over the last few days of the month and the first day of the new month. If you are going to work expireds, get ready to make those days very long work days. I followed this routine:

I'd arrive at the office around 6:00 a.m. and immediately print out the expired listings. Some days I'd end up with more than a hundred listings on my desk.

At 6:30 a.m. one of my staff members, who on other days arrived at 7:30 a.m., came in to start researching phone numbers that weren't listed on the MLS printout. We searched four different sources for missing numbers. We first searched the Coles Directory. Then we would move on to the MLS Metro-scan search. If we still did not acquire the phone number, we would go to the Internet through Yahoo and People Search. Finally, we would package up the rest for the title company to search the tax records and have the material back in to us before 9 a.m.

In certain instances I would call the previous agent to ask for the seller's phone number—and offer them some of the commission if they would give it to me. The reason is if I got it and few other agents have it in the market I would have a higher probability of securing the listing.

Based on gut instinct, market knowledge, and the information contained in the MLS printout, I'd sort the properties, quickly determining why each didn't sell and putting the ones that offered the highest probability of listing conversion and sale on top. Also, I'd move promising properties located in areas where I really wanted listings to the top of the list.

I would then practice my scripts and dialogues, anticipating the objections I might hear from the seller and practicing how I'd overcome the barrier. I knew before placing a phone call to the owner that my objective was to move beyond any objections and to secure an appointment.

After half an hour's practice, by 7:45 I was on the phone, aiming to reach people before they went to work and before other agents began to make contact later in the morning. Today, your schedule is dictated by limitations stipulated by state and national Do Not Call regulations.

If you cannot secure the phone number because of the Do Not Call laws or you simply cannot find the number, go to the door directly. Most people are better face-to-face anyway. You will see fewer people but be more effective because you are face-to-face.

My goal was to be the first to get through to the owner of every expired listing, but obviously that isn't always possible, especially on a day when the pile of listing printouts numbers a hundred or more.

Once I got through, scheduled an appointment, and established a good connection and sense of trust, I'd warn the owners about what to expect over the course of the next twenty-four to forty-eight hours, suggesting that to avoid interruptions they could unplug their phone for the day. I knew that if the owner could dodge the calls over the first day or two following the listing expiration, most agents would quit trying to get through.

The key to success with expired listings is to work them consistently and with commitment. Most agents who "work" expireds do so only at the end of the month and, even then, only sporadically. I never took a vacation at the end of the month, because I didn't want to miss the flood of expireds when they came through. And, in between, I also watched for the three, four, or five listings that expired on a daily basis. Only a small group of agents work expireds as a way of life, but I can vouch for the fact that those who do build great businesses.

New Technologies for Expireds

Expireds really are a way of life. It has become much easier to secure the information you need than when I was chasing and listing expires. One service that has made a huge change is RedX, the Real Estate Data X-Change.

RedX has really transformed the information collection and the information management process for expireds. It is a wonderful service that helps you invest greater amounts of your time in direct revenue providing objectives and helps you streamline the production supporting activities.

With all the time and effort you save using RedX you will have more time to invest in your next level of activities with waiting expireds, which is talking with a prospect face-to-face or phone-to-phone. The more you invest in either of these two activities or both of them, the higher the results you will achieve.

RedX will research all the phone numbers for expireds, keep track of your leads, and integrate with your MLS so you know if a property has been relisted so you don't call them. It reduces your personal labor of researching and follow-up by 90 percent!

Some benefits of RedX include

- Searches multiple databases to deliver the most accurate and up-to-date contact information for expired, cancelled, and withdrawn listings;
- Cross-checks expired leads against the active MLS listings to ensure the property has not been re-listed with an agent or sold;
- Screens contact phone numbers for expired leads against the National Do Not Call Registry (DNC) for your convenience;
- Delivers up-to-date expired leads directly into the lead manager
- Organizes all your leads, creates notes and tasks, and sets reminders or to-do's; and
- Customizes the lead manager to maximize the features and functions to accommodate your prospecting needs.

For more information go to http://theredx.com/signup/dirkzeller.html.

Defusing the Expired and Lowering Resistance

With some expireds you can defuse them through humor. It's easy to take ourselves too seriously when we have an angry expired. Making a funny comment or telling a funny story or pointing out a comical item on their listing agreement can break the ice. Telling a story of one of your other clients that had it worse can often defuse the expired.

Calling the Seller: What to Say and How to Say It

When you call the owner of a home with an expired listing, you have one objective: to secure an appointment for a face-to-face meeting. Remember, the owners will likely be contacted by dozens, if not hundreds, of other agents, so you need to move quickly and skillfully by following this advice:

- **Address their situation.** Quickly convince the owners that if they choose to work with you, the outcome will be different from the last time. Explain why working with you provides them a higher probability of sales success than they'll receive by working with any other agent.

- **Be proactive.** The most serious sellers will re-list their home within a couple of days of a listing expiration. To land the listing, you can't be low-key with your dialogue and delivery. These owners are ready for action. You must convey power, conviction, and belief in your ability to succeed.

- **Leave yourself wiggle room.** At this stage in the game you may not be aware of all the factors. You don't know the condition of the home, the neighborhood layout, the level of access the owners are granting to buyers, the price and time frame they're trying to achieve, the probability that their expectations can be met, and what the previous agent really did over the course of the listing term.

  Because so much is up in the air, you have to leave yourself a little wiggle room by not overcommitting to what you can and can't do for the client. You also don't want to commit to what you would charge in terms of commission. You need to be flexible depending on the market and motivation of the prospect.

- **Turn the most frequently asked questions to your advantage.** "What will you do differently? Why did my home not sell?" You can say something like: "Are you asking me to guess, or do you really want to know for sure?" When they say, "I want to know for sure," you book an appointment to see the house and have a friendly discussion. With that helpful move, you get your foot in the door.

- **Gain information.** The owners need to understand clearly that without firsthand knowledge of their situation it's impossible for you to determine which specific approaches would achieve their desired outcome. You need to see their home in order to review its features, benefits, condition, and curb appeal.

You also need to figure out the previous agent's marketing strategy. Ask the seller what the other agent did to market their property. If you can, get the previous agent's flyers, ads, and brochures. Taking a look at the previous agent's Web site may also help. Finally, you need to gain an understanding of the owners' expectations regarding time frame, listing price, sales price, and access for showings, as well as their interest in your evaluation of the competition they face in the current marketplace

- **Differentiate yourself.** Use your track record (or your firm's track record if you're new in the business) to gain credibility with the owners. As you present your success story, do so with the caveat that your success is based on your outcome with clients who sought your counsel, accepted your recommendations, and implemented your advice. Tell the owners that you want to contribute to a similarly successful outcome on their behalf. You may even want to supply references of satisfied clients—especially those clients whose listings were also expired before you began working with them.

  Provide the option of an easy exit. The sellers with an expired listing most likely wanted to fire the other agent long before the listing term was up, but in most cases they were bound by the contract terms to wait out the agreement. Acknowledge your understanding that the owners feel cautious about tying their home up for another long period of time. To put the owners at ease, offer them an easy-exit listing agreement or include a 100 percent satisfaction guaranteed clause. Either approach allows the owner to sever the agreement any time before it expires.

Enticing them with a guaranteed sales program or added bonus can really help them to listen more attentively to your offer for service. You don't want to explain the program in depth at this stage. You want them to understand that you offer a guaranteed process to sell their home, to test the level of motivation of the prospect. Don't go into the fine print of the program of commission charged, percentage of acquisition charge between market value and purchase price, or any of the steps of the program. You need to push for the appointment and qualify then.

Sales Scripts

When you encounter a challenging prospect, I really believe an empathetic but firm approach is really best. It establishes you as a professional with them. Scripted approaches like the ones I will share with you right now really work to bring about a positive conversation or reveal the real truth about the prospect so you can move on to another prospect.

"Because we have just met over the phone, I at this point don't know enough about your situation to guarantee I can help you, and you don't know enough about me to know that I can't help you, so wouldn't it be worth a few minutes to know with certainty?"

"_____, here's the truth, I don't know enough about your goals and objectives to know 100 percent that I can help you like the 50 other expired clients I have successfully helped in the past, and you don't know enough about me and my process and the results I achieve for clients to know that I can't help you, so why don't we both invest a few minutes to find out if I can help. Would [insert date] or [insert second date] be better for you?"

"_____, the truth is I couldn't possibly help everyone that I speak with in a given week, month, or year, and I wouldn't want to. I operate an exclusive practice and am selective in the clients I represent. I believe I can help you as I have hundreds of others in my career. Are you willing to invest a few minutes with no obligation to find out if you can still achieve what you set out to do a few months ago?"

By admitting you don't know if you can help them but also getting them to acknowledge they don't know that you can't, you defuse their fear of being sold. By also positioning yourself as a professional who only works with clients that you select you go against the grain of the typical view that most consumers have of real estate agents.

When you tell them there are no costs and no obligation, you are in effect telling them there is no risk. In fact, in a subtle way you are saying to them that they would be stupid not to consider your "no lose" offer. You could even say to them, "I hear your hesitation, but you really have nothing to lose and everything to gain by spending a few minutes with me. I mostly want to ensure that all the decisions you make are based on solid knowledge." The truth is when they give you a "reflex no" after you ask about their going back on the market, their response could be based on the media reports of real estate nationally, regionally, or locally. It could be from third parties such as neighbors, friends, and relatives' junior market analysis of what they have heard or read about the market. It could be from their previous agent's view. That's right—the unsuccessful agent who didn't get their home sold. It could be just out of general frustration that they didn't get what they wanted. There are really a host of factors that can influence a seller's decision not to list or just not to listen to you. Your job is to cut through that fog to be heard.

One of the biggest mistakes that real estate salespeople make consistently is to overstep or overreach in their approach. When they first get on the phone with a prospect, instead of establishing a relationship they jump to set up a listing presentation, or qualify the prospect, or position themselves as the best agent. At this early stage you should only be trying to book an appointment, which will allow you to have an honest conversation with your prospect about their goals and expectations. Only after you secure an appointment does the phone conversation change from an outsider discussion to an insider conversation where you are trying to serve.

Questions For a Reluctant Prospect with an Expired Listing:

- If you wanted to make a change in your real estate agent, what would need to happen next?

- Provided you would be willing to consider a change, what would you need to know to be assured you are making a sound decision?
- What's the typical procedure or process you would use for making a decision like this?
- What standards do you apply in considering a real estate agent?
- What were the criteria you used in choosing the agent you currently employ?
- If we could create the ideal situation, what would it look like?
- If you could have exactly what you want from an agent, what would it be?
- At the bottom line, what do you want?
- How will you define outstanding results?

Using an effective script process for expireds is a must. You have to keep the conversation with an expired moving, and the best way to do that is to use a sequential script like the one below.

Expired Script

Hi, I am looking for _____ *(state the name). This is* _____ *with* _____.

Is your home still available?

    OR

When do you plan to meet with agents about the job of selling your home?

    OR

I noticed your home was no longer on the MLS. I was calling to see if you still wanted to sell?

Main Questions to Ask:

1. *When you sell this home, where are you hoping to move to?*
2. *Did you have a time frame to get there?*
3. *What do you think caused your home not to sell?*
4. *How did you select your previous agent?*
5. *What are your expectations of the next agent you choose?*
6. *Has anyone shared with you the real reason your home failed to sell?*
7. *There are only a few reasons homes fail to sell: exposure, changes in market competition, and price. One you control, one the agent controls, and one no one controls. Which do you think it is?*
8. *Let me ask you . . . do you want to know which one for sure?*
9. *All we need to do is meet for fifteen or twenty minutes and take a look at your home. Would _____ or _____ be better for you?*

You will also need some additional questions to ask to make sure the dialogue continues to flow. These questions should be used when you feel an extended pause or hesitation on the part of the expired prospect. These questions will allow you to reignite the conversation and move toward an appointment booking question. Once you ask these, pause and listen. The prospect will usually respond in a manner that will give you an opening to sell the value of an appointment with you.

Ten Ways to Increase Your Success in Calling Expireds

1. **Always use a headset.** A professional salesperson always uses a headset. Being hands-free allows you to be more effective in taking notes. You know what has been said because you have recorded it on paper. You can reconfirm, review, and summarize like a professional salesperson.

   Using a headset can reduce fatigue because you aren't holding a phone to your ear for a segment of your day. It also eliminates the chance you will drop the phone while talking to a prospect. Nothing kills a sale faster than an expired prospect getting their eardrum blasted by the thud of the phone hitting the desktop.

Psychologically, when you put on the headset, it prepares your mind . . . it is game time. It's like a football player putting on his helmet before running out onto the field!

2. **Stand up when making calls.** Your body, in the standing position, will convey more power, authority, energy, enthusiasm, and conviction. Too many real estate salespeople make calls in a poor posture position with their left elbow on the desk slumped over with the phone held to their ear. They are curled up like a question mark.

   The range of communication is narrowed over the phone. That is why you must stand up to transfer more energy and intensity through the phone line. You will feel better and be sharper mentally when you stand up to make calls. With over 55 percent of all communication being through your body, you are dramatically reducing your results by not energizing your whole body in the communication process.

Sales is a process of doing something with someone, not doing it to someone.

3. **Create variety in your delivery.** You must vary your tone, volume, and pace of delivery to keep a prospect's attention. The expired prospect already has a preconceived idea of who you are because you are in real estate sales. You have to create variety in delivery and provide a compelling reason that you aren't like their previous agent and all the other callers. Sales is a process of doing something with someone, not doing it to someone.

   This is especially true for expireds. You must balance your tone, volume, and pace of delivery to a prospect.

   A. *Tone.* The tone of our voice consists of the rhythm of how we talk. Each person has their own rhythm to their words and delivery. When you vary your rhythm, you cause the client to listen closely—even when your call is longer. Everyone from PeeWee

Herman to Jimmy Stewart to John Wayne has a different rhythm to their voice.

Inflection and intonation are also a part of tone. These two characteristics allow you to convey your personality in the call. Without inflection or intonation, you will sound like every other real estate agent—and you will sound like you are reading through your script for the first time.

B. *Volume.* Most prospects gain a mental picture of the salesperson by the volume of their voice. If our voice is too soft, they assume we are incompetent in our job. If it's too loud, we can be typecast as the pushy agent.

We don't want to be typecast in our role as a salesperson solely owing to the volume of our voice. If I had the choice I would rather, when working with an expired, be more forceful in volume and intensive than coming off as too meek. We need to vary the volume of our speech to align with all types of prospects. Many times, this typecasting happens subconsciously and after just a few minutes of dialogue.

C. *Pace of delivery.* The prospect will recognize your pace as either being pleasing or repelling. If you are a fast-talker, slow down from time to time. If you speak too quickly, people will pigeonhole you as a fast-talking, smooth operator who convinces people to list just to make a quick buck. People will assume you are just trying to make a fast sale and move on—they won't trust you, and the listing and sale will never happen.

If your pace is too measured and deliberate, you risk coming off as inexperienced. The expired prospect will feel that you lack confidence in yourself and your recommendations. If your speech is really bad, your prospect will become bored. A bored prospect isn't a client who will list with you any time soon. Worst of all, if the expired prospect is a fast-talker and fast thinker, they will think that you are stupid! Listen for their pace of delivery. Listen for how quickly they talk and respond to your questions. Then modify your pace to better align your speed of delivery to theirs.

4. **Talk less . . . listen more.** Right now, you only know what you know . . . which is part of the reason that you are reading this book and "listening" to the written words to acquire more knowledge. In the same way, you need to *listen* when working with an expired prospect—to learn more about the prospect, what they want, what their needs are, and what specific problems they currently have. You will separate yourself from the other real estate salespeople and increase your results quickly by listening more.

Take the time to listen for key words, phrases, and concepts. Listen intently for other people's names and how they will influence the future decision. Listen for the facts and also for the emotions behind the facts or problems.

5. **Stay focused on selling or go home!** We walk a fine line as we try to both pay attention to new listings and new sales and also service our current clients. Make sure that you balance this equation: Do not lose sight and provide poor service to your clients. But also don't fool yourself into thinking that marketing and closing a property are actually "servicing" your client. Focus on delivering what you sold with integrity.

6. **Practice before the game begins.** Every salesperson—let me say that again . . . EVERY salesperson—should practice their base scripts and dialogues before they pick up the phone because the twists and turns of prospecting expireds is more complex, challenging, and competitive then most other facets of lead generation in real estate. I recommend at least fifteen minutes of practice before you begin a calling session. Doing the practice aloud is preferable. You might sound funny to other people, but they won't be laughing when you lead the sales board soon.

You want to practice your opening statements, prospecting scripts and dialogues, appointment objection handling, lead follow-up scripts, and closes. Any professional in athletics or entertainment will practice to properly warm up before the contest or performance.

Before you complete your day, be sure to role-play with someone. Investing the time to improve your skills in role-play situations will help you sound more like a professional.

7. **Bundle your calls together.** Planning and bunching your calls into blocks will improve how you sound on the phone, and your results will improve. Don't make a new prospect call, then a lead follow-up call, and then a presentation call. Don't make one expired call, then a lead follow-up call, then a past client call to ask for a referral. If you are going to prospect expireds then bunch them all together at one time. If you are going to make expired prospect calls, make at least ten in a row. You will improve your performance with each call. The tenth call will be much better than the first. The same is true for all of the calls that you make grouped by type and where they are in the sales cycle.

8. **Always ask for commitment.** It's impossible to make a sale on every phone call. It is also impossible to turn every call to an expired into an appointment. But it's not impossible to gain some level of commitment. Even if it's a low level of commitment on their part to book a preview appointment to review the information you are sending to them. Champion salespeople ask for and require a commitment; marginal salespeople wait for the prospect to commit themselves.

   "If I send you the literature, will you review it?"

   "Do you like the idea of _____?"

   "It seems that I have answered all of your questions, correct?"

   "Is it worth four minutes of your time to investigate if you could still achieve your objectives?"

   "If it was solely up to you, would you go ahead and book an appointment?"

9. **Persistence has a big payoff.** There is no substitute for persistence. Most salespeople quit long before any sale is made. This tendency is enhanced when dealing with a potentially harder prospect to convert, like an expired.

Your talent, skill, attitude, service, marketing pieces, and so forth, will not make up for a lack of persistence and perseverance.

The average sale is made after the prospect has said no four times but most salespeople quit asking long before then. These statistics say it all:

44% quit the first time the prospect says "no"

22% quit the second time the prospect says "no"

14% quit the third time the prospect says "no"

12% quit the fourth time the prospect says "no"

92% of salespeople quit after four tries or less for acquiring the order from the customer.

Only 8% of salespeople ask for the order more than four times.

60% of all sales are made after the prospect has said "no" four times, before they say "yes."

8% of the salespeople control 60 percent of the business . . . just for asking!

10. **Know the threshold moment.** You have to record your prospecting calls regularly if you want to learn to recognize the threshold moment with prospects. It's almost a sixth sense. You will develop it faster if you are willing to record and replay your calls as a learning experience. There is a yin and yang to persistence. I believe that in most sales calls, and especially when you're calling expireds, there is a threshold moment that you reach when the sale will either be made on this call or it won't. One of the most glaring mistakes I hear when I listen to salespeople's recorded calls is their prolonging the call after they reach the threshold moment when they cross into the "no

sale" territory for that particular call. The threshold moment doesn't mean a sale won't happen; it just means it definitely won't happen on that call.

Once you know that, wrap up and get off the phone. I often hear salespeople on the phone another ten to twenty or even thirty minutes after they reach the threshold moment. All they have done is reduced the number of dials, contacts, and sales they will make that day. The extra time invested in the call won't make the sale rise from the dead like Lazarus. It's over at the threshold moment. Wrap up the call, set up the next call well before you hang up, and shout the four-letter word of sales . . . NEXT!

11. **Bonus—tape your calls.** The absolute best way to sound like a sales professional is to tape your calls. The problem is few salespeople actually do it. My sales team at Real Estate Champions is required to hand in a tape of their opening statements, benefit statements, appointment setting calls, and their presentation calls for coaching, seminars, and product. They also have objection-handling segments and closing segments on their weekly tape . . . it's required, with no exceptions. Of the people who *do* tape their calls, fewer still actually listen to them. It's almost as if we fear hearing how we really sound on the phone.

Listen for openings you missed.

I really recommend listening to your calls twice through. The first time through listen for only one thing: Listen for the openings you missed. Focus only on the sales openings that you missed that the prospect gave you.

Was there an opportunity to insert a strong trial close or closing statement after their response that could have started the movement to a booked appointment?

The truth is I have listened to literally hundreds of prospecting tapes from top-notch salespeople. I have never listened to one that was not littered with missed opportunities. These missed opportunities translate into real lost sales and real lost commission dollars for the agent.

A great salesperson will wait patiently to seize the right moment to help the prospect and at the same time position themselves as the best agent to provide the service needed. It really is a fine balance between patience and action. The best way to learn that skill, and it is a skill, is to listen to your tapes. You could learn it through trial and error by making more calls, but that is really a high price to pay for learning.

Once you have reviewed your taped calls for missed opportunities or missed openings then you need to review the whole call.

How effective was your opening statement? Do you need to adjust it?

How was your pose and tonality driving the call? Did you read the prospect well enough to align yours with theirs?

Did you build trust and credibility?

Do you think the prospect recognized you as being different from other agents?

Did you get an appointment booked, whether over the phone for another call, or for a preview of the home, or a full listing presentation appointment? If you didn't, why not?

Was there anything you should have done differently?

Take the time to do an honest review of your taped calls. You might have to invest a few hours a week to really accelerate the learning by reviewing your calls. The time you invest will be worth it because you will be raising the conversion rate and your experience.

If you really want to be the best and provide yourself and your family with unlimited opportunities in life . . . tape your sales calls always!

CAPITALIZING ON FSBO PROPERTIES

The most important thing to do when working with FSBOs is to understand the profile of the FSBO seller. They have a specific reason for trying to sell on their own. We as agents need to find out that reason. In nine out of ten instances the primary reason is to save on the commission. The other reasons are low motivation, the belief that real estate agents as a group are incompetent, or their ego (because their neighbor or friend got lucky it must be easy). Some of these reasons are hard to get around. In many cases, low motivation and ego are cause enough to move on to another potential client.

Remember, your first objective in every selling situation is to gain the interview.

Be Picky

In working FSBOs I subscribe to the three Ps theory: picky, patient, and persistent. You must work these three *P*s in some combination to be successful in FSBOs. The first, and I believe the most important P, is being picky. You must be highly selective in working FSBOs. One of the first mistakes I made early in my career was trying to work too many FSBOs at a time. They must be screened very carefully and completely.

The more you exclude the difficult or unreasonable FSBOs, the more time you will have to devote to the enjoyable people you can work with. You are not going to list them all. Focus on the really motivated and good people you will enjoy working with. This will allow you to do more business with less effort. Life is too short to work with people whose expectations for you will always be unattainable.

How Strong Is Their Motivation?

The FSBOs need to be screened for motivation. You are looking for the ones who *have* to sell, not those who just *want* to sell. They have to be moving for a valid reason, not just because they feel like it. The feeling may not be strong enough for them to invest 6 to 7 percent of their equity in your fees. This is clearly their mind-set. This mind-set is false, but often they feel that it is very valid. They feel they would be losing money. The truth is they were never going to get the money in the first place. They need to be motivated to sell because they are transferring, having a new child, divorcing, needing a one-level house due to health, or some other clearly defined reason. They have no option but to sell and sell *right now.*

Will They Require High Maintenance?

Once you have motivated sellers, you need to determine their maintenance level. You must decide if the sellers are high maintenance or low maintenance. High maintenance FSBOs will cause you to lose money. You need to be able to spot them and exclude them from your client base. Otherwise they will call you at all hours of the day and night and bother you incessantly. They often will try to tell you how to do your job. This pestering can be an ongoing drain of time and energy for both you and your staff. This is only one deal—what are you willing to do for one deal? FSBOs often know just enough to be dangerous to themselves and others. They, however, do not realize this fact until it is too late. You must evaluate the owner before you take the listing. Do you want to be associated with this person for at least 60 days and more likely 120 to 180 days until the deal is closed and you are paid?

How Great Is Their Integrity?

The next evaluation I make is based on integrity. Do the sellers have the integrity to tell the truth regarding the condition of their home? Are they going to be honest with you or are you the enemy just looking for a commission? You do not need to do business with people who have this attitude. Rarely will you create a win-win situation with people who have this philosophy of life.

Be Patient

Another key to success in working with FSBOs is patience. You need to patiently wait them out. They will all run their course. They all have a certain length of time they will endure in the process of selling on their own. The key is to find out that length of time and be there at the appointed hour.

Most of the FSBOs will not think about listing until they have tried selling for three to six weeks. They want to give it a good try before giving up. The higher the motivation, the shorter the time they will try the FSBO route. Therefore your follow-up will need to be more aggressive with the motivated ones.

Your patience factor needs to be great because you know you can help them. You have to let them fall and then help them get back up. It is almost like watching your children go through the process of taking their first steps or riding a bike for the first time. Early on I wanted to teach FSBOs and help them before they were ready. It was painful to watch them create all these problems for themselves. But they did not want my insight or help at that stage of the game. If you move in too early and too hard, you are out the door. You need to patiently wait till they go through the whole cycle. When they finally realize they cannot do it themselves, then you can step in and help. At that moment you must step in aggressively and decisively. You cannot hesitate once they get to this point.

Your goal is not to convince them to list with you, but just to interview you.

Be Persistent

The last principle is persistence. You must hang in there with calls, letters, updates, and other communications. The goal of persistence is to be one of the three or four agents they interview for the job. Your goal is not to convince them to list with you, but just to interview you. Just like expireds, they get fewer calls from agents as the weeks go by. If you maintain a steady professional level of contact for three or four weeks, you will usually get an interview. Continue to contact them and continue to follow up on their progress. Let them know you are there to provide a quality service if they have the need for it.

The Importance of Qualifying FSBOs

If you have been picky and have qualified FSBOs well, you can be less patient and less persistent. This means that if they are more motivated, you will spend less time and money on follow-up mail pieces and phone calls to them. Their window for marketing the home as an FSBO is small. They will try for a few weeks and then turn it over to you.

I cannot impress upon you enough how critical qualifying can be. The biggest loss is the client you list who turns out to be a nightmare. She can disrupt or ruin the whole day for you. You also lose all the time and money you have invested when they do not sell or when you release them because they are not worth it. Make that selection very wisely. You are going to spend time, effort, and energy on every listing you take. Make sure you get compensation for your efforts.

FSBOs can be a wonderful source of income for many of you. You must look at them as a valid set of clients who truly need help; they just do not know it yet. By applying the three Ps, you will be able to add a fourth P—high *profit!* That fourth P is the most important P in any business.

An FSBO Script

To make personal contact, begin by asking the FSBO seller if you can come by and see their home. You can ask them in a few different ways. You can explain that you want to keep abreast of the regional housing inventory, you can say that you are working with buyers who may be interested, you can present yourself as a potential investor, or, when you can, you can use the "reverse-no" technique. Following are sample scripts for each approach.

Script for Keeping Up with the Inventory

Mr. Seller, your home is located in my core area of sales. Because of this, I would like to come by and preview your home. Would there be a time on _____ or _____ to do that this week?

Script for Working with the Prospective Seller

Ms. Seller, I understand you are selling your home on your own. Let me ask you this: Are you cooperating with real estate agents? What I mean is, if a real estate agent brought you a qualified buyer at a price that was agreeable to you, would you be willing to pay a partial commission?

We are working with a few buyers for your area whom we have not been able to place yet. May I come by on _____ or _____ to see your home?

When you use the above approach, understand that you are not interested in reducing your commission. What you're really trying to do is achieve a face-to-face appointment to collect more information on the sellers' motivation in order to determine the probability of securing a listing in the future.

Script for a Potential Investor

Mr. Seller, your home is located in a solid area for real estate investment. I was wondering if I could come by to see your home as a principal for possible purchase, to see if it is a property that would meet my investment needs. Would _____ or _____ be better for you?

In using the above approach, realize that the key phrase is "investment needs." You will rarely find an FSBO that will meet your investment needs. My personal investment need is a home that can be acquired at a 70 percent discount below fair market value. Most FSBOs are trying to sell their home at 110 percent of fair market value. This technique does get you in the door to see the home and talk with them.

Script for a Reverse-No

Ms. Seller, would you be offended if I came by to take a quick look at your home?

The reverse-no technique can be used with any script. It capitalizes on the normal reflexive human reaction of "no" in order to achieve a positive response. It opens the door to you to then set an appointment.

The FSBO Survey Script

Surveying can be a very effective way to gain face time or phone time with an FSBO prospect. Below is an example:

> Hi, this is _____ from _____. I am looking for the owner of the home for sale.
>
> Your home is in my core area. I am doing a quick survey of the FSBOs in this area. May I take a few minutes to ask you some questions?
>
> The ad in the paper said that you had _____ bedrooms and _____ bathrooms.

1. Do you have a two level or one level home?
2. Are all the bedrooms on the same floor?
3. Are they good-sized rooms?
4. What is the condition of the kitchen?
5. Are the bathrooms in good condition?
6. Would you describe your yard for me?
7. Is there anything else you feel I should know?

Then ask questions aimed at learning their motivation for selling and their openness to using an agent.

1. It sounds like you have a great home. How long have you lived there?
2. Why are you selling at this time?
3. Where are you hoping to move to now?
4. What is your time frame to get there?
5. How did you happen to select that area to move to?

6. *How did you determine your initial asking price for the home?*

7. *What techniques are you using for exposure and marketing your home?*

8. *Are you aware that over 86 percent of the buyers for properties begin on the Internet now?*

9. *If there was a clear advantage for you in using me to market and expose your home, and it cost you very little, would you consider it?*

10. *Let's simplify. Set a time to get together for fifteen to twenty minutes, so I can see your home and understand your objectives. I have time available _____, or would _____ be better for you?*

ADVANTAGES OF FSBOS AND EXPIREDS

1. Most agents don't work them, so there is little competition.

2. They have announced that they want to sell.

3. They will force you to acquire sales skills. Many agents overlook this point. People who are successful in these disciplines are the best sales-people in real estate. They have the ability to make convincing and compelling presentations. They also have the skill to overcome the objections of the seller. If you truly want to be the best in the real estate field, these two areas will forge your skills like no others.

4. Once you master these two groups, you will be marketproof. Many agents' income is tied to an increase in the market. If the market goes up, they make more money. If the market softens, they make less. Being successful in the expireds and FSBOs creates success in all market situations.

When the market is up and inventory for listings is tight, there will be few expired listings because all the listed homes are selling. This will cause more people to try to sell their home on their own, so there will be an abundance of FSBOs. When the market is falling and homes are difficult to sell, there will few FSBOs. Most people will feel that if the agents can't sell them why should they try on their own? In that market there will be a lot of expireds. There will be many homes that failed to sell. If you master FSBOs and expireds you can earn a fantastic living in any market.

CHAPTER 9

MASTERING YOUR SALES SKILLS, PART II: LEADS AND EFFECTIVE LISTING PRESENTATIONS

LEAD GENERATION

We are in the lead generation business. If you want to take control of your life and your business at a greater level, you must set up a lead generation system. This system should be designed to generate large quantities of leads. By always having great quantities of leads, you can be highly selective in the people you work with. You will be able to help only a handful of people with regularity. These few people should be the best and most motivated clients and the ones who are sold on you and your service.

What Is a Lead?

One of the critical questions to ask yourself is, What is a lead? What is your definition of a *lead*? Each person's definition will tell a great deal about where he is in the business. When I first started, my definition of a lead was someone who wanted to buy or sell. It was a very simple definition. It was also a very broad definition and excluded very few people. My definition today would be someone who wants to buy or sell in the next fourteen days. My definition has changed dramatically over the years. How did I get from a very broad definition to one that was quite narrow? Let's take a look at the process.

You Can Have Too Many Leads

Like most new agents, I had very little knowledge of the business. I was chasing after any and every deal I could find. Because my definition of or philosophy about a lead was so broad, everybody on the face of the earth qualified as a potential client. Because everyone qualified as a potential client, I had too many to work with. Most of my potential "clients" honestly would never buy or sell a home, let alone one through me.

> *When I first started, my definition of a lead was someone who wanted to buy or sell. It was a very simple definition. It was also a very broad definition and excluded very few people.*

I spent a tremendous amount of time trying to persuade people to buy or sell who really never were going to buy or sell. I decided to tighten my definition to anyone who would buy or sell within a year, then to anyone who would buy or sell within six months, then within sixty days, thirty days, and finally fourteen days. If I had tightened my definition from the beginning, I would have saved myself a lot of mistakes, anguish, and lost income.

Cultivate Now Business

Do not hesitate to clearly define a *lead* in terms of *now* business. Spend the additional time working to find more leads through prospecting. Having a few good leads is better than having a bunch of marginal ones. Quality versus quantity is the name of the game. If your desire is to sell a home a week, you need only two to three *now* leads weekly to accomplish your goal. Think in terms of qualified people who want to do something *now!*

Having a few good leads is better than having a bunch of marginal ones. Quality versus quantity is the name of the game.

All the time I spent working with people who were too far out cost me a lot of money. We have all spoken with many people or even shown them property when they did not have the motivation to buy or sell *now!* Do not continue that process—change today!

Hang On to the Good Leads

There are people who want to buy and sell today; our job is to find them and help them do it. My goal was to list or sell a home every day. My job every morning when I got up was to find that person every working day. It is no more complicated than that. I would find people who were two weeks away, ten days away. If I filled my pipeline with these people, I always had great leads to work with. I did not have lots of leads, but the ones I had were highly motivated and I was confident I would get a listing or sale in the next week or two by combining sales skills and effective follow-up. You might call it relentless follow-up. Do not let go of a good lead. Have you ever tried to get a bone away from a big dog? Develop that attitude with good leads.

Know the Difference Between Now Clients Versus Project Clients
You must clearly state your definition of a lead. Here is a little hint for you: It should be someone who wants to buy or sell in sixty days or less. Any further out and you are not creating closings for the near future. You are investing your time, your most precious commodity, in someone who may not buy or sell. Do not waste your time for anyone or anything. We are all given only so much time in life. You and I have only so many days, so do not waste them with people whom you cannot help.

If you have too many potential clients rather than *now* clients, you will have a high level of frustration and no control of your business, not to mention the financial losses you will face. Keep your number of long-term or "project clients" down so you can invest your time in finding people who need help now. I define *project clients* as those who are

1. Looking for the "perfect house." I guarantee they will never find it.
2. Looking for a "tremendous deal." The deal rarely is good enough for them to move today. If the deal is so tremendous, some other smart agent has bought it already.
3. Waiting for the right house so they can put their home on the market. If they do not become motivated to sell after you show them a few houses that meet their criteria, you need to reevaluate whether they will sell in the near future.
4. Still not motivated after you call them back a few times.

We have all spent large amounts of money on mailings to people who are not moving. We have also spent large amounts of time following up on poor leads. Stop working with people who are not committed to doing something *now.* The old belief that "great salespeople should be able to sell ice to an Eskimo" is false. Great salespeople have clear definitions of what constitutes a lead. They clearly follow their narrow definitions. They prospect enough to keep a constant supply of leads flowing, so they can qualify and define them carefully.

Separate the Wheat from the Chaff

As it says in the Bible, Jesus would have us separate the wheat from the chaff, gathering wheat into the barn and burning up the chaff. We must separate the good kernels of *now* clients from the chaff of unmotivated sellers and buyers. The kernels of wheat have value, the chaff has no value. The wheat will feed your body and mind. The chaff will provide zero nourishment.

When you do not separate effectively, you get too bogged down with future business that never happens, or worse, you miss the *now* clients or do not have the time to find them because you are hoping this future business will work out. You often feel like you have so much invested in future business that you cannot just cut your losses even though in your heart you know doing that would be right. Always remember the least painful loss you will take is the one taken today.

Stick to Your Definition of a Lead

Take the time today to reflect and clearly define what a lead is to you. Review your definition every quarter to see if it has changed. Stick to your guns. Do not compromise because most of the time you will be burned. There is nothing more painful than to compromise and then not get paid for your effort. Once in a while you will find that the person you excluded will buy or sell with someone else. More often than not, you just saved yourself time and frustration.

> *Great salespeople do not worry about the transaction or the closing they never had. They focus on the key four-letter word in sales,* next.

Above all do not be concerned if you made a mistake by overqualifying or overdefining, which causes someone to use another agent. Great salespeople do not worry about the transaction or the closing they never had. They focus on the key four-letter word in sales, *next.*

THE 80/20 RULE

There is another way I use to categorize people and leads. It's a rule I used early on in my real estate sales career. It will help ensure that you select the correct people to work with. This is the Pareto principle or the 80/20 rule.

We have all been exposed to the 80/20 rule—80 percent of our results come from 20 percent of our labor, or 80 percent of our income will come from 20 percent of our prospects. When this rule is learned and applied, it is a powerful tool for success.

THE 20/50/30 RULE

Another rule is more powerful but less known than the 80/20 rule. It is the 20/50/30 rule. Let's take an in-depth look at this rule.

The 20 Percent: People Who Already Trust You

In the 20/50/30 rule, the 20 percent are made up of the people who will do business with you easily. This 20 percent represents people with whom you have already built trust and rapport. They have faith that what you say is true. They believe that you are skilled at what you do, and they would be pleased to work with you. They often treat professionals in other fields with respect. This type of client and prospect is like gold. This 20 percent is a pleasure to do business with. They can come from any source, such as open houses or prospecting. They could also be past clients or referrals.

The 50 Percent: People Who Are on the Fence

The next group is the 50 percent who are on the fence. This group, upon receiving a solid presentation and systematic approach, move toward your side of the fence. But it takes sufficient data and reasoning to get them to commit to buying or selling a home. This group, after careful evaluation of the data, will make a decision based on how it will benefit them. Having a benefit-based listing presentation is crucial to landing this type of prospect. You just need to apply solid sales skills and these prospects will become like the "golden" 20 percent.

The 30 Percent: The Highly Demanding People

The final group, which is the group 30 percent of people fall into, is the most challenging and dangerous group. This group demands tremendous amounts of energy and time to convince them to join you on your side of the fence. This 30 percent is highly demanding and often has limited respect for the services provided by others. Even if you give them a solid service presentation, they often demand more from a salesperson than the other two groups do.

Once I had determined an individual was in this 30 percent, I would disregard the lead because the conversion rate in this group is very low. A large amount of time can be invested on people in this 30 percent, but it will equate to low payoff and high frustration. I doubt if this group can be satisfied even if everything goes perfectly. My advice is run away from prospects and clients in this group, fast!!

Concentrate on the 20 Percent and the 50 Percent

We, as salespeople, cannot help everyone. Why not simply focus first on the easy 20 percent, the 20 percent who are truly in your corner rooting for you? In addition, move to the 50 percent, which will require a little selling of yourself and the benefits of working with you. These two categories will provide more income, less frustration, and more enjoyable experiences.

Next time you speak with a prospect or client, ask yourself three questions. The first question is, Which category is she in? Next ask how you can move her into the 20 percent if she is not already in it. And finally, how much effort and energy will you have to invest in moving her to the 20 percent? Once you have asked these questions, determine what the odds are that she will convert. Ask yourself, is the effort worth the reward? By asking these questions you will be applying the 20/50/30 rule effectively.

Categories of Leads

AA Lead = the prospect will buy or sell in 30 days or less

A Lead = the prospect will buy or sell in 60 days or less

B Lead = the prospect will buy or sell in 120 days or less

C Lead = the prospect will buy or sell in 120 days to one year

CLASSIFY YOUR FOLLOW-UP

Now that you have defined all your leads, your next step is to build a follow-up system. The follow-up system needs to be focused on contact by phone, mail pieces, and e-mail correspondence. The higher the motivation of the lead, the more frequent and personal your contact with them. Personal contact is to be completed either by phone or in person.

AA Leads—Will Buy or Sell in Thirty Days or Less

Call them at least three times a week.
Send at least one e-mail or mail piece weekly.

Repeat the process until they purchase or list their home or until they drop to another lead category. You can't follow up enough on these people. Even if you were to call a buyer lead just to say, "I looked twice today on the multiple listing service and nothing came up that matched your criteria for homes. If I can do anything for you please give me a call," your client would appreciate your persistence and feel he has the best agent on the job. Make sure you call, call, and call again on these AA leads.

A Leads—Will Buy or Sell in Sixty Days or Less

Call at least once a week, just to check in and ask for an appointment.
Send a piece of mail weekly.

These are the people you are percolating so they can move to the higher category. Make sure you don't neglect them, as they have a high probability of becoming an AA lead.

B Leads—Will Buy or Sell in 120 Days or Less

Call them every three to four weeks.
Send a piece of mail to them once a month.

In many cases, these B leads need to be realistic about the value of their property and pricing or what they can afford to purchase. The people who are forever in this category must be avoided; for example, those who are trying to find the perfect house will rarely find it. There are people who look at homes regularly who would move if they could sell their current residence for $30,000 over market and could buy at $25,000 below market. Often these people will even feel they are doing you a favor by having you look for properties for them. My advice is simply this: Don't waste your time. These people rarely buy or sell. The conditions will never be "just right."

C Leads—Will Buy or Sell in 120 Days to One Year

> Call them every two months to see if their plans are still on track. Send them any regular mailing you do, for example, your quarterly newsletter.

For C leads to be any good, they need to be planning to buy or sell at a specific time in the future. We can fill our databases up with pseudo-leads who are "thinking" of selling next year. To be a qualified C lead, there should be a specific reason. For example, they are retiring and want to downsize, or their last child is graduating from high school. There should be some event coming up in their life that will trigger the move. Because someone "feels like moving" is not a good enough reason for you to keep the lead long term. People who say, "We are thinking about making a move next June," and there is no reason given, don't warrant very much attention!

Because someone "feels like moving" is not a good enough reason for you to keep the lead long term.

CREATE AN EFFECTIVE LEAD FOLLOW-UP SYSTEM

Lead follow-up costs you time, time that could be spent prospecting, creating strategic alliances, or practicing your skills. Your ability to categorize your leads and follow-up will help you control the leads you have right now. Creating an effective lead follow-up system can be the backbone to a consistent real estate sales business. The more effectively you handle the leads you generate, the more production you will achieve.

Too many agents spend too much time trying to find the leads they generated. They know the leads are on their desk somewhere. You need to be able to put your hands on your leads immediately when needed.

Software for Tracking Leads

One of the best ways to track leads is by contact management software programs. These programs are designed to help you keep information that will enable you to sell more efficiently and effectively. There are many on the market; some of the best are ACT!, Top Producer, Goldmine, and SharperAgent. Select a system you are comfortable with and be certain it will grow with you and your business. My recommendation is Top Producer. Here is their Web site so you can evaluate them: http://www.topproducer.com/partner/real-estate-champions/8i.

Your broker may already have a system for the whole office, as many companies are now providing this service to agents. The most important element is knowing how to use it fully. Get the training you need to master this technology that will allow you to handle the leads you generate easily and quickly.

A Low-Tech Tracking System

If you are unable to afford a computer and software, you can track leads manually with 3×5 note cards in a shoebox. I tracked my leads this way when I started in real estate sales many years ago. Sometimes we can get too fancy and technical for our own good. We become excited about all the new technology and gadgetry and forget "old-fashioned" sales skills. The key is to meld the technology with quality sales skills. By doing this you will achieve spectacular results.

If you have to do lead follow-up manually, get a set of cards for the twelve months of the year. Then get another set of cards for the days of the week (Monday through Friday) or dates (the first through the thirty-first). Use the two systems together. Use the month cards for the month you have to call the prospect back. When that month arrives, use the dated cards. Move your leads to the date that you want to call them. Then write notes on your conversations and information about the client or prospect on the 3 × 5 card.

QUALIFYING SELLERS AND BUYERS

Understanding what are leads and what are not leads will keep you on track for your daily prospecting. Qualifying will also ensure you are always working with people who can buy or sell today.

The process of qualifying is a lost art in the sales profession, and this is especially true in real estate. We often work with people who have low motivation, hoping we can convince them to do something. In the end we spend large amounts of time working with people who don't buy or sell. Then we de-motivate ourselves because the outcome is not what we desired. We beat ourselves up because of lack of success and lack of income. We put ourselves in such a negative state that when a good buyer or seller comes along we are not prepared to seize the moment and help him. This causes us to miss another opportunity to grow our business and provide for our families. It is a vicious cycle, one that must be broken.

The Problem with Too Many Leads

Qualifying effectively determines whether the leads are good or bad. Most people don't realize that leads can be bad. Ultimately, having too many leads can be bad for your business. It can cause you to get bogged down in lead follow-up and never get back to generating new leads through prospecting.

Having too many leads can cause you to become complacent—comfortable with the probability of future income. For example, we have twenty-five leads that are uncategorized and unqualified. Most agents would feel very good. Some would stop prospecting for leads and they would just work those twenty-five. The mistake is that we have not qualified them. We really don't know if these leads have any value.

Determine Who is Going to Act Now

The best agents are highly skilled at qualifying. They can quickly separate the wheat from the chaff when it comes to prospects. Being able to determine who is going to act now versus act soon versus never act at all is critical. Most new agents are just trying to do a deal rather than make sure it's the right deal to do.

Most agents treat all leads the same with the result that the most motivated ones are missed. We don't want to annoy anyone, so the most motivated people slip through our follow-up system and buy or sell with someone else. Now we are down to twenty-two leads. These twenty-two leads are still not motivated enough to do anything. But because we lost the others we don't want to lose these so we hold on to them for dear life. The problem still remains because they are never going to do anything. We spend too much time working with unmotivated people. We have stopped prospecting, so there are no new leads. We have now come to a dangerous point in our business. For these reasons, you must make sure you qualify every prospect and client to ensure you gain a return from your time invested and never stop prospecting.

To Qualify a Seller

To qualify the seller effectively you need a series of questions to ensure their motivation is right and to prepare you for the listing presentation. Here are the key questions we recommend:

1. **How soon do you want to be in your new home?** This question focuses on time frame and motivation. It also gives you an opportunity

to create a sense of urgency. If they say "in sixty days" and the average market time in your area is seventy, you have an opportunity to talk about the urgency of listing tonight and getting going because they are behind. They need thirty days to close the deal once they are under contract and seventy days on average to sell it. We are forty days behind where we need to be. We don't have a minute to waste!

2. **How much do you want to list your home for?** This question reveals the motivation of the client. The higher the price over what is fair market value, the lower the motivation. Sometimes clients will not tell you. They feel they don't want to tip their hand. If that is the case, then ask: What are you planning to invest in your next home?

3. **What are you hoping to net after the sale of this home?** This will give you what you need. We are trying to understand their feelings of value for their property. It is rare when someone does not have an idea of what they want to sell for.

4. **So I can prepare a new sheet, how much do you owe on the property?** I want to be able to use the net profit to help them. I also now know how much they want to list their home for even if they don't tell me. It's a great way to learn their price.

5. **Have you thought about selling yourself?** This will tell you if you are going to face the commission objection. Also they may just want a price opinion from you and never want to list. We don't need to waste our time with this information-service type of client.

6. **Are you interviewing other agents?** It's important to know the agents and the firms you are competing against. By knowing your competition you have a competitive advantage. You can accentuate the services your company provides that the other companies don't. If you are up against a very successful agent, you can sell personal service and attention. You can assure your clients that you can spend a greater amount of time accomplishing the sale of their home.

7. **What are your most important criteria for selecting an agent?** You want to know what they feel is important. People have different reasons for hiring agents, and you need to know theirs. Often they will tell you the price of the home or the commission. You want to make

sure you go beyond those two. Get at least two criteria to address on the presentation.

Qualifying the seller before the appointment is a nonnegotiable component in successful selling. Don't waste your time going to an appointment with the wrong type of seller. These questions should be asked over the phone twenty-four hours before the appointment to list their property. Practice the qualifying scripts and process daily. Don't be one of the many agents who struggle with selecting the right client in the first place.

To Qualify a Buyer

We invest large amounts of time with buyers. There is nothing more frustrating than spending a lot of time with buyers and never getting paid for our efforts. The key component to successfully working with buyers is the qualifying process. Qualifying is the lost art of the sales process. Sometimes we get so excited when we have a lead that we fail to determine its value. That is why the process of qualifying is focused on determining the value of leads. Here are some questions to use in qualifying a buyer.

Separate the Motivated Buyers and Sellers

The key in sales is the ability to separate the unmotivated buyers and sellers from the motivated ones who want to do something now. Top-producing agents know how to do this quickly and efficiently. They have a specific step-by-step series of questions that remove the unmotivated people from their lives.

1. **How long have you been looking for a home?** The object is to find out their time frame and level of passion to move. The longer the time the buyer has been looking, the lower the motivation. We have to wonder why a buyer has not been able to find a home in six months. Are they looking for something that doesn't exist? Are their expectations too high for the marketplace? Do they just enjoy the pro-

cess of kicking foundations? When someone says to me that she has been looking for more than ninety days, I want to know what she is looking for and the reasons that she hasn't found it yet.

Sometimes we get so excited that we have a lead that we fail to determine its value. That is why the process of qualifying is focused on determining the value of leads.

2. **Do you need to sell your current home before you can buy?** The follow-up question is "Are you currently on the market?" Most people need to sell their home before they can buy another one, but a great percentage of them want to find a house before they put theirs on the market. This approach seems to be backward. Most sellers truly can't buy anything because they have to sell first. They often want us to invest a large percentage of our time in finding them the perfect home prior to listing theirs.

3. **Are you committed to another agent?** Too often we rush out to show one of our listings only to find out the clients are working with another agent. We just spent thirty minutes of our time and never got compensated.

Buyers Become Sellers

One of our rules when I was an agent was that buyers had to list their property with us for us to work with them. We did not want to work without the opportunity of getting paid. Because the buyers have to list their home sometime, why not now? Why delay the inevitable if they truly want to sell? If their plans changed we would withdraw the listing.

In my career I have received some unbelievable responses from prospects regarding why they hadn't contacted their own agent about showing them property. Responses ranged from "My agent is out of town" to "I did not want to bother him." They wanted to bother me and then get *their* agent to write the sales agreement if they decided to purchase it. Our policy was, if buyers are working with another agent, he can show them the home. That is what their agent is getting paid to do.

4. **Have you met with a lender yet?** This question will start the process of determining their ability to purchase. Truly motivated purchasers meet with lenders. If they have not and they have been looking for six months, are they motivated buyers? I don't think so.

Next, determine if they have been prequalified or preapproved. There is a world of difference in these terms, and buyers don't know the difference. The focus needs to be to get them to meet with your lender. If they meet with your loan office, you will have solidified your position with them.

Determining the time frame and motivation are critical to earning a paycheck now. If a buyer doesn't want to move for six months, then realize that your commission check is also at least six months away. How many prospects can you afford to work with when your commission is six months away? How much time can you invest in someone who will pay you six months to a year from now or perhaps never?

Set Up an Appointment

The best way to qualify people is to ask for an appointment. In this one question you can separate the motivated ones from the unmotivated. The people who are unmotivated will fight not to meet with you.

This appointment should be at your office where you have control. Do not set the appointment at a property. The prospect knows that you are serious about creating a relationship and helping him. If he doesn't want to or is not ready, he will avoid the appointment.

Here is a simple, straightforward script for this appointment, which I call the buyer interview:

*In order for me to provide the highest level of service to you and all
my clients, we always set up a meeting prior to showing the properties.
Would Tuesday or Wednesday be better for you?*

Then the big question is, "If we could find a home in the area that you desire, are you prepared to purchase it now?" If you get a favorable response, set an
appointment with them to help them find their new home.

LISTING PRESENTATIONS

Basic Tips on the Listing Presentation

The listing presentation is your moment to show a prospective client all that
you're worth. With the value of your services and the relationship you hope to
have with a client on the line, it's hard to believe that the less said, the better.
But it's true—the longer a listing presentation takes, the worse it gets. The client's mind begins to wander, and the agent begins to promise more in marketing and advertising to keep the client's attention and to procure the listing.
The commission rate will have a tendency to decrease and the listing price to
increase. This will lead to longer marketing, less profit, or eventually, an expired
listing. Truly, the longer your presentation goes the weaker it becomes; a short,
focused presentation is the one that will speak volumes for you.

Design Your Questions Today

Top producers have a specific set of questions they ask. Their success is not based
on chance; it is based on a well-designed system. Develop your system today.

Keep It Short

Many speakers and trainers have been teaching agents for years how to do a
two-hour listing presentation. But think about it: In today's busy society, does
anyone really want to listen to an agent talk about himself and his company

for two hours? In the seller's position, after an hour or so, wouldn't you find yourself thinking about what you would rather be doing with your family? Once the owners begin to think about things other than listing their home with you, it becomes very difficult to get them refocused on signing a contract or agreement. Remember that the length of your listing presentation is critical to your success.

Ask Questions

One key to making the most effective presentation in the shortest amount of time is to ask questions. To be an effective agent, you need to find out the desires and expectations of the prospect. The only way to do this is by asking questions, and one of the biggest mistakes I see agents making is not asking enough of them. The person asking the questions is the one who controls the conversation. Develop a series of questions to help you to stay focused on your presentation. By asking each client similar questions, you will learn to evaluate each client's motivation, compatibility, and expectations. Working with a standard set of questions will also help you to remember to ask all of the necessary questions. You will be able to standardize your presentation and control the time that your presentation takes. Without a standardized presentation based on a set series of questions, you will have a tendency to take listings at too high a price, for too short a term, or with people whose expectations are not compatible with what your skills and experience can offer them.

To be an effective agent, you need to find out the desires and expectations of the prospect. The only way to do this is by asking questions, and one of the biggest mistakes I see agents making is not asking enough of them.

Direct the Presentation to Price

As you gather information from the sellers and present yourself to them, keep in mind that presentations should be directed, first and foremost, to price, rather than to secondary issues such as marketing or advertising. Price is king in real estate; it is the dominant reason a home sells or fails to sell. Our presentations need to accurately reflect this reality. Rather than focusing on marketing, stick with the issue that will really affect the sale of the home. I advocate rolling up your sleeves and getting down to the business of price, sooner rather than later. If you and the seller cannot agree on price, then nothing else you might say is going to make this relationship work; you should politely excuse yourself and move on to the next prospect.

Plug Yourself

Above all, you need to show the clients the benefit of working with you. This is, after all, what the clients will be paying you for. You need to show them how your skills, experience, and strategy will benefit them. They need to know and understand the benefits of your approach to selling their home. Determine a few of the advantages you offer and share them with the listing prospect.

If you create a step-by-step presentation that is well prepared, concise, focused on price, and clear about what your business offers to the client, you will reduce the time you spend on each presentation. You will also see an improvement in the number of listing presentations that lead to signed contracts. And your clients will thank you for demonstrating respect for their time. You may even have a few minutes left over to spend laughing with your new clients at their stories of "the real estate agent who was here for two hours doing a listing presentation."

Elements of a Dynamic Listing Presentation

The listing presentation is one of the most misunderstood areas of real estate sales. There are as many theories about this presentation as there are licensed agents in North America. Although the listing presentation has been altered dramatically in the last five to ten years, an efficient and professional presentation will enable the agent to control his clients properly. What are the elements of an efficient, professional listing presentation?

First, it is necessary to clearly define a purpose for the listing presentation. Now I know that you are thinking, "Of course, the purpose is to take the listing." You would be partially correct. Certainly the objective is to get the contract signed. The true purpose, though, is to identify the clients' problem in an efficient manner and convey to the clients that you are the person who will provide them the best opportunity to solve their problem in the marketplace. That is really the objective of a professional's listing presentation.

Focus on the Issue of Price

The actual problem that needs to be solved in a listing presentation is the problem of price. Price will fix everything else in the equation. The price is like the known variable in an algebra equation. You need to search for the other potential issues or potential problems, but they all flow through the known issue, price. By lowering the price, you can sell a property with problems like poor condition, poor location, busy street, functionally obsolete, a "buyer's market," or poor marketing. The list of fixable problems is never ending. Price has a direct correlation to all of these issues. These issues or problems may or may not be interconnected, but price is the only guaranteed connection to all of them. Your presentation should be focused on price, so that you will have an opportunity to get a sale rather than just a listing. Both you and your client want the sale. Neither of you just wants the property listed.

You and your client must have a mutual agreement on price. The stronger you are regarding the price, the better chance you have of a sale. Many agents will delay the hard reality, hoping it will go away. Deal with it up front rather than thirty days down the road. You must have the integrity to tell the client the truth: "It won't sell for what you want. You need to lower the price." Do not hedge or mince words. Tell the client directly that it will not sell. Get an agreement with the client on price before you move on. There is no point in continuing if you and the client do not agree on price. You will be wasting your time. I urge you to have the conviction of your skills as an agent to truthfully interpret the market. Be honest. Most agents want the listing and are unwilling to risk losing the listing even though they know the property will not sell for the client's desired price.

Get an agreement with the client on price before you move on. There is no point in continuing if you and the client do not agree on price.

Sell Yourself

Once you have resolved the pricing issue, you are in the home stretch. Your job now is to convey that you are the real estate agent for the job. Brevity is crucial to success in this arena. Most people do not want to listen to someone talk about how great he is at selling homes. Ask specific questions to see what kind of services they are looking for from their real estate agent. Most people will just say, "We want someone who can sell our home." This is the perfect opportunity to demonstrate your confidence and conviction that you are the one for the job. Look them straight in the eyes and tell them your track record of success and ask them if they are looking for an agent of your caliber. If you do not have a track record, sell your company's record. You may even need to sell a little of both. Finally, ask the clients to sign the paperwork.

Use Trial Closes

This section of your presentation should last less than ten minutes unless your clients ask a lot of questions. All during this presentation pepper them with trial closures, for instance, "Do you want a lock box or appointment only? Are there times that would be inconvenient to show the home?" If you are concerned about the condition of the property, ask the clients if they could fix certain items. There are a million trial closes; use a few to test the water. Most people will answer them and proceed.

Ask for the Order

When you have set up a few trial closes and you have already agreed on the price, you have arrived at the moment of truth, so simply ask for the order. It does not have to be elaborate, just ask. Here are a few examples: "I think I have all the information I need. Can I have your OK in the box?" or "Do you believe I can sell your home?" When they say yes, ask them to sign. If they say no, ask them to tell you why and listen to their answer. Once you have heard their answer, address their concern, and ask them for the order again. Do not give up after the first setback. Did you know that the average sale is made after the fifth or sixth customer refusal? Be persistent; do not give up. If you firmly believe that you are the agent for the job, that belief will come through. People want to select winners to sell their homes.

Debrief the Client After the Signing

Lastly, once the contract is signed spend a few minutes debriefing the seller. If you have staff, introduce them to the seller. If you have a routine of communication or a system you use that may be unique, fill them in. A few minutes of explanation will save you the frustrated seller's phone call in thirty days. Let them know you care and appreciate the opportunity, and move on to the next appointment.

Keep It Brief

Many agents do not understand the concept of brevity. They have a two-hour listing presentation. What in the world are they doing for two hours? The seller wants to know each agent's version of the problem, how that agent can solve the problem, and which one is the best agent for the job. The seller really does not care about the rest of the presentation. If you want to be the chosen agent, focus on the problem and the solution. Spending endless amounts of time on other matters or past victories will simply weaken your presentation.

A truly dynamic presentation is short and to the point. Do not break your momentum by going too long or not staying focused during the presentation. Stay directed, focused, and solve their problem.

The Listing Appointment Routine

A successful seller's interview or listing presentation starts before you show up at the house. Top producers have a specific routine they go through before they arrive to obtain a listing. Before you even begin your presentation, follow the five steps below to ensure that you will also obtain more of the listings you seek.

1. **Prepare a solid prelisting package.** This presentation should give the client a brief overview of who you are and what your track record is in sales in their market area. It should clearly focus on the benefits of doing business with you rather than with any other agent. This piece should not be the big "Brag Book" that many people used in the eighties and nineties. Sellers in the new millennium are busy. They don't have the time to read thirty pages about how great you are.

   If you are new to real estate, your book will need to be focused on your company and the benefits it offers its clients, such as the marketing plans and other services the client can expect from doing business with you. Your track record will be nonexistent in real estate sales, but if you have relevant experience in other sales or customer service, I would share that. Present that information in a clear, concise fashion. You will want to incorporate graphics that show current market trends with regard to amount of inventory, average days on the market, average list price to sales price, and your company's statistics of success.

   Lastly, your pricing sections should be clear so the client understands the dangers of overpricing her home. The biggest battle you wage is getting a home priced properly by the seller. By starting that discussion early, before the appointment, you create momentum for discussion at the actual listing appointment. You also have more credibility when you explain to the seller that the price she wants is too high for the marketplace.

2. **Qualify hard before the appointment.** Have a specific set of qualifying questions. The goal is to check the clients' level of motivation to sell. You need to know if their desire to sell is greater than their desire to achieve a certain price. You want to know where and why they are moving. You want to know their desired time frame for moving. That information is related to motivation, and motivation and price are intertwined. The higher the motivation, the lower the price the seller will accept. The lower the motivation, the higher the price the seller will want.

If you are new to real estate, your book will need to be focused on your company and the benefits it offers its clients, such as the marketing plans and other services the client can expect from doing business with you.

In my qualifying I always wanted to know who else the seller was interviewing. This information really gave me an edge over the other agents. It allowed me to bring or send the seller multiple listing service data about the agent or firm. It also gave me the ability to compare services. (Please understand that you don't want to say anything to trash the other agent or company. You do want to point out the differences in your approach and track record compared to theirs.) Most sellers think agents are all alike. I was there to show them that I provided the best opportunity in the marketplace for the sellers to achieve a sale on their home.

If you provide a compelling list of benefits over another agent or firm, sellers will select you almost every time. The only way you will lose a listing is to get outpriced or out-commissioned. It never bothered me to get outpriced or out-commissioned. Those kinds of agents won't last long in most markets. When a potential client makes a selection based on those two issues, are they a client you want to do business with? My answer was no. They didn't have enough respect for me, my team, and real estate agents in general to warrant my investment of time, money, and emotional energy.

3. **Develop a preappointment routine.** Developing a preappointment routine is essential for success in sales. We need to make sure we are taking all the materials necessary to do the job well on the listing appointment. We also need to make sure we are heading out the door in the right mental state.

Since there is a "zone" in basketball and golf, why not in real estate? What are the steps to enable us to enter the zone? We have all been in it at one time or another, such as the day you have a few appointments booked and they all sign the contract smoothly at your price and terms with little effort, or the day you are prospecting and every call seems to end in an AA lead or an appointment. We have all had days like this. The question is, How do we get more of them?

The first step is to develop a preactivity routine. If you watch professional golfers hit a shot or make a putt, they will do the same things in sequence through the completion of their shot or putt. If something breaks their concentration during the preshot routine, they start all over again. Basketball players at the free throw line do the same thing. They bounce the ball so many times or flex their knees the same way every time they shoot a free throw.

If you developed a preactivity routine before you went on a listing appointment, your results would improve. You should create a checklist and make sure you are following it. Here is an example of a preactivity routine for a listing appointment.

a. Review the Competitive Market Analysis (CMA) for thirty minutes before you leave the office. The CMA is your evaluation and report of the value of the property.

b. Determine the exact price at which you want to set the listing.

c. Practice the objections you expect will come up based on the responses the sellers gave to you after you qualified and confirmed the appointment earlier today.

d. Practice your presentation before you leave the office.

e. Select music to listen to in the car that relaxes you and focuses you on your task. Review the presentation again.

f. Take control before you knock on the door.

If you develop a solid preactivity routine, you will find you will enter the zone more frequently and with more intensity. You should also develop a preactivity routine before prospecting, lead follow-up, negotiating of contracts, and so on.

Don't let success be based on chance. Prepare well before the appointment. Great teams win championships in practice. They win them before the big game is played. Preparation is essential for smooth and successful seller interviews. Start your routine today.

Great teams win championships in practice. They win them before the big game is played.

Closing the Contract

If you really want to take your listing presentation to the professional level, there are two things that separate the really high producers from the other agents in the field. The first is that they ask for the order at the end of their presentation, and the second is that they tape their listing presentation (this will be discussed later in this chapter). The best producers ask the client to sign the contract. The very best agents don't leave until they get a contract signed. They continue to work with the client, handling the objections and asking for the order until they get it. Many agents fail to ask for the business at the completion of the presentation. You will not get contracts signed unless you ask.

Trial Closes

One technique to help you with asking for the order is inserting trial closes in your listing presentation. These trial closes create agreement on small items before you gain the big commitment of a relationship. The trial closes will help you achieve "yes" momentum. When your clients continue to say yes on the small items, it will be very hard for them to say no at the contract signing. You will also gain confidence as a salesperson, which will make asking for the order at the end easier.

Some trial closes you could use are:

Do you want an open house this week or would next week be better?

Should we put the For Sale sign on the right side or left side of the driveway?

Would it be better if I took the pictures of your home today or would you prefer I come back tomorrow?

Clients would have to really struggle to say no to these questions, which are designed to give them a choice, and either choice is good for you.

Tag Lines

When you get ready to close for the contract, another technique is to insert "tag lines" before you ask for the order. A tag line helps build your position as the authority. You hook it or tag it on before you ask your final closing question. If you receive a positive response, you have the green light to close. If you receive a red light, you must ask the prospect why.

One of the great tag lines you can use is "Do you believe I can sell your home?" If they say yes, you have nothing more to talk about. In that case you can begin filling out the contract and ask for the order. If they feel you could get the home sold, you have little else to discuss.

If they answer no, that's an indication that there is a concern as to your ability. You then have to follow up by asking them why. "Why do you believe I couldn't sell your home?" They will share a reason or two. Your job is then to answer those concerns and ask for the order. The tag line will help you ferret out the bottom-line objection and why the client is not moving forward. Using tag lines effectively will enable you to close with greater ease.

The Close

The closing on a listing appointment is a natural ending to a great presentation. We have a tendency to hesitate at the moment that is most crucial. We must be bold and step forward to ask. Try this authorization close:

Mr. and Mrs. Seller, if you just OK this right here, we will get started for you right away.

The authorization close has a couple of key components. One is that you ask them to approve the paperwork. It's a much softer way of saying, "Sign here." Their bodies can often tense up when you say the word *sign*.

People like things done right away.
They want definite action now for the
commitment they have made or for the
money they have paid.

Another key component is that you tell them you will start right away. People like things done right away. They want definite action now for the commitment they have made or for the money they have paid. We live in an instant society where we expect everything right away.

Focus on asking for the order in every presentation you go on. Even when you think you didn't do well, ask for the order. You might be surprised to get the contract signed.

How Effective Is Your Listing Presentation?

What separates the very best producers from the rest is that they tape their listing presentations. They elevate their skills by taping and reviewing their presentations.

Do you know of any sports team that doesn't watch films of themselves and their opponents? Athletic teams and individual players are constantly evaluating their performance by viewing videotapes of the game. If you want to be truly professional, you need to take the step to record your presentation, at least on audiotape.

1. **Make the commitment to tape your listing presentations.**
2. **Buy a small cassette recorder that uses regular-size cassettes so you can listen to the tapes in your car.**
3. **Prepare a statement to inform your clients why you are taping the conversation and how it benefits them. Example:**

Mr. and Mrs. Seller, I am taping our conversation today for two reasons. The first is to help me follow through on each and every item we discuss regarding your desires and our commitments to you regarding the sale of your home. The second is that I am constantly working to improve my skill in selling real estate, just as a golf professional at the top of his game continues to study his swing. My speaking and selling skills are like my golf swing. By working to be the best, I become even better able to serve you, my client.

4. **Listen to the tapes!** This is the most difficult part. For some of you it will be one of the most painful experiences you have had in some time. The value to your career, however, will be immeasurable. You will identify things that you are doing right. You will also find out a few things that you are doing wrong.

   By listening to the tapes, you will increase your confidence because you will know what your strengths are. You will build stronger rapport with your clients because you will know the areas in which you need improvement.

   The tape will also reveal where you are wasting time in your presentation. The listing presentation can almost always be more effective if done in less time. No matter how good you are at the listing presentation, you will find that you talk too much and don't ask enough questions.

5. **Evaluate yourself.** Ask these questions:

   What are two or three things I did well?
   Did I listen to my client's concerns?
   How much time did I talk?
   How much time did my client talk?
   Did I stay on track during the presentation?
   What is one area I could improve on?
   What did my client get most excited about?
   What steps do I need to take to stay on track better?

6. **Give the tape to a mentor or associate who will review it.** Ask for
    an honest evaluation. Tell your reviewer what to evaluate. Receive the
    feedback and make the adjustments that are necessary.

We Really Make Three Presentations

The old saying that we always make three presentations is a valid one. The first
presentation is the one we make on the way to the appointment. Then there is the
actual one that counts. Finally, we make the best one on the way home, when we
replay the presentation and get a chance to answer the questions we missed and
make the best responses. If you tape your presentations, soon your best ones will
be made in the moment that counts, in front of the client.

It takes a courageous person to tape presentations and review them. There
is always a difference between the truth and our perception of the truth. It takes
courage to look the truth in the eye and to look for ways to improve.

THE BUYER INTERVIEW

Another key presentation skill is the buyer interview. The buyer interview is
the first step in the buying process. It should happen before you run to the
computer to find the buyer the right home. You may be competing with two or
three other agents for the same buyer. Why compete when you don't have to?
Let the other agents in the marketplace compete and waste their time with dis-
loyal buyers. "Top gun" agents invest their time only with people who are loyal
and who will buy through them.

Determine the Buyers' Values and Needs

The buyer interview is separated into three sections. The first section is determining the buyers' values and needs. You want to find out what their needs are
in a home, such as the number of bedrooms and bathrooms and the layout of
the home. To be able to best fulfill their needs, you want to obtain all the information about the property they want to own.

Then you will need to find out the values they are attaching to this new home, the why behind the move, the emotions they are using to make the buying decision. We all buy things because they appeal to our emotions. We then rationalize our emotions through logic. To create long-term satisfied clients, a great salesperson makes sure the buyers' emotions are met.

Understand What Level of Service Buyers Are Looking For

You then must understand the benefits the buyer is looking for you to provide. There are some specific beliefs these people have about real estate agents. They want you to provide a certain type of service. You need to know their expectations of service.

When I was in a buyer interview with someone who wanted me to be available at all times including nights and weekends, we had a problem. I needed to know if my service model of being available only at certain times was acceptable. I also needed to know why the buyer felt I needed to be available twenty-four hours a day, seven days a week for him. If I could not persuade him that we would be able to provide him with the highest quality of assistance, I would disengage the appointment and refer him to another agent in the office who was willing to provide the service he felt he needed.

Present the Benefits of Your Services

In the second section of the buyer interview present the benefits of the services that you provide for all your buyers. Have these services on a written form for the buyer so you can show him the benefits he would receive from working with you. People make decisions in the selling process based on emotion and the benefits they receive. If you don't show them their specific benefits, they will not buy. Examples of services and benefits:

1. I will enter into the multiple listing service system your requirements for a home. I will be notified any time that a property meets your specific criteria.
2. I will arrange to get you preapproved with a lender. With preapproval, your offer will be stronger because you have the ability to perform.

This eliminates the guesswork for the seller. You will also know the maximum dollar amount that you can purchase.

3. I will give you my professional opinion regarding the price, location, and condition of any property that you are considering purchasing. My opinion of price, location, and condition is detached and less emotional.

4. I will review and explain all the forms that you will be signing, disclosures, disclaimers, rights of recession, and so on. You will have an explanation and reason for every form that you sign.

5. Once we have successfully negotiated a purchase agreement, I will help you select a home inspector. After the inspection, I will review the report with you to determine if any negotiation is needed with the seller regarding the repairs.

6. When the appraisal is completed, I will review it for accuracy.

7. If there are any lender-required repairs or conditions resulting from the home inspection or appraisal, I will negotiate these items with the seller. I represent you, the purchasers, and your best interests are always my number one concern.

8. Prior to signing all the closing documents, I will review them for accuracy and determine if all the conditions of the purchase agreement have been met. This will protect you from any last-minute surprises and ensure a smooth closing.

The last service listed acknowledges the fact that the seller actually pays our fee. The buyer would receive all these services and benefits free of charge. We would ask for only one thing from him to receive all of these services: his commitment to work with us *exclusively.*

Get the Buyers' Commitment

Next comes section three of the buyer interview. This section I call "The Client Commitment." You don't have a client until he has committed to you. Until then he is only a prospect. This section of the buyer interview separates the "top gun" agent from the rest. You must lay it on the line. The buyer needs to understand that this is your job and how you provide for your family. You owe it to your spouse and children to work only with people who are 100 percent committed to working with you. A buyer's commitment may be something like this:

1. The buyers agree to work with _____ of _____ to find and purchase a home. By working together as a team, purchasers and real estate agent will be able to successfully complete the purchase of a home.

2. If buyers drive by or see an advertisement for a property they are interested in viewing, buyers will call me. I will then obtain all the information regarding the property and set an appointment to view the property. This will eliminate looking at property that doesn't meet the buyers' requirements or needs. Also I will be able to obtain complete information about the property.

3. In order to conduct my business as a business, my business hours are from _____ to _____. In an emergency, I will return your call within 1 hour, when possible.

4. Buyers will contact me if they see a property that is For Sale By Owner that they are interested in viewing. I will contact the owner and obtain all the information about the property and set an appointment to view the property. Many properties that are For Sale By Owner are willing to work with a real estate agent.

5. Buyers are to be prepared to make an offer when we have found the "right" property.

    Real estate is how I make a living; it is my business, my only business. My commitment to you is to do the best job I possibly can through finding the "right" property and by making your buying experience as pleasant as possible.

It's About Commitment

You can provide a high level of service to only a selected number of clients at a time. You cannot help them all. Make sure they want to be helped by you. If they cannot give you a commitment, thank them and refer them to someone else. Invest your time finding another person who will commit. It's all about commitment; either you are committed or you aren't. "Top gun" agents ask for the commitment, and if they don't get it, they will move on to the next prospect.

Because you are providing all these services for no cost to anyone till closing, you have to ensure that a closing will happen. Draw the buyer in by asking him to visualize being in your position. He wouldn't work for a month hoping his paycheck wouldn't bounce at the end of the month. He would find another job.

BECOMING COMFORTABLE WITH OBJECTIONS

Objections are a real part of sales. An objection is that statement or question that stalls a sale temporarily at the moment before you get the contract signed. When most agents hear an objection in the sales process, they often react like deer caught in the headlights: They freeze in terror, moving only at the last second before the buyer or seller runs them over. It doesn't have to be that way.

Often agents view an objection as a big wall between them and the sale, a wall so formidable they can see no way around, over, under, or through. But objections are really like a two- to three-foot-high picket fence. They have lots of openings. You can climb over them or walk down the fence's length and find the gate. We all want the people to whom we are trying to sell a home to just "roll over and buy." Even a neophyte agent finds it easy to make such a sale.

Objections Are Opportunities

An unskilled salesperson fears hearing an objection, but a great salesperson views objections as opportunities. Your mental approach to an objection will determine your success or failure. You have to want to love objections. You have to view objections as opportunities to make the sale. In the end, there are no sales without objections.

Objections in the selling process indicate interest. If your clients have no objection, they have no interest in your services. We have to adjust our mind-set so that we see objections as wonderful. The objection lets you know you are less than a couple of steps away from making the sale. Your ability to handle the objection or solve the problem will put you at the doorstep of making the sale.

There are many real estate sales trainers who claim they have invented the objection-free system. The truth is it doesn't exist, even if you are working 100 percent referral or past client-generated business. You will get asked to cut your commission. They will tell you, "I want to think it over." They will explain to you how "the other agent will list our home for a higher price." We all need to be prepared to handle these objections with focus, conviction, and intensity.

Objections give you the opportunity to close for the sale. If you handle the "Will you cut your commission?" objection, you then get to ask for the order. You could say, "Because we have resolved the last issue, do you want me to handle the sale for you?" Always follow up your objection-handling techniques with a closing question or tag line. You want to go on the offensive right away. You are playing defense in objection handling, but your position can change to offense in a second. Make sure you take advantage of this opportunity.

Listen Carefully to Objections

When you get an objection from buyers or sellers, make sure you hear clearly what they are saying. If you interpret the objection incorrectly, the answer you give, no matter how eloquent, will not be sufficient to overcome their area of concern.

Let me give you a few techniques I have used to turn objections into dollars. I would pause to make sure I clearly understood, and then I would repeat what they said or ask them to explain further. This technique would do a few things for me. When I confirmed what their objection was in order to ensure I had understood it, I bought myself a few seconds to prepare an answer. I was able to respond in a powerful, well-planned manner. I would avoid the big mistake of trying to answer the objection before the buyer or seller got the objection out of her mouth, as if stopping her from stating the objection completely would stop the objection. The objection is legitimate to that person, no matter how ridiculous it may sound. She feels it is legitimate; therefore it is! Interrupting can cause the seller or buyer to become irritated with you. It may not matter how well you handle the objection if you interrupt.

Why Do Objections Arise?

Most agents dread hearing an objection, but most objections result from one of two situations. The first situation occurs because the seller or buyer has legitimate concerns regarding the property or your skills to sell her home.

The other situation arises because your presentation was not good enough. You did not convey the confidence that you are the person for the seller to hire for the sale of her home; you did not make a convincing enough presentation for the buyer to purchase the home you showed her. The client's desire to work with you is a natural ending to a good presentation. If the presentation is weak, the objections will flow like a river.

Practice Objection Handling

NFL teams spend four to six hours a day practicing football. The players and coaches spend a couple more hours a day reviewing film and studying their playbooks during a two-month span in spring training; then they play four practice games in preseason to prepare for the real NFL season. During the season the players and coaches spend a few hours a day practicing and watching films five or six days a week to prepare for *one* sixty-minute game. They will spend forty to fifty times more time practicing and preparing for the game than actually playing the game. How skilled in sales would you be if you adopted that regimen? How about if you practiced even one hour a day on your skills at overcoming objections? You would become an unstoppable real estate salesperson.

There are really only about forty possible objections in the selling of real estate. If you wrote them all down and practiced them for half an hour a day for the next six months, you would know them automatically. You would be prepared for any situation in selling. You would then have the confidence to say, "Bring them on. I am ready for them." About ten to fifteen of the most common objections will stop unprepared agents in their tracks 90 percent of the time. How difficult would it be to learn just those ten objections in the next thirty to sixty days?

Solve the Problem, Then Close

Objections are an opportunity to get a signed contract. When a buyer or seller gives you an objection, he is presenting you with the opportunity to close. He is basically saying, "I like this, but there is one factor I do not like." The buyer might say, "If the home you are showing me had a larger patio, it would be right for me." All you have to do is get him a larger patio and you have made a sale! You must put your problem-solver hat on. If you solve his problem, then you get the opportunity to ask him to buy. The client can say yes or give you another objection. If he gives you another objection, you get another opportunity to solve the problem and ask him to buy. This procedure may continue for a few objections. Do not give up; you are getting closer to a sale. As long as you are able to continue to solve his problem, the client will buy. Remember, you are the problem solver.

What to Do About Price Objections

When the seller feels that her home is worth more than the marketplace would support or more than you would recommend, this is your signal to go back to the price. Reemphasize the importance of proper pricing. Show her that she will be the highest bidder for her home. Remove the emotion from the discussion and look at the facts. The more emotion you allow into the discussion, the higher the price the seller will want. You must have conviction and belief in your price. Remember this is your opportunity to overcome the concern and then ask for the order again.

What to Do If a Seller Is Concerned About Your Abilities

If the seller's concern is about your abilities, this objection stems from your presentation and conviction. When this problem arises the great agents will go back and focus on their track record. They will focus on telling the seller about their ability to get the job done. Once they have done that they will ask for the agreement from the seller. This can be done in many ways. I often used a question such as "Do you believe I can sell your home?" If they said yes, I asked for the order. If they said no, I used the most important and powerful word in sales, "Why?" It allowed me to get to the bottom line of the objection.

The Most Common Objections

There are about forty possible objections you will encounter in real estate. You can learn to counter them all. The most common are

> Will you cut your commission?
> I want to think it over.
> The other agent will cut his commission.
> The other agent will list my home for more money.
> We want a shorter listing term.

If you learn to handle these few you will be far ahead of your competition. I have found that even ten-year veteran agents struggle with these on a daily basis. You can be better than they are in a short time by mastering this process.

Let me share with you how to handle each of these objections:

1. **Will you cut your commission?** "I realize that you are trying to save money. I can appreciate that. Which of the services do you want me to cut out of the marketing of your home? Or do you want our full marketing program?"
2. **I want to think it over.** "I agree that evaluating a decision is important. If you had to make a decision right now, whether to list with me or not, what would you decide? Why don't we go ahead? Do you realize it takes a week to ten days to alert the world that your home is for sale? Can we really afford to wait?"
3. **The other agent will cut his commission.** "Mr. Seller, I realize you can get someone to list your home for a lower fee. Here is my concern for you . . . if they can't even negotiate their own brokerage fee, how can they negotiate a good sale price for your home? When they are not skilled enough to protect their own money, how quickly will they try to give away yours?"

4. **The other agent will list my home for more money.** "I can understand why you would be led in that direction. Here is the truth. A lot of agents will tell you anything you want to hear just to get your listing. Are you just interested in having your property listed or are you truly interested in getting it sold? The question that you have to answer is, Who can get your home sold? Do you think I can get your home sold?"

5. **We want a shorter listing term.** "I can understand how you feel. The truth is, in our market today, it often takes three to six months to get a home sold. Did you know that? Do we need to list your home tonight at 10 to 20 percent below fair market value to ensure a sale within your shorter listing period? Then we will keep the longer listing period of six months. Will that work for you?"

Objections allow you to have the success you want in your sales career. Don't be like most agents who fear and avoid them. Resolve to practice and meet them head-on.

Your sales skills will dictate your level of success in real estate sales. You must develop a game plan to increase your sales skills today. What are you waiting for?

"We are all paid in life based on our ability to sell."

—Earl Nightingale

CHAPTER 10

MASTERING YOUR SALES SKILLS, PART III: REFERRALS

It should be every salesperson's goal—whether a total novice or a seasoned veteran—to build a referral-based business. Now, "referral-based" doesn't mean a "sit back and let the dough roll in" type of business. Building business based on agent referrals is hard work, especially for a new agent. If you are entering the real estate business from another industry in which you dealt with customers or clients, you have an advantage over most beginning agents, and you should seize the opportunities your experience presents to you.

When it comes to building a referral base, size does matter! The larger the group of contacts you have the better. If you have 100 people you have done business with in the past plus another 250 people you know as family, friends, or acquaintances, you should generate more business than another new agent who doesn't know and communicate with 350 people regularly.

While quantity does influence the number of business referrals you create, quality should be your ultimate goal. A smaller but well-educated and mobilized group of advocates will make up for any quantity deficiencies you might have.

When it comes to building a referral base, size does matter!

Later in the chapter I will elaborate on the best ways to generate *quality* referrals, and teach you how to communicate with, engage, and coach referrals.

Too many agents seek out a referral-based business for the wrong reasons. Really, they just want to build an *easy* business, so they can sit back with their feet on the desk waiting for the phone to ring. While building a referral-based business is the best approach to long-term sales success, doing it right, for the maximum benefit and reward, isn't easy. If all you do is send mail and e-mail to your clients as most agents do, you will go broke as a new agent.

Building a referral-based business takes time. You should not expect referrals for up to ninety days after starting the process to build and expand your referral base. The referral lead generation model is a long-term rather than short-term strategy. By directly prospecting highly motivated prospects—doing things like calling expireds or FSBOs—you will generate more transactions more quickly than basic referral prospecting. It's also worth noting that historically, referrals are more weighted toward buyers than sellers (that is to say, you will receive more referrals of buyers than sellers). In any case, referrals are essential for your long-term career success. They just take time to build.

THREE GOLDEN RULES OF REFERRALS

To be effective in generating referrals early in your career you must follow the three rules of referrals. They may seem obvious if you have been in a customer-centered business before, but even experienced agents frequently fail to master these golden rules.

1. **Outstanding Service = Referability.** Our objective should be to provide outstanding service before, during, and after the transaction. Outstanding service is really the first step to generating referrals. (It doesn't guarantee you will get referrals, but you won't get referrals without it.) The biggest challenge in generating referrals is that much of the service we provide to consumers is intangible. They can't see, touch, or feel it. They do know when we fail, but they don't always appreciate when we've done an outstanding job. Much of what we do as real estate agents is behind the scenes and unrealized or unrecognized.

For example, an agent should invest time in getting to know the marketplace. You do this by regularly analyzing the marketplace, attending seminars, listening to CDs, or reading books like this one. Your clients and prospects don't see the hours you invest to acquire skill and knowledge, but they clearly know when an agent falls short, because the service quality is lower.

2. **Go the extra mile to find out your client's *intangible* needs.** One of the ways to increase referrals is to determine the prospect's and client's expectations early. A skilled salesperson explores the client's needs, wants, desires, and expectations. New agents tend to focus too much time trying to determine the client's tangible (i.e., home) wants and needs. They focus too literally on bedrooms, bathrooms, and square footage, rather than on intangible (i.e., service) wants. The truth is that a real estate agent doesn't sell homes. What we sell and provide is representation services. We sell communication, expertise, and the competitive advantages our company provides. Let me ask you an important question: Who defines outstanding customer service? The truth is, your customers and clients do! Most agents think a client merely wants to buy a home or to sell a house. Those end results may be the finish line, but there are a number of ways to arrive there. The benefits and service you provide en route is what really creates advantages for the clients. It's a lot easier to sell to someone what they want to buy rather than what you have to sell them. The question is what do they want to buy from you beyond four walls and a floor and roof? We have to ask questions to assess their service wants and needs:

- What are the top three services I could provide that would add value when working with you?
- How frequently and by what method do you want me to communicate with you? (According to a number of studies by the National Association of Realtors, the most common complaint from consumers about agents is frequency of communication. Find out how often you need to talk with your clients.)
- If you've worked with other agents in the past, what did you like best about them, and what did you like least?

It's a lot easier to sell to someone what they want to buy rather than what you have to sell them.

To achieve referability, you must service the client even after the sale. You must be in constant communication with your past clients through mail, e-mail, phone, and in person about market trends reports, interest rate updates, and regular valuation services (at least every few years) of how their home has appreciated.

3. **Ask and you shall receive.** Too many agents, especially new ones, fail at the easiest way to generate referrals . . . ask! You will not generate referrals without asking and asking directly.

   To a new agent the "referral ask" is challenging and cumbersome. You don't have a track record of successful sales. Your friends, family, and acquaintances know that as well. You are unproven in the real estate profession, and the only people who don't know that is people you don't know. Despite all these obstacles, you *will* have to ask for business unless you are willing to prospect relentlessly.

   When I was a new agent in real estate sales, I started my practice in an area of Portland, Oregon, where I knew few people. Looking back some twenty years, it wasn't the smartest decision I've ever made. Because my prospects for referrals were limited, I was forced to learn how to prospect and generate business from people I didn't know rather than from people I did know. Don't make my mistake. Ask regularly for referrals—even if you lack experience—or else you will make the same error I did of constantly relying on strangers.

   Let me give you a bonus rule #4, which might be the most important of all:

4. **Always say thank you.** Service providers rarely think to say "thank you" to the clients they are servicing. When was the last time your

insurance agent, attorney, dry cleaner, or even the gas station attendant said "thank you" to you? Customers and clients, regardless of the service they are seeking, have lots of people to choose from when it comes to finding a service provider. This is especially true in the real estate industry. As such, every "thank you" you send to your clients sets you apart from your competitors. Express your "thank you" verbally but also in handwritten notes. After all, these clients are the people who put gas in your car, shoes on your kids' feet, dollars in your retirement account, and provide memorable vacations with your family. They do merit a "thank you" after all.

We are paid well in the real estate profession, but we also assume a lot of risk. Not all "buyers" buy, nor do all "sellers" achieve a sale, so we don't always get paid for all our hard work. We don't have a base salary, health insurance benefits, or a retirement pension. This decreases our job security, but agents who effectively manage the risk can achieve very high incomes. We live in an instant-access, rush-rush world. There is little time for the professional courtesies afforded to previous generations. Our mailboxes are stuffed with junk mail, and we are slammed with spam. As such, the handwritten note carries more power than ever before. I remember my mother sitting her three boys down every Christmas and birthday, forcing us to write handwritten thank-you notes. I have to say, thank you, Mom . . . I know it wasn't fun for you. I know because I am doing the same thing with my now eight-year-old son Wesley. He probably hates it as much as I did, but I am grateful that I am now in the habit of physically putting a pen to paper to thank people—which in real estate is one of the most powerful marketing techniques available.

CREATING A CONTACTS DATABASE

As a new agent you must create a list of business and social contacts. These people might never become clients, but they could refer you to people who will be clients. When working business and social contacts you must *give* referrals to expect them in return. Be a referral resource for your business contacts and they will do the same for you.

When constructing your list of business and social contacts, don't assume everyone you know will be a valid source of referrals. Use an organized listing process like the one that follows so you have sorted your contacts by their area of expertise and/or profession. This way, you can see at a glance who among your contacts will likely be a source of new business for you. Most real estate agents have never strategically organized their contacts, and they have no easy way of assessing who can help generate business prospects. Use this sheet as a guide to think about all the people you know who work in these industries. Start the process by brainstorming all these occupational areas for people you know. Then once you have listed all the people, sit down to research each one's address, phone numbers, and e-mail address. Create a list of contacts in each category who may be willing to refer prospects your way.

Referral Database Worksheet

Accountant	Baseball	Colleges	Firemen
Advertising	Beauty Salon	Computer	Fishing
Aerobics	Beeper Service	Construction	Florist
Airline	Bible School	Consulting	Furniture
Alarm Systems	Boats	Contractors	Gardens
Animal Health/Vet	Bonds/Stocks	Cosmetics	Golfing
Apartments	Bookkeeping	Country Clubs	Groceries
Appraisers	Bowling	CPAs	Gymnastics
Architects	Brokers	Credit Union	Hair Care
Art	Builders	Day Care	Handicapped
Athletics	Cable TV	Delivery	Handyman
Attorney	Camping	Dentists	Hardware
Automobile	Carpet Cleaning	Dermatologists	Health Club
Babysitters	Cellular Phones	Doctors	Health Insurance
Banking	Chiropractors	Dry Wall	Horses
Barber	Church	Electrician	Hospitals
Bartender	Cleaners	Engineering	Hotels

Hunting	Newspapers	Preschools	Software
Insurance	Nurses	Printing	Spas
Investments	Nutrition	Property Mgmt.	Sporting Goods
Jewelry	Office Furniture	Rental Agencies	Surgeons
Laundries	Office Machines	Resorts	Tailors
Lawn Care	Optometrist	Restaurants	Teachers
Libraries	Orthodontist	Roofing	Telecommunications
Limousines	Pediatricians	Satellites	Tennis
Loans	Pedicures	School	Theaters
Management	Pensions	Secretaries	Title Company
Manufacturing	Pest Control	Shoe Repair	Training
Mechanics	Pets	Siding	Typesetting
Medical	Pharmacies	Signs	Universities
Mortgages	Phones	Skating	Video
Motels	Physician	Skiing	Waste
Museums	Plumbing	Skydiving	Weddings
Music	Podiatrist	Soccer	Wine
Mutual Funds	Pools	Softball	

Segment Your Database for Success

It is important to identify the people with the highest referral potential—people who can help you the most in your career. Don't waste your time and effort and energy by treating everyone in your database the same. Divide your contact database into three segments according to their referral probability. Evaluate the people in your database first by these following traits:

1. People who previously have sent you referrals (especially in your previous careers),
2. People who really like you,
3. People who understand your need for business referrals—such as someone in a professional sales career. For example, your insurance agent knows the value of referrals. They also have a database to draw from to send referrals.

People who meet all three of these criteria should be considered your top-tier referral sources. You might call this a level 1 group. This is your best group for referral alliances, and as such you need to keep in regular, personal contact with them.

Establish a monthly mailing or e-mail newsletter for all of the people in your database—but this is just a baseline, minimum standard. Your level of personal interaction (frequency of calls and handwritten notes, birthday cards, anniversary cards, Christmas cards, calendars, and all other forms of marketing and personal promotion) is how you differentiate among the four levels of clients.

Level 1 Group

The level 1 group is the highest level. This group will generate more referrals than all other areas combined. I recommend a call at least every other month to this group, but once a month is better. Call them until you reach them or call and leave messages at least three times for that month. Don't make the mistake most agents do. They are inconsistent in executing calls to the people they know and have done business with.

Level 2 Group

Your second tier, or level 2, contacts are the people who met only two of your three criteria. Your personal contact frequency with this group should be quarterly. Personal contact again should be face-to-face or phone-to-phone. Leaving a voice mail message when you don't reach them can be effective. Don't rely exclusively on leaving voice mail; work to reach them. Leaving a voice mail for the people in this group is acceptable for up to 50 percent of your calls in a year; but remember that the level 2 group is still a solid source of referrals.

Level 3 Group

This group may refer someday, but the jury is still out regarding when and if. Nonetheless, these people still deserve your attention and follow-up. You need to understand that their excitement will be muted. They might be people who struggle to give referrals to anyone, no matter what the quality of service. Often they can be demanding in their expectation of service, and that puts the brakes on their willingness to share referrals with others.

CREATING LEVERAGE THROUGH YOUR REFERRAL RELATIONSHIPS

Referral relationships don't have to rest in the business sphere. You can and should establish referral relationships with the people in church, at the athletic club, and at the kids' sports events. Don't be a "secret agent" with the people you know. Secret agents are embarrassed to ask for referrals, so they don't. You need to leverage the relationships you have by communicating what you do. Share your service, benefits, success stories of satisfied clients, willingness to work hard, and your commitment to your clients.

Don't be a "secret agent" with the people you know.

As you move forward in your career, set a high standard for yourself in communicating with these new people. Don't expect a quick payoff. You have to plant, water, and protect these acquaintances before you can expect a referral garden. There is a lot of plowing and planting before a referral harvest. You must be willing to be both persistent and patient.

Generate Referrals from People You Know

Some of us view asking for referrals from friends, family, and others as pestering or bothering. You need to approach the referral process with the correct mind-set, the right skills, and the proper timing. Some of selling is being there at the right time. The process of asking for referrals is all about timing, too—you won't be pestering your personal contacts if you approach them at a time that maximizes their opportunities as well as your own.

Respect the Referral Process

When you ask someone you know for a referral, you are asking them to share with you their most valued relationships and intimate personal space. There is a proper way and time to ask. For example, the closing table is not really the place to ask. Many agents have been taught otherwise—but it is not very strategic to ask at the end of a transaction. Your client is not focused on giving you referrals—your client is focused on moving. If you get any response at all, it will likely be a mumbled reflex response: "I don't know anyone." In essence, "Thanks for asking, but I really do not want to think about helping you right now." Better to call or see them after they have settled into their home, and start a referral discussion a few days or weeks later.

Your client is not focused on giving you referrals—your client is focused on moving.

You may encounter trainers who will teach you gimmicky throwaway lines like "Oh, by the way" before you ask for the referral. This tactic cheapens the referral process, and I guarantee your client or contact can see right through it. A quality referral request should take at least five minutes, and ten would be better. You need to start with a solid framing like "I have a very important question to ask you." This technique causes a pause, builds anticipation, and sets the tone for a valuable conversation.

When You Are Stuck, Ask for Help

A referral is a request for assistance. There is nothing wrong with soliciting the help of someone who cares about you! You are asking your friends, family, current clients, and business partners for help. "I value your help" or "I need your help" are key phrases that will start a good referral discussion and they are not gimmicky.

Ask Permission to Explore

You want to ask permission to explore people they know who might benefit from your service. You are trying to discover friends and associates you might be able to help. You can ask permission to explore using a script like this one:

> *I'm delighted that I've been able to serve you. I am wondering about others you might know in your life who would also benefit from my service. Could we explore for a few minutes who else we might be able to serve?*

Ask for Referrals Specifically

Too many agents stay in the general referral area. As a new agent, create the habit of being specific and lead the contact to talk about specific areas of their life. Don't stop with "Who do you know that wants to buy or sell?" This approach is akin to the department store clerk who asks, "May I help you?" The clerk, well over 90 percent of the time, receives what is called the "reflex no" response. It's the automatic response we use when we, as consumers, are on autopilot. Let me give you a hint: Autopilot referral contacts are not good for salespeople. An autopilot or reflex response to that clerk would be, "No, just looking." How many times have you said that to clerks to get rid of them?

Generate a better referral request by narrowing the field of choices. If you give people the whole world to choose from, it's easier for them to say no. Explore with them niches or areas of their lives in which they have relationships. Ask them about people in their immediate family, their small group at church, the people in their department at work, Bobby's soccer team, and Susie's second-grade class. If they are involved in social service organizations or clubs, take the time with them to pull out the roster and invest some time talking about the names on the list.

SEND, CALL, SEE TO SUCCESS

The most effective referral strategy in sales is to send, call, and see. You should be sending something to your contact list at least monthly. Call your sources on a set schedule based on the ranked categories we established earlier in the chapter. See them periodically in person to enhance the relationship. The frequency of being face-to-face is again based on category and likelihood of referrals. Coordinating all these in a comprehensive plan really ramps up referrals. Most agents send out their monthly mail via bulk mail. The problem with bulk mail delivery is, by the end of the month, when you are making your final calls, the contacts have no idea what you sent them. They don't remember because it has been weeks.

Mail out this week only to those you can call next week. This ensures a better bang for the marketing dollar and better return on investment for the call. They will remember you and what was sent to them. The mailing will also create an opening for the phone call in case you are challenged by how to begin.

CURRENT CUSTOMERS ARE THE MOST NEGLECTED REFERRAL SOURCE

Too many agents put zero effort into current client referrals. We often wait to ask for referrals until after we have completed the job. You can get referrals the night you list the home. I have done it a handful of times. You can ask and get referrals when you first start working with a buyer. In some of the markets that are challenging, where the client will probably realize less profit than they had hoped, get the referrals sooner rather than later. Later they may not be happy with the outcome, through no fault of your own. The market might dictate the negative feelings. It's never too early to begin building referral relationships. You can start during the first meeting or phone call with any prospect, using a script such as:

> *Fred, I build my business primarily based on referrals from clients. The benefit to you is my focus will always be to give you the best service possible. The reason is I want to earn the honor to talk with you in the future about who you know who would benefit from my service. The only way I deserve to have that conversation is based on the job I do for you. I know that if you are delighted with my service, you will want to help me and your friends out.*

Ask for referrals during the process of finding or selling a home for a client. After all, this is the time when they most have real estate on the brain—probably every conversation they have with friends, neighbors, and relatives is about the home they are buying or selling. Even if you do have the referral conversation during the transaction, don't forget to call and ask for other referrals during and after closing. Call them a number of times right after the closing. The most fertile time for referrals is from the time they decide to buy or sell up until around forty-five to sixty days after the close.

Call them at least four times in the first thirty days after they close. Remember, in their view every call you made up until closing was because you wanted to get paid. Every call you make after you close is because you care.

CREATING A STRATEGY TO UPGRADE REFERRALS

Most new salespeople are so excited to receive a referral they can't wait to get off the phone once they get the lead. They get the name and contact information and then try to get off the phone immediately so they can call the prospect. I urge you not to make that mistake.

Pause to thank the referral source. Don't get ahead of yourself. Thank them for their confidence in you and for the referral. Assure your contact of the quality service their referral will receive. Give them your personal guarantee of service. Before the end of the today, handwrite a thank-you note. You can use gifts or other inducements as well, but with the handwritten note, you don't necessarily need them.

Determine the quality or level of the referral and work to upgrade it. You are trying to increase the probability that the referral will be productive. The first step is to work to secure more information before you make the call to the referral. The first call will either lead to conversion of the lead or trash of the lead. Don't rush and make a mistake. Determine which of these four categories the referral will fall under.

Cold referral. This referral has the lowest conversion rate. These referral sources have given only the name and phone number of a potential prospect. They do not want you to use their name to create an opening or connection.

Cool referral. The odds are improving on this referral, but still the chance of conversion is probably less than 50/50. These referrals have given you the prospect's name and phone number, and they have given you one thing the cold level did not: permission to use their name as the referral source to open the door. That certainly helps the connection on the first call.

Warm referral. Again you have the prospect's name and number, but you have also been granted permission to use the name of your referral source to open the dialogue door. In addition the warm referral source has granted you time to ask questions. They are willing to give you five or ten minutes of their time to discuss the referred individual, to probe and help increase the odds of connecting with the prospect. They allow you to ask these types of questions to better know who you are calling:

- How do you know this person?
- How would you describe your relationship?
- Is there anything that you can see that this person and I have in common?
- What type of a personality will I encounter?
- What organizations does this person belong to?
- What are a few of this person's personal interests?

Hot referral. This is the level to shoot for. It's the premium of referrals. It has all that the warm referral has and more. You have all the information that you have with a warm referral, but these referral sources are willing to open the door for you themselves. They are willing to make an introduction or call personally for you. This call doesn't replace your call. It only makes it easier for you to call and raises the chance of a quicker positive result. You might find that a really effective referral source can set up a lunch or breakfast meeting with everyone involved. Even as a new agent I would buy lunch for the referral and referral source to improve my odds of earning a commission check.

Referrals are what we all want. But of course, most agents make giving and asking for referrals more complicated then it really needs to be. When all is said and done, you just need to be warm and caring—and ask. The real key is to ask. You cannot receive referrals without asking.

CHAPTER 11

STAYING ON TOP IN TODAY'S REAL ESTATE CLIMATE, PART I: OPEN HOUSES

USING OPEN HOUSES TO GENERATE LEADS

In the first edition of *Your First Year in Real Estate,* I did not write about open houses at all. Agents frequently commented on my omission of open houses as a lead-generation technique—but honestly, back then I didn't like them. I rarely held open houses—and if I did it was under protest. I told myself that I didn't need them, but mostly I wanted weekends off with my wife. I was selling 150+ homes a year and took Friday, Saturday, and Sunday off—all days of the week that are prime open house times. Joanie and I would get in our car between 3 p.m. and 5 p.m. on Thursday and head to our vacation home and not come back until late Sunday. I was totally disengaged from real estate and especially from open houses.

After reading this you must be thinking, "Three-day weekends at a vacation house? Sounds great! So why the change of heart?" Well, since I wrote the first edition of *Your First Year in Real Estate,* it has become increasingly challenging to get face-to-face with a prospect. Many buyers are starting their searches on the Internet and remain in stealth to the real estate salesperson. That said, they still do go to open houses. In some markets open houses have a huge traffic of prospects. They are one of the few remaining ways for an agent to actually get face time with their prospects, and I've had to adjust my views and accept that open houses are not only a viable lead-generation strategy—for some agents and in some markets, they are one of the best.

Before I launch into strategies for open houses, I must deal with a few myths that new agents have about them. The biggest myth is that open houses sell homes. Even experienced agents make the mistake of thinking an open house's primary purpose is to sell the home being held open. According to National Association of Realtors' numerous studies over many years, fewer than 5 percent of all buyers purchase a home they visited during an open house. So don't assume that the house you're standing in that Sunday afternoon is the house you're going to sell.

What you can assume is that by hosting an open house you are creating a solid opportunity to generate prospects. Prospects, as you know, are the lifeblood of a real estate agent's business success. So as a new agent, you should rewrite your definition of an open house: It is not the best vehicle for selling a home, but rather a fruitful means for prospecting. The open house is really a neighborhood storefront from which an agent can do business for a day. Each time you host an open house, you set up your storefront, hang out your shingle in a client's home, and create an opportunity to meet prospects, establish relationships, and expand your real estate business.

Don't assume that the house you're standing in that Sunday afternoon is the house you're going to sell.

Even if you don't sell the house being held open, the greatest benefit of an open house is that it allows an agent to generate leads.

Providing a face-to-face opportunity. Not only does an open house bring in buyers to preview the home; an open house provides the opportunity to meet neighbors and friends of the home's owners—all of whom may end up in the real estate buyer or seller market in the future. Ask questions of each visitor to learn the needs, wants, time frame, and motivation behind each person's reason for visiting that home. One of the best things about an open house is it's harder for someone to reject you as "just a salesperson" once they've met you face-to-face.

Generating buyer leads. Many open house attendees will decide that the home you're showing doesn't meet their wants or needs. Don't tie yourself solely to the home you are in for the day. Have some other options and services to offer.

Generating seller leads. Sellers come to open houses for many reasons. They check out the competition, they are move-up buyers, they are curious, they come for a friend or coworker or family member. If the home you're holding is in a move-up price range, it will attract buyers who have to sell another home before they can make the next purchase. Don't neglect to ask questions and probe for sellers as well as buyers during an open house.

Real estate agents seek a magic formula for success in all areas of their business. As in most areas there is no magic formula for open houses, merely rules to improve the odds.

Setting Objectives and Standards for Your Open Houses

Before each open house, set your prospecting objectives, including

- The number of visitors you hope to meet and greet
- The number of contacts from whom you hope to collect information for mailings and other forms of follow-up
- The number of buyer interviews you hope to schedule

As a new agent, your number one objective at an open house is to book face-to-face interviews with a prospect later that same week. It is almost impossible to have a substantive discussion about your representation services while conducting an open house—better to do it in your office. Remember you are in the lead-generation and appointment-booking phase of your business at an open house.

INCREASE YOUR EXPOSURE THROUGH PLANNING

Open house success follows five clear rules:

1. Feature an attractive home in a low-inventory, high-demand area.
2. Choose a home with great street appeal.
3. Engage the neighbors.
4. Play the risk/reward odds by selecting a home in the upper-middle price range.
5. Choose a home in the right location—and lead your prospects there with easy-to-follow signage.

The following sections explain these five key points in greater detail.

Feature an Attractive Home in a Low-Inventory, High-Demand Area

People come to an open house to see an appealing home, and your role as the hosting agent is to make that house the star. They are not coming to meet you. Your goal is to create, attract, and convert prospects. If you happen to sell the home, it's a bonus. Choose a home with star power, curb appeal, and an attractive price by following this golden rule: Scarcity is a well-proven marketing strategy. People will show up at your open house in greater numbers if the home you're showing is one of only a few for sale in a well-regarded neighborhood. If it's really priced well, the traffic level will increase as well. Doing an open house for an overpriced home for a seller who is squawking they want one will do little for the seller and even less for you.

Choose a Home with Great Street Appeal

Experienced agents have seen and witnessed the drive-by buyer. A prospect pulls up alongside an open house, slows down, pauses to look, and then drives off without ever going inside. The house or neighborhood lost the curb appeal test. It's your job as an agent to counsel the home sellers to turn the house's curb appeal into a "10."

The three significant areas for visual appeal are landscaping, design of the home, and paint color and quality.

When landscaping reaches maturity after about six to eight years, it needs to be thinned out and reshaped. The landscaping can turn into a "jungle" and block the view of the home from the street. The drive-by prospect views only bushes and trees from the street, rather than a home.

You must convince your seller to trim and remove overgrown or excessive plants. Planting seasonal flowers that add color and warmth, and invite the prospects can help curb appeal. A few hundred dollars of seasonal flowers can dramatically change the appearance of the home and increase traffic on your open house.

Adding decorative features to the exterior can also slow down and stop the drive-by prospect. You could have the seller install painted shutters in an accent color to change a monochromatic ranch home. By adding an additional texture such as fish scale siding or a shake siding accent on a wood area or over the garage gable can transform "blah" into "wow!"

> *Adding decorative features to the exterior can also slow down and stop the drive-by prospect.*

The exterior paint color and condition is often the first thing a buyer sees. Many buyers are unable to visualize the home in another color if the home is robin's egg blue with pink trim. (Don't laugh. I once sold a home with exactly those paint colors.) The prospect who can see beyond what *is* to what *could be* is a rare find.

Engage the Neighbors

You can achieve greater open house results from neighborhood marketing efforts than from public exposure. As you plan and implement your open house marketing strategy, pay special attention to your nearest potential prospects by marketing to, calling, or seeing those who live in close proximity to the house you're holding open. Follow these steps:

Hold a neighborhood "sneak preview." Invite neighbors to an early preview an hour before the public open house. This will expand your reach in the neighborhood. It allows for more leisurely discussions as well.

Send at least twenty-five invitations to the closest neighbors to increase neighborhood response. The best strategy of all is to hand-deliver the invitations. Before you allow yourself to assume that door-to-door delivery is too time-consuming, realize that this simple touch will increase your invitation response rate dramatically. The people you meet will be impressed by the way you "go the extra mile" for your clients, the sellers.

Use the neighborhood sneak preview open house in restricted-access neighborhoods. Restricted-access neighborhoods would include gated communities or condo complexes that require the public—including real estate agents—to gain permission before entering. This entry barrier makes prospecting in these areas difficult at best. The good news is that other agents are facing the same challenges but few will put in the extra effort. When you get a listing in this type of area, leverage the opportunity to stage an open house neighborhood preview that allows you to meet and establish relationships with surrounding homeowners.

Select a Home in the Right Price Range

Doing an entry-level open house will attract buyers in solid quantities. The question is, Will it attract the type of buyers you want to work with—buyers who will be profitable for you to work with? I recommend working open houses in the upper-middle price range or even the middle price range. When you work only low-end houses you will attract buyers but rarely sellers because the buyers coming through will not have to sell a home in order to buy. They will typically be first-time homebuyers or investors. Both of those groups are good for business in certain ways; but you will create greater leverage and return on your business if you work that middle or upper-middle "move-up" neighborhood for your open houses. You'll get more bang for your buck and steadier returns for your time.

As a new business owner you have to think strategically when you are using your energy, money, and time resources. A home in the middle or upper-middle of the marketplace could be a $300,000 sale that would generate a $9,000 commission check for your efforts. An open house home that attracts buyers in the entry level could generate half that amount of money. The work is mostly the same but the income is vastly different.

Choose a Home in the Right Location—and Lead Your Prospects There

Open house advertising isn't the most important aspect of an open house. The real skill is selecting the right open house. Consider these rules:

1. A home near a well-traveled street will increase exposure. Be careful that the home isn't too close to road noise or you'll get traffic *by* the home but not *to* the home. Remember that buyers are reluctant to live right on or directly next to a thoroughfare or busy street. They do want the ease of access but not the noise pollution or safety issues.
2. Hold your open house in a home that is no more than three turns off a well-traveled street. Home buyers don't want to feel like they are going through a maze. There is no cheese at the end for them.
3. Ads are not essential, but when using them select standard times for your open house. Start times should be on the hour if possible unless you are doing multiple open houses in the day. The standard start time enables prospects to fit your home into their schedule of open houses for the day (and yes, the open house buyer *is* looking at multiple homes that day). Your job is to get your home on their list for that day.

Another winning strategy is to do multiple open houses in a day. Shorten the time frame for an open house to ninety minutes rather than the standard three to four hours. Select two homes in two different price points and locations so you won't have buyer overlap. Not surprisingly, you will generate almost twice the buyers with two houses.

STEPS TO HOLDING A SUCCESSFUL OPEN HOUSE

Research the Inventory in the Area

When organizing your open house, you should always look before you leap. Study the inventory levels in the neighborhood you're considering for your open house. How many homes are for sale in that area and range? What are the sales per month? How robust is the buyer pool? Obtain the prices of recent sales to be sure that your home is within the acceptable range. Research the number of days that recent sales and current listings have been on the market. Then compare your findings with research on nearby neighborhoods to be sure that the home you're considering competes well. These are statistics you should be tracking anyway. If you rule out the home you're studying as a candidate for an open house, the time you spend on the effort will be worth it. After all, you won't waste your time pitching an unmarketable house! What's more, you'll end the day with greater market knowledge.

This research will also aid you *during* the open house. You should always know the competing inventory of other homes. It will give you some additional homes to suggest, show, or just talk about with the buyers that come to your open house. I would suggest taking it a step further by previewing at least five competing homes in the general area that are similar in price, amenities, neighborhood, and geography, so you can talk specifically about the buyers' other options in the marketplace. The best approach is to take an hour and preview each one of them personally. You can tell the buyers you have been inside and seen these homes and know how they really compare to the open house home. When they express to you that this home you are holding won't work because the backyard is too small, you will be able to describe this other house you previewed and its larger backyard.

Because you will sell only one out of twenty homes you actually hold open, you must be ready with other properties you know well that your prospects can consider. Create flyers or feature sheets of the open house property as well as the other properties you have previewed. Keep the feature sheets simple with a picture of the home and the information about bedrooms, bathrooms, square footage, and amenities. Place your picture along with your contact information on the feature sheet, so buyers know who to follow up with.

Ask the Seller to Take a Hike

Most sellers want to help. The truth is by hanging around they aren't helping, only hurting. The best help they can provide is not to be there. All too often sellers spill the beans, telling prospective buyers how desperately they need to move—which of course lowers initial offers. Sellers might also say something that creates fear and caution about the condition of the property. Having the seller underfoot in an open house only causes barriers between you and the potential prospects.

What to Do During the Open House

Your primary objective during the open house is to meet guests and sell them on a future face-to-face meeting at your office.

Get Prospects to Leave a Trail

A few years ago, Joan and I were on a vacation in the La Quinta, California, area. We were considering purchasing a second home in the Coachella Valley. We went to look at open houses. It was a fascinating afternoon. We entered and exited the first eight homes without once being asked to sign a guest register. Not a single agent requested our name and contact information. After the eighth house, I was on a mission to see how many more agents we would encounter before someone asked us for our name and contact information. We made it to eleven homes.

Always ask everyone who comes into your open house to sign in. Use the seller angle if you have to by saying the seller has requested everyone to sign in. A sign-in register should have a place for name, address, phone numbers (work, home, and cell). Also be sure to collect their e-mail address. Getting complete contact information leads to higher conversion ratios. Your sign-in sheet should also have the approved Do Not Call list clause at the bottom that guarantees that if they sign in you can call them.

You also want to write a couple of names in the first couple of lines of your sign-in sheet. Nobody wants to be first, so make up a few names. It says to the buyer that it's safe; someone else has already done it. Do not use single prospect sign-in forms. Those put everyone in the position of being first because only

Welcome to Our Open House!

Please let us know who we have had the opportunity
to serve today by signing in.

Sales Associate: _____

Date: _____

Address: _____

Name (Please Print)	Address	City	State	Zip	Phone (Home, Office, or Mobile)	E-mail Address	How did you hear about this Open House? (Signs, Internet, newspaper, etc. Which site/newspaper?)	Do you own a home? Yes/No

Thank You!

By providing us with your name and telephone number,
you grant us permission to contact you via the telephone.

one person can sign one of those sheets or cards. I have included a form that works effectively as an example.

Don't forget your business cards. When you hand a prospect your business card, you leave a professional impression on them. You also open the door to dialogue, because by giving a prospect your name, you are in a position to ask their name as well.

Book Appointments

Your measurement for success in an open house is how many appointments you book. The appointments are for buyer interviews, which are meetings during which you determine the prospect's motivation, time frame, wants, and needs— and the prospect learns how you work and what services you provide. Successful buyer interviews conclude with a prospect committing to work with you on an exclusive basis. The single best way to obtain a buyer interview is to convince the prospect when you are face-to-face at the open house that you are the best real estate resource based on

1. Your high level of professional service,
2. Your superb knowledge of the marketplace,
3. Your commitment to delivering the quality representation that the prospect truly deserves,
4. Your ability to deliver a buyer advantage in the marketplace, and
5. Your experience saving buyers money in the short run via lower sales prices or initial down payments, or in the long run via reduced payments.

Your measurement for success in an open house is how many appointments you book.

What to Do After the Open House

The first step after an open house is to send handwritten thank-you notes. Send the handwritten note to anyone who attended who provided contact information. If the prospect requested additional information, or you offered to send them something, send it separately from the handwritten note. Send the additional information after you mail the handwritten note. If you are going to send additional information, confirm that they will review it. Ask for a face-to-face if you can't get that assurance, then ask for a phone-to-phone appointment to review the information with them.

Don't assume your home was the only open house they attended. The truth is it's a competition between you and the other agents they saw that day. The competition is on sales skills and lead follow-up. Whoever wins that contest wins the client.

You want to call the prospect the day your handwritten note arrives. The call objective is to book a buyer presentation appointment at your office. Call them later in the week on Thursday or Friday. Tell them you found a property that is similar to what they described they wanted. Again go for the appointment in your office, but if you can't get that, book an appointment to show the new property. The competition is still on with other agents to get them to visit your office. Whoever gets them into their office first dramatically improves their odds of acquiring a commission check.

> *Don't assume your home was the only open house they attended. The truth is it's a competition between you and the other agents they saw that day.*

You want to repeat this process of checking in for a few weeks. If you have not been able to get them into your office in that amount of time, then the quality of the prospect is probably lower than initially anticipated. It's time to cut them loose and move on to more motivated buyers.

GETTING THE MOST FROM YOUR OPEN HOUSE

A successful open house requires a well-chosen and presentable home, a well-organized real estate agent host, and a stellar follow-up plan. Your strategies *after* the event are almost as important as the work you did *before* the open house. The following checklist will help you standardize your open house planning before, during, and after the actual event.

Open House Checklist

ADVANCE PLANNING

Select the right property:
> High-demand area
> Attractive home
> Curb appeal (Get seller to enhance curb appeal if it is lacking.)
> Proximity to a major street

Set objectives:
> Number of visitors
> Number of leads
> Number of buyer interviews

Set the open house hours.

Plan neighborhood events:
> Organize a sneak peek.
> Send a set number of invitations.
> Mail or hand-deliver them to neighbors.

Plan the directional sign strategy.

Write open house ads.

DAYS BEFORE THE EVENT

Place open house ads.

Preview five to six similar properties in the area.

Remind seller to leave during open house.

Prepare feature sheets.

THE DAY OF THE OPEN HOUSE

Set up

> Put out a guest book or sign-in sheet.
>
> Set out your business cards.
>
> Make your feature sheets available.

AFTER THE OPEN HOUSE

Handwrite thank-you notes.

Send them to all attendees who left contact information.

Call people the day they receive their notes.

Confirm that people who expressed interest in supplemental materials still want them.

Send supplemental materials.

Work to schedule face-to-face follow-up meetings.

CHAPTER 12

STAYING ON TOP IN TODAY'S REAL ESTATE CLIMATE, PART II: TECHNOLOGY

LEVERAGING TECHNOLOGY TO CREATE BUSINESS

The real estate industry has been over the moon for technology, and especially for technology that has the potential to create leads. Technology has increased lead generation drastically since the first edition of *Your First Year in Real Estate* came out in 2001. Today, buyers search the Internet rather than newspapers and home magazines for real estate listings; interactive voice response systems have increased lead volume on current listings; and social networking tools have become indispensable to the business world. All these factors have created a changed world in the real estate industry.

Before you read this chapter, I caution you to be very careful in balancing your "high-tech" approach with "high touch"—that is to say, do not neglect a solid sales skills base. No matter how high-tech you get, you should never forget your fundamental sales approach: send, call, see. Most salespeople using technology to generate leads or to follow up on leads forget the "call" and "see" parts of this equation. They tend to send and send and send via e-mail and wonder why they don't convert the lead or prospect.

Be very careful in balancing your "high-tech" approach with "high touch."

Whether the avenue of your lead creation is Twitter, Facebook, an interactive voice response, or IVR, system, or any other new media option, you still must use fundamental sales techniques, strategies, and systems to drive the prospect to meet with you face-to-face. Using technology *as a substitute for this face-to-face contact* is the mistake that too many agents are making in today's world of real estate sales.

The Internet is the cause of almost every change in the real estate industry since I wrote the first edition of *Your First Year in Real Estate*. The Internet has fundamentally changed the way buyers buy, and has fostered a new breed of do-it-yourself lookers entering the marketplace. This trend will continue on and grow. According to the National Association of Realtors, the first step to home-ownership for 87 percent of buyers is an Internet search for homes.

An Internet strategy is a must for an agent intending to attract buyers and make sales. But the Internet is not what some make it out to be—a magic pill that will solve all your sales ills. The Internet is not the savior of real estate agents; it won't miraculously help bad agents survive or thrive. The truth is, the Internet will make good agents better because they will have more leads. The real estate business is still a personal service business. Personal services must be sold; they don't just magically get bought. The error I frequently see is agents glued to their computer screen in an effort to avoid prospecting or lead follow-up. It's easier to take sales rejection from a computer screen than from an actual person. You won't reach your full potential as a salesperson or a business person by having a love affair with your computer.

> # The Internet is not what some make it to be—a magic pill that will solve all your sales ills.

There has been a massive shift in the way agents market properties, away from traditional media such as print advertising. While I agree that print advertising's effectiveness has drastically decreased in recent years, you should still invest your marketing dollars where prospects can see your inventory of listings and services. Print advertising may not be the way to go in today's world of technology-based marketing and new Internet companies, but real estate agents must be savvy about new media. Beware of someone selling you something they claim generates leads without any effort on your part. That's like someone trying to sell you their magic pill for weight loss.

USING THE INTERNET AS A TOOL

The Internet is a great tool, but that is all it is—a tool. For some agents, it is an essential tool for their business success; they generate large volumes of business from their Web site or Web sites. For others, the Internet is a very minor piece of the puzzle; they engage in a more traditional real estate model. There are a lot of ways to generate revenue in the real estate business, and the Internet is one of those ways. One of the best aspects of real estate sales is there is a wide variety of strategies and sources to tap for leads. The Internet is one of those sources. There are also expireds, FSBOs, open houses, notice of defaults, bank-owned properties, investors, orphan clients, cold calling, public seminars, divorce attorneys, real estate attorneys, door knocking, representing builders, small 'plexes, geographic farming, sphere contacts, past clients, leads groups, social networking, call capture ... I could go on for pages.

The big problem with most agents' approach to Internet strategy is they forget that to generate leads online, those leads must be driven to a fundamental sales channel. A fundamental sales channel could be sending them something, calling them to book a face-to-face appointment, and ideally going to see them. Most Internet leads don't sell themselves. If you are waiting for someone to call you when they hit your Internet site or call you when you send them information on properties, in most cases you will be waiting a long time. Those type of leads call back at a rate of about one time out of a hundred. Those are not the odds on which to build a business.

These odds sound dire, and you may be wondering why it's even worthwhile to have an online presence. What's important to realize is, the low conversion rate is not actually the fault of the technology—it's caused by the agent's poor lead follow-up strategies. It's important to at least try to connect with consumers online, because the Internet allows us to access consumers earlier in the cycle. In the old days when someone wanted to get information about homes, property, home prices, pictures, neighborhoods, and homes for sale, they had to make personal contact with a real estate agent or company. They had to pick up the phone or go in to see the agent. Today the consumer can visit any number of Web sites and remain anonymous for an extended period of time while they ponder their options.

Therefore, the goal of your Internet strategy is to get the consumers to reveal themselves to you quickly and efficiently so you can serve them and raise the odds of earning a fee. Even if they are not ready to become clients, if you serve them well, they will come back to you when they have digested the information and made some decision to move forward. It is this integral step of serving potential clients—that is to say, prospects you have netted online but who are not presently ready to commit—that agents forget. This is the reason that the conversion rates for Internet leads are so low.

Dealing with Stealth Consumers

In today's wired world, real estate consumers no longer need to reveal their identities before acquiring information about available properties. They can cruise and click through hundreds of sites, requesting additional information via e-mail from scores of agents without ever making a personal contact.

As an agent, your only option when you receive an online inquiry is to hit "reply" and send back an e-mail missile of your own. In doing so, though, you face the unavoidable barriers that are part of cyber communication:

It's hard to distinguish yourself via online correspondence. Your e-mail note will look very similar to the notes the consumer will be receiving from dozens (or more!) of other agents.

If the consumer forgets that he requested your response, your reply may be perceived as a spam mailing. A Penn Institute survey found that 22 percent of people have reduced their use of e-mail and 53 percent are less trusting of e-mail owing to spam concerns.

E-mail provides a quick, convenient, cost-efficient way to answer a prospect inquiry. But when it comes to determining the desire, need, ability, and authority of a buyer prospect, or determining the prospect's motivation and time frame, or distinguishing yourself from the countless other agents in the realtor community, e-mail provides few opportunities for differentiation.

The real objective and initial challenge with the Internet is getting prospects to reveal their full contact information, so you can call them back. This raises the conversion ratios substantially. Additionally, because of the Do Not Call act, you have that ninety-day window of opportunity for future phone contact. The National Do Not Call act—DNC—was adopted in 2003. There are more than 150 million consumers in the United States on the registry. It has affected the way that salespeople in all industries call and make contact with consumers. In essence, salespeople are not allowed to call people who have not contacted them through some medium whether it is an Internet inquiry or an inbound call or letter.

Most agents are chasing a lot of low-probability prospects through the Internet. They have an e-mail address and are sending property match searches daily. While this is an automated process in most cases and only costs you time to set up initially, it is not performing sales functions—so don't wait for your prospects to contact you themselves. Further, if you put a prospect on an electronic newsletter list, this may keep a base level of communication, but don't think for a second that when you get an Internet lead you are the only person that knows about this prospect. If they hit your site, they hit others. Also if they hit your site, it's most likely that they are not with another agent. It's a competition: Whoever gets committed face-to-face with them wins.

I encourage you to use a newsletter or other standard e-mail communication pieces. Just don't expect all recipients to open them, read them, and call you. According to the Direct Marketers Association, the open rate for a double-opt-in e-mail is currently less than 19 percent. To clarify, a double-opt-in is a person who asks you for something, after which you send a confirmation e-mail that basically asks, "Do you really want what you asked for?" The requester has to reconfirm their desire by replying or clicking and confirming. That level gets an average open rate of only 19 percent. That 19 percent open rate doesn't even factor in if they actually read what you send them or if the value and copy of your offer is good enough to get them to respond.

It's a competition: Whoever gets committed face-to-face with the prospect wins.

Generating Internet Prospects and Profits

The two main concerns with Internet leads are quality and quantity. You want to drive visitors to your site so you can increase the odds of generating leads from it. You want to increase the quality of the prospects so you can separate the really good buyers and sellers from all the rest. You want to achieve a reasonable conversion rate, which is much higher than the 0.5 to 1 percent conversion rates we are seeing nationally.

Balancing quality and quantity is a delicate act. Which is more important? Before you answer, let me tell you one thing about the Internet: The volume of traffic is important. At the end of the day, the one who has the most visitors usually wins. You may build a beautiful Web site, but you have to drive traffic to it to make money with the Internet.

Once you have traffic, you have to convince people to stay and to leave a breadcrumb trail so that you can connect with them later. You could send a couple thousand people to your site monthly and still end up with only two or three prospects. I am not talking about clients; I am talking about *prospects*. A prospect is someone who has given you an indication of wanting to take action to buy or sell but has not yet committed to using you exclusively to represent them. You now have to do the work of moving them up the loyalty ladder to becoming a client by converting them from visitors to buyers. This is where the challenge comes in. Most agents don't have a set strategy to move the lookers to buyers—to take the stealth leads and get them to reveal themselves.

To do this, you can offer a free report, foreclosure list, market trends report, a newsletter, or something that a buyer or seller would deem valuable enough that they would be willing to give you at least their first name and e-mail address. You need to walk them up each step of the conversion track. With each level or step they take, your probability of earning a commission check grows. The object is to move the visitors to prospects, the prospects to clients, and the clients to referral sources. You can even inform them that by meeting with you they are guaranteed to receive the highest level of service, to buy a property for below market price, or to acquire a low-interest-rate loan. Be sure to explain to prospects that the most satisfied clients who enjoy their homes most and get the best buys all met with you face-to-face at the office.

> *Be sure to explain to prospects that the most satisfied clients who enjoy their homes most and get the best buys all met with you face-to-face at the office.*

The more complete contact information you can get people to leave or that you can acquire in a few e-mails, the higher the probability you can move them up to the client category. More information increases the opportunity of moving them to a fundamental sales channel of send, call, and see. There are some leads that will want to remain stealth, giving you only first name and e-mail address. The most motivated leads will give you full contact information if they see the benefit of doing so. Many trainers and agents believe the hands-off, don't rush them approach is correct. I don't share that view. If you can't get prospects to reveal themselves after asking a few times through e-mail, I don't advocate taking them off the automated property program, but I do say that you should understand your conversion rate will be less than 1 percent. I wouldn't expect to build my whole business model around these prospects. I wouldn't even expect to make enough money monthly to make my mortgage payment from this "hands-off" strategy.

Listing with Realtor.com

According to the National Association of Realtors, Realtor.com is the most visited Web site for real estate in the world. At a minimum, you must put all your listings on Realtor.com to expose them to buyers and generate leads. If you need some of the enhanced services for your market and listings, Realtor.com charges extra. If you are spending money on premium exposure services through Realtor.com® or any other Web site, it is critical to track the number of leads, the conversion rate on those leads, and the dollars you generate from the leads. This is the only way to find out if your investments are paying off.

INTERNET SITES AND STRATEGIES THAT WORK

What You Should Know About Image or Brand Web Sites

Agents often invest dollars trying to build a brand or image. Branding is a fairly standard term to marketers of all types. It basically means that you'd like to establish a memorable or at least recognizable position with your potential prospects and customers. Ideally, you'd like all of the people in your given market to think about you when they think about buying or selling a home.

But there are a few aspects of branding that don't make it the best solution for many agents. As a new agent you must understand that branding can be expensive. It also can take a long time to establish a brand. Finally, it is almost impossible to quantify the effectiveness of branding. All three of these aspects are contrary to what most people think the Internet is all about—low costs, immediacy, and easy ways to quantify traffic. Even though branding is not always the easiest choice for an agent, I still suggest that every agent participate, to some extent, on a main company Web site. Connecting yourself with the company you work for will brand you with the company, and that is the easiest way to start to cultivate your image as an agent.

On the Internet, you can have a Web site up and running within days or even minutes, with barely any costs at all. The advantage of a Web site is you will be able to find out all kinds of data about your visitors. Basic requirements for this type of site are a clean and organized look, company logo, professionally placed photos of agents, bios of the agents, and several means of contact for the visitor. The main purpose of this type of Web site it to make it easy to reach you. As a new agent, it's fine to send your traffic there because the sole purposes of the site are to show that you are legitimate and to help the prospect or customer get in contact with you. The site will also include properties that can be viewed.

Determining When to Use Property Information Web Sites

These types of sites are focused solely on one property and can be very effective in systematizing the sales process of individual properties. They will allow you to expose an individual property or listing. You can attach numerous pictures, video tours, and information that is specific to the property. A property information Web site is often used for featuring a high-end listing. Frequently the URL is a derivation of the address of the property to enhance search engine optimization. You can purchase these sites for as little as $30 per month for three individual addresses, or you can spend up to $99 per month per address. You must treat these sites as part of a sales and marketing process.

Let's say you have a house listed at 123 Main Street. You fire up one of these sites, and you can include a virtual tour of the home, all the particulars about the home, all of your contact information, and many more details. The site, by itself, really has no value, but if you run a classified ad in the newspaper talking about the home and include the 123MainStreet.com link, now you've gotten somewhere.

The problem with these sites is that the prospect may make a negative decision based on a bad photo on the virtual tour, or the fact that the paint color was wrong. You can't answer a prospect's objections, and you may never have the opportunity to even know their name.

So these sites can be a valuable way for you to gain exposure for your properties, but the lead volume will likely be small. Use this type of site as *part* of your arsenal, to gain exposure for specific properties.

Benefiting from Lead-Generation Web Sites

One of the biggest problems with the activities we find ourselves involved in as real estate agents is that we often forget why we are doing them. If I had only one choice for what a Web site would do for me, it would be to generate leads—not some leads, but a ton of them; not just any leads, but very qualified (ready-to-do-business-with-me) leads.

This brings me to my favorite kind of Web site, the lead-generation Web site. The sole purpose of this site is to generate a large volume of a specific type of lead, whether for buyers or sellers. This Web site is designed for a very targeted audience. This could be buyers and/or sellers of homes in Anytown, USA, or it could just be buyers and/or sellers in general. The narrower your focus, the more targeted your niche, the better. The best choice among the prior examples would be a site dedicated to *only* buyers or *only* sellers in Anytown, USA.

For buyers, you need to have the site loaded with content that is extremely valuable to only your target prospect. The Web site must be focused solely on things that (1) are very valuable to buyers in Anytown, USA; and (2) will help buyers in Anytown, USA, to accomplish their objective, which is to buy a home in Anytown, USA.

The site also must have Internet data exchange, or IDX, technology. IDX technology integrates with your local multiple listing service (MLS), enabling the visitors to your site to see not only the inventory of homes you have listed and the company's listings, but all properties that are available for sale in your marketplace. The information a visitor to your site receives through this search is complete with all the information and pictures that the listing agent put on the MLS. But it omits the listing agent's contact information and replaces it with yours—so if buyers are interested in the property, the only contact they have is you!

Using Your Web Site to Persuade the Prospect

Having high-value content for a targeted audience isn't enough by itself. You must, through persuasive sales copy and Web conversion elements, persuade the many people who visit your Web site to become prospects. For this, I recommend that you contract a good copywriter—preferably one who has Web site design experience. You can find them online at www.elance.com or any other contract labor source. The key is to find one who is good at persuasive copywriting and design for the Internet; asking them for a portfolio or examples of their previous work always helps. A great copywriter could make you hundreds or thousands of dollars for every dollar you spend.

Getting Interactive with Your Internet Prospect

As mentioned previously, the two goals of a Web site are to interact with the visitors and to get them to leave a trail. You also want them to come back to your site again and again. That is why IDX is so important. IDX allows visitors to access all the homes listed for sale in your area—not just the ones that you or your company has listed. It makes your site a resource—a portal through which visitors will find information on all properties in the area. IDX helps you lure visitors to this resource—and when they leave a trail, you will have to get their phone number and other contact information.

Offer Free Reports

Again, get them to take information that is valuable by offering free reports. Offer access to information (e.g., "The Ten Mistakes Sellers Make When Selling a Home"). Such a report lists mistakes and solutions. Someone who requests that type of a report is at least considering a sale. Another report (e.g., "How to Guarantee You Get Your Home Sold and for the Highest Price Possible!") could lead them through the steps to ensure the sale at a top-dollar sales price. There are similar reports on the buyer's side as well. You are trying to generate a volume of leads at this point. Free reports are a good first point of contact. There are thousands of reports already available, so don't waste your time sitting down to write one. My own company has some reports that you can use for free at www.realestatechampions.com. Most Web site providers also have sections of free reports as part of the Web site. You can also use reports from your local Board of Realtors, MLS, or the state or national real estate associations.

Offer Free Newsletters

Free newsletters are also an effective means of communication. There is immense power in having an e-mail list of people who read your material regularly. Your job is to provide value in that newsletter. I encourage you to do a newsletter monthly. Start with a generic version or template version. Don't work to create one on your own—it wastes valuable time. I started my newsletter eleven years ago with a few hundred readers. I now have over 300,000 people who read my weekly *Coach's Corner* newsletter. If you want to receive it, sign up for it at www.realestatechampions.com.

Expanding Your Reach in Cyberspace

Filling your Web site with valuable content is paramount to getting search engines to rank you high. When you get ranked high it means that when someone searches for "real estate in Topeka, Kansas," your Web site comes up first, second, or third. One way to increase your value is to link to other similar sites of value. You can do this by exchanging or even buying links. Hiring an expert to go out and buy links to other sites will help you rank higher and generate more traffic and leads. When doing search engine optimization, one of the keys is finding ways for other Web sites to link to your own site. The more links or high-quality sites that link to you, the higher in the search engines you will appear. The higher you are in the search engines, the easier it will be for buyers and sellers to find you on the Web.

If you sell real estate in a resort area, linking with agents who sell resort real estate in other areas can drive traffic. Linking with resort Web sites, tourism Web sites, and local chambers of commerce can help to drive traffic to your site. The objective is to link strategically to increase your Web site traffic.

When it comes to linking, there is a difference between quality and quantity. Search engines give weight to the relevancy of a link. If you go out and link to anyone and everyone, it probably will not be very beneficial. Your links should be focused on real estate and/or on your specific market area.

When it comes to linking, there is a difference between quality and quantity.

Achieving Top Ranking: Search Engine Optimization (SEO)

The goal for every agent should be to have a Web site that is optimized for the search engines. The value of being ranked high in the search engines continues to grow. The major search engines Google, Yahoo!, and MSN represent about 90 percent of all Internet search traffic. If you aren't ranked with them, you won't be found. If you are not on the front page with them, you won't be found. Most people do not go beyond the first page after they type in a particular search. In fact, even the first page is astounding. If you are number one on a search engine, you can expect to get about 40 percent of the people to click your link. If you are number two through number five, you can expect to share the next 40 percent. It pays to be number one. The next four ranked sites have to share the same traffic that the site that is ranked number one gets all to itself.

A word of caution: Before you run out and hire someone to implement search engine optimization for your site, be careful! Implementing SEO strategy is tricky business. You need to make sure you are working with a reputable firm that will stand behind its work. You also can't have the philosophy of once and done—fix it once and it will last forever. Effective SEO strategy is never ending. Everyone is fighting for that front-page position. It changes each day, so you have to work to maintain your ranking.

Knowing When to Use Pay-per-Click

More and more agents are getting into pay-per-click as an answer to their online marketing. Pay-per-click advertising on the search engines and other sources can be effective, or it can be a bust. Most search engines have pay-per-click areas on the right-hand side of their Web page. People bid for the spots on a pay-per-click basis, which can range from a few cents to a few dollars each. The truth is, only about 10 percent of searchers go to the pay-per-click section. The vast majority of people use a search engine to search a specific phrase and then select the top-ranked sites to click on.

Keep in mind, you are not paying per *prospect* but per *click*. A click doesn't mean that you are going to get anything. Pay-per-click can be used effectively if you know the conversion numbers of your Web site, meaning that you know how many people take a free report, sign up for your newsletter, ask for more information, identify themselves as a lead, or are willing to book an appointment with you once they get to the Web site. To make pay-per-click profitable, you need to know your numbers, both online and through your standard sales process. Until then, you will only be guessing whether it works and is profitable.

USING SOCIAL NETWORKING EFFECTIVELY

Recently, social networking has been the buzz in the real estate industry. There are numerous training classes and courses on social networking and its uses in lead generation and branding.

I am not an expert on social networking online. I have researched its use and have come to some conclusions. The first is that social networking warrants some investment of time, energy, and dollars. Engaging in social networking to build your brand and create a community or following is becoming more and more useful, assuming that the social network resonates with your target demographic. If you are targeting a retirement community for seniors as a mainstay of your business, social networking will be a limited lead source. The people you are targeting to service are not linked in to social networking. If you are targeting Generation Y, or Millennial Generation consumers, social networking will continue to evolve and grow into a lead-generation strategy. The segment of generational prospects will determine how effective your social networking will be.

My biggest concern with all the hype on social networking was and still is that it's the latest, greatest in a long line of magic pill answers to building a successful sales career. It's the most recent silver bullet that agents will buy hook, line, and sinker so they can avoid prospecting activities, using the phone, or having face-to-face conversations that carry more personal results but also entail the risk of more personal rejection.

The jury is still out on the number and quality of leads that are generated through social networking. This lead-generation avenue is too new for anyone to have accurate numbers tracking the cause-and-effect connection between hours and dollars invested in social networking and number of transactions, commission income, lead conversion rates, or percentage of leads from buyers or sellers.

As an agent you will be approached repeatedly in your career by other agents, your broker, speakers, and salespeople advocating that they have a better mouse trap to increase your business and income. Their mouse trap is easier, faster, and better than the current one. This is especially true in the technology lead-generation environment. Always ask the hard questions, such as

- Is there proof of the return on my investment?
- What are the lead conversion rates?
- What percentage of leads created are buyers or sellers?
- What is the lead volume?

- What is the time frame to payoff?
- What level of ongoing time commitment is necessary?

The verdict is still out on social networking. Even so, many agents spend vast amounts of time "prospecting" using it. I encourage you to invest time in social networking—but not *hours* each day, as so many agents are doing. Really, they're just fooling themselves into thinking they are prospecting.

I would advise investing only thirty minutes a day in social networking. Real estate sales are not accomplished by spending hours in front of your computer screen. Your computer will not buy a home from you. As with all real estate sales, our objective must be to get face-to-face with the prospect.

USING CALL CAPTURE TECHNOLOGY EFFECTIVELY

Another lead-generation strategy with solid lead quantity is call capture or interactive voice response (IVR). These two terms are used to describe an 800 number that buyers access using a code to hear information about a particular property you have listed. This way, they can hear the information about a property without having to call a real estate office.

The best part of the interactive voice response system is that the system captures the phone number of an inbound caller—because the caller is dialing a toll-free number, and because you are paying for the call, you have a right to their phone number.

Another advantage of these toll-free numbers is that you can record caller-specific messages that are stored in separate voice mail boxes. Advertise your call capture toll-free number everywhere you would normally advertise and market. This includes such things as your mailings, Web site, classified ads, and FSBOs or expireds campaigns. You can put it on property flyers outside the home or hang sign riders on the for sale signs. The goal is to create lead traffic so you can capture phone numbers to call. More people will access information about homes if they can do it anonymously.

One of the reasons the Internet has had such explosive growth is that it allows prospects to be stealthy. The problem with stealthy prospects is that they are hard to convert. You need to focus on creating leads that you can then trans-fer to a fundamental sales channel of calling, and IVR is one of the best tech-nologies available to remove the stealth barrier between you and your prospects. Go to the Web site www.callcapturesuccess.com to look more closely at specific IVR services.

In addition, IVR produces more leads because most prospects don't under-stand that they may get a call from a salesperson. The key word is *may*. I know too many agents who have IVR technology and call the leads back inconsis-tently at best. You won't convert leads without making a call. The consumer feels safe to call your number to get information. They know a live salesperson will not be answering the phone. But the system will notify you so you can fol-low up on the lead or inquiry.

The volume of leads you generate from an ad in the newspaper or a home magazine will usually increase fivefold when you use IVR technology. For example, if you would normally receive five calls on an ad, you will receive twenty-five when using an IVR system. All your ads direct prospects to the 800 number and the code. Call capture technology is also very effective when coupled with advertising in home magazines. An ad in a home magazine with a one-month shelf life will often see a greater increase in lead generation than a classified ad in a daily or weekly newspaper. It is not uncommon for agents who have high-single-digit inventories of homes to get a couple hundred calls a month to the IVR system with the right marketing approach. I have found IVR to be effective in most markets across North America. I have had a few clients who said that it did not work in their market because the prospects didn't use the service—but that was rare. When you get a listing inventory it's worth the investment to try.

An IVR system is like a twenty-four-hour marketing department that churns out leads for you to follow up. More leads and twenty-four-hour service sounds too good to be true. Of course, there are obstacles as well; it's not all rosy, but the benefits are significant. Nothing is better than a system that creates leads for you while you sleep.

A call capture or IVR system gives you leverage with people on the federal Do Not Call Registry, since when these Do Not Call prospects call your system about a home, your free reports, podcasts, or general real estate information, the system secures their phone number. You then fall under the ninety-day inquiry period provision of the law. This inquiry period allows you to contact the prospect for up to ninety days after the call was first made, even if the prospect is on the Do Not Call list. This gives you the opportunity to connect, establish value for your service, and ultimately ask permission to continue to follow up with them beyond the ninety days if you need additional time to serve them.

Specifically targeting people on the Do Not Call Registry is an effective strategy, because you know they are having limited personal contact with real estate agents. When you connect with a high-probability source like expireds (a seller who was previously listed with another agent but who is no longer listed), you have created a wonderful combination to generate listings. You are combining a limited-access strategy with a high-probability prospect. You can effectively combine these strategies by offering free information to that expired on your call capture system. You could call and leave them a message to call you IVR system and get a report or listen to a report on "Why Homes Don't Sell," or the "Ten Mistakes that Most Sellers Make When Selling a Home," or "How to Guarantee Your Home Gets Sold in Today's Marketplace." Of course, you could simply use direct mail to offer these services, telling prospects that all they need to do is call an 800 number to receive or hear about your benefits. Some IVR systems have fax or e-mail back on demand functions. There is a tremendous amount of marketing flexibility with an IVR system.

One of the best benefits of IVR technology is that you alleviate the hassle of the Do Not Call Registry: having to document that they called you first. Your IVR system takes care of noting when the first call was made. A word of caution when working people listed on the registry: The ninety-day inquiry period can be cut short if they tell you not to call again. If they do that, you can't call back unless they engage you again through your IVR system or call you back for information.

I think the biggest mistake agents make with the IVR technology is not contacting all the people who call in. We get busy, and we fail to schedule the time to return a prospect's call. It's as though the prospect called the office inquiring about a property, the receptionist took a handwritten message, and we just didn't call them back. I doubt you would do that, but countless agents, every day, fail to call their IVR leads.

One of the challenges with using IVR technology in your marketing is that the volume of leads increases without your being able to assess the quality of the lead. If you ran a standard marketing page in a home magazine directing prospects to call you for more information, the number of callers would be less than with the IVR, but the quality would be higher. When people call a real estate agent's office, they are expecting to talk with a sales agent. The likelihood that they are not represented by an agent when they call in is very high. Your conversion ratio on that type of a lead should be very high as well. Ad calls and sign calls generate a higher probability of making the sale. Since we are in an odds-based business, probability leads are better than possibility leads.

If you are driving everyone from your ads and signs to your IVR number, you are combining into one large pool of warm and cold leads most of the people who would have picked up the phone and called you directly. The only way to find those golden, high probability leads is to call everyone who uses your IVR system. I required my buyer's agent to call them all—no matter what. I watched and monitored her progress in this area. I didn't want to lose the easy ones. They can get mixed in with the more challenging ones.

You must be careful not to focus solely on buyers who call in, since some buyers must sell as well. I have seen agents secure a relationship with the buyer but lose the buyer's listing because they forgot to ask for it. People will call who want to sell as well. Calling everyone back is the only option for success. Calling them back immediately will dramatically improve lead conversion.

On most call capture systems, when a phone number has been captured, the phone number and voice mail are sent to you instantly via your pager or cell phone. The best rule to follow is to call people back in less than fifteen minutes, which increases the chance that they are still at the phone number they called from. Do anything you can to raise your reach percentage. Your reach percentage is the percentage of people that you call back and talk to rather than just leaving a message. Selling via voice mail is less effective then actually talking with someone phone-to-phone. The higher the reach percentage, the higher the income you will earn. That's why establishing a time frame for yourself is important.

A portion of these people might be startled by your quick response. In most cases they are not expecting you to call. A number of techniques are effective in getting prospects to open up. Once I call them back, my favorite technique is what I call the customer service call. I approach them softly: "This is a customer service call to the person who recently called our real estate information line.

Were you the person who called? How did you like the service? Did you get all the information you needed?" Once you get through those early questions, just move into a standard buyer script to convert the lead and book a face-to-face appointment. I really like the customer service call approach. It is softer and it will produce fewer negative responses, such as "How the heck did you get my number?"

You will need an inventory of about half a dozen listings before you should consider investing in a call capture service. You need that level of inventory to balance value and cost. Most systems will run you less than $100 a month for all expenses, so it's a small investment with a large return. For more information, visit www.callcapturesuccess.com.

CHAPTER 13

MAKING GOOD THINGS HAPPEN

One of the best things about being in real estate sales is there are no limits. There are no limits to the money you can earn. There are no limits to the investments you can own and control. There are no limits to the time off you take. However, as a brand-new agent, you can often feel like there are limits on you every time you turn around. The truth is there are no limits on your earnings in your first year. I have seen agents make $100,000 and beyond in their first year in the business. If another person has done it, so can you! In this chapter we discuss some practical things you can do to accomplish your goals.

WHERE WILL YOU BE IN FIVE YEARS?

The biggest limit we set is our undefined outcome, which occurs because we don't have goals for what we want to accomplish. Well-defined and well-set goals allow us to go beyond where others are today. When President Kennedy set the goal in the early sixties that in the following ten years we would be placing a man on the moon, everyone thought he was crazy. We were nowhere close to accomplishing that feat. Miraculously, within that ten-year span, Neil Armstrong made that small step for man and that giant leap for mankind. Man walked on the moon because it was a goal that was focused on and embraced by many. Your goals will have that same power in your life. In five years you will end up somewhere—the question is, where? The decision of where you end up is up to you. In five years you will have a certain lifestyle. The question is, What will it be? That decision is yours.

In five years you will end up somewhere— the question is, where? The decision of where you end up is up to you.

Take Fifteen Minutes to Dream

What do you want in the next five years? I am going to help you find out with this exercise. Get a piece of paper right now. This is the most important decision you will make this year. Take fifteen minutes to write down at least fifty important things you want. Let me give you a couple of hints:

1. What do you want to earn?
2. What do you want to own?
3. Where do you want to travel?
4. What do you want to become?
5. What do you want to learn?

Write as fast as you can. Keep your mind free-flowing. Don't limit yourself. Don't allow the negative voice to say, "You can't have that!" Put this book down right now and make the list!

Select Your Top Goals

Now that you have your list, let's review it. Next to each item write the number of years you think it will take you to achieve it. For example, if you wrote that you want a blue Porsche Boxster, and it will take you three years to get one, put the number 3 by it. If you wrote $100,000 income and you believe you can do it in one year, write the number 1. Repeat this process for each item that you have written down.

> ## The Power Source Behind Goals
>
> If your desire to earn $100,000 is tied to a great enough reason, you will accomplish that goal. If you are a parent and one of your children has to have a $100,000 operation and there is no other way to raise the money but sell a lot of homes, would you make that $100,000? I don't know too many parents who wouldn't find a way around the roadblocks to make the money needed for their child. The "why" behind the goal is ultimately the power source. It's the power source that pulls you toward the accomplishment of the goals.
>
> One of my goals in real estate was to make $100,000 my first full year. My "why" was my passion for financial independence and early retirement. My father retired at fifty-seven from dentistry. I wanted to make sure I did it much earlier than that. I had something to prove. I entered real estate on a mission of wealth. The fire of that passion got fanned by the agents in my office. They were experienced and they often laughed at my coming in at 7:00 a.m. to set up my day and begin prospecting at 8:00 a.m. They felt what I was doing was a waste of time.
>
> I resolved then to show them by becoming the top agent in my office and fulfilling the prophecy of the old saying, "Massive success is your best revenge." Maybe there is someone who said to you, at one time, that you couldn't do it or that you would never amount to anything. Here is your chance to create the success you want and to have the life you want.

Now select the three top one-year, three-year, and five-year goals. Then write a paragraph on each of these goals describing the reason you want to achieve this specific goal. For instance, you may want to know how it feels to possess and drive a Boxster or what it will feel like to be a millionaire. You must have strong and compelling reasons that you want to accomplish these goals.

Although the written goals will not remove all the roadblocks to your success, they will make you resolve to discipline yourself to meet or exceed them. When there is something we truly desire, we find a way to obtain it. What you want is a huge motivator only when it is linked to the compelling reason that you want it.

Although the written goals will not remove all the roadblocks to your success, they will make you resolve to discipline yourself to meet or exceed them.

MAKE $100,000 IN YOUR FIRST YEAR

Here is a plan for making $100,000 in your first year in the real estate business. This plan, if followed every day for 240 workdays this year, will make $100,000 for you, provided you work twenty days per month.

> Goal–$100,000
>
> Yearly Income–$100,000
>
> Quarterly Income–$25,000
>
> Monthly Income–$8,333
>
> Weekly Income–$2,083
>
> Daily Income–$416

The average gross commission check for most markets is $3,500. Let's figure out the number of homes you need to sell:

> Goal–$100,000
>
> Yearly Income–$100,000–29 homes
>
> Quarterly Income–$25,000–7 homes
>
> Monthly Income–$8,333–2.5 homes
>
> Weekly Income–$2,083–.625 homes

For you to make $100,000 in a year in most markets you need to sell a little over one home every other week. You can take four to five weeks off during the year and still make your goal of $100,000. You also can work a normal schedule of hours—forty to fifty hours a week. The key is focusing on the activities that pay you the most money. For you to make $100,000 working forty-five hours a week and only forty-eight weeks a year, you have to focus your time.

$$\text{Value of time equation: 48 weeks} \times \text{45 hours a week}$$
$$= 2160 \text{ total hours worked}$$
$$\$100,000 \div 2160 = \$46.00 \text{ per hour}$$

Your Step-by-Step Plan

Here is your plan for earning $100,000 your first year in real estate:

1. **Be at the office early.** No later than 8:00 a.m. Most agents don't show up until the day is half over. Your day should start no later than 8:00. You have the opportunity to get a lot accomplished before everyone else starts to distract you. Your broker will also be impressed with your commitment to excellence.

2. **Start working on your sphere of influence.** These are all the people you know. Your main job the first week is to construct a database of people you know or could know. First, write down all the areas of your life on the form we have provided at the end of the chapter (see Figure 1). If you are involved in a church, a bowling league, your spouse's work, or your children's athletic teams, write them all down—as many areas as possible. Don't forget your old job. List people you know who play key roles in your life. These might include brothers, sisters, or parents. All these people know other people. And remember that studies have shown that most people know at least 250 other people.

Your main job the first week is to construct a database of people you know or could know.

Once you have all the areas of your life defined, list all the people you know from each area. You can use the form we have included at the end of this chapter (Figure 2). If you don't know all the information, you will need to research it. If you are missing an address and have the phone number, call your future clients and ask for it. If you have the address and no phone number or no address at all, you have a couple of options. You can get your title company to do the research if you work in a state that has title companies. Ask them to search a certain address or even a specific name for phone numbers. They will see if the phone number is on the county records. You could also go to a crisscross directory. This directory is usually arranged by streets and addresses and also by names. You can often pick up phone numbers that way. You can also do a search for people on the Yahoo! Web site (www.yahoo.com). You need to have complete information for all your spheres of influence. Your job this first week is to get as many people as possible in your sphere right away. You will continue to add people every week (Figure 3). Remember, however, that in order to get your career off to a great start you need as many people as possible in the first week.

If you are going to use a computer database, such as Top Producer, ACT!, Goldmine, or SharperAgent, your objective is to get all your names into that database this week. If you are not skilled at typing, hire someone to input the data into the program. You must get this done in the first week. I meet agents regularly who have been in the business for ten, fifteen, even twenty years and they have never done this. Do you want to be like one of them a few years down the road?

3. **Study the marketplace.** It's imperative that you know the marketplace. In the end, it doesn't matter whether you are in a good market or a bad one. It's the one you are in and it may not change. You have to know the marketplace statistics so you can react properly to the marketplace. However, it's not the marketplace that has the greatest effect on your income; it's what you do with the marketplace you are in that matters. If you make a career of real estate sales, you will experience both good and bad markets. Knowledge of trends in the marketplace helps you react appropriately.

Your job in week one is to know the multiple listing service statistics for the board and, specifically, for your company. Use the form "Statistics You Must Know" (Figure 4), found at the end of this chapter, to help you. You will also want to look at the numbers for at least three to four months prior to the start of your sales career. You need to memorize these statistics so you can insert them into your conversation with prospects, clients (both buyers and sellers), and other agents. This activity must be done monthly so you are ahead of the market trends. You can receive this data from the multiple listing service. If you are having difficulty finding this information, talk with your broker.

These statistics will also give you power when you go in for listing appointments and buyer interviews. If your company's average list price to sale price is higher than the board, you will be able to show the seller you will make her more money. If you see the actual number of homes coming on the market increasing, while the number of sales is staying constant, you will be able to counsel your seller that price is a big issue, because buyers have more to choose from now than sixty days ago. You become much more of an expert because you have researched the trends of your marketplace.

4. **Preview property.** To really know and understand the marketplace, we need to preview homes. We need to see what someone can buy for a specific amount of money in the areas in which we work. We need to know what someone can buy for $100K, $150K, $200K, $250K, and all the way to the upper ranges of the marketplace.

A new agent should preview at least fifteen homes a week. This preview process must continue for six months. At the end of six months you will have seen enough properties not to have to do it daily. You might want to preview once or twice a month to keep up on the inventory.

When working with buyers you should preview all the homes that you plan to show them. This allows you to be prepared before you enter the home. It shows the buyers that you are knowledgeable about the marketplace and the homes in their price range. When you preview, you will not be embarrassed by showing a home that is substandard. You can cross that home off before you show it.

A new agent should preview at least fifteen homes a week.

5. **Take top agents to lunch.** You can learn a great deal from other agents who are successful. They can share with you how they got to the top. The top agents in your office have gotten where they are for a few specific reasons. You need to find out what they are. Here is a list of questions to ask them:

> What are the three least effective things you see new agents do?
>
> What three things did you do early in your career that made you successful?
>
> What were the three big mistakes you made early in your career?
>
> If you were starting over tomorrow, what are the three things you would do?
>
> What are the biggest time wasters in our business?
>
> What one skill do I need to acquire to be successful right away?
>
> What do you see our market doing in the next six months, one year, and three years?
>
> Is there anything I can do for you for taking the time to meet with me?
>
> May I ask you for advice from time to time?

6. **Write ten personal notes a day.** The personal, handwritten note is one of the most powerful tools in selling. For decades it has been the staple of great salespeople in terms of time and involvement and in importance to the receiver. Most salespeople do not send personal notes. They don't take the time for that type of correspondence. We need to make the time because it will prove to be time and money well spent.

   If you receive vast amounts of junk mail as I do, you probably sort it all right over the garbage can. I am very quick to throw out everything that is unnecessary. I then arrange the real mail. The bills and other letters that are in those #10 envelopes go in one pile. Then I see that wonderful invitation-size envelope. I get excited and open that one first.

The way to really get noticed is to send personal notes. They are even more important today because most communication is by e-mail. People who are in business use e-mail heavily because of the instant communication and the cost . . . it's free! That is why a handwritten note today has more power than ever before. It is uncommon, so make sure you send out ten every day.

Send notes to people who provide you service. Send them to your sphere and past clients. Send them to people who call about a property. There is no limit to whom you can send a note.

Here are a few sample starts and finishes to personal notes:

- "I don't know the last time I said thanks, but thanks!"
- "I tried to call you today; unfortunately I missed you. I needed to tell you . . ."
- "I was thinking of you today and ran across this information. I thought you might find it helpful." (Send quote, property, news article, and so on.)
- "Thank you for taking the time today. I know that you are very busy so any time you spend is valuable."
- "I wanted to personally thank you for the referral of _____. It is a delight to have clients like you."
- "Thank you for the referral of _____. Being recommended by you means a lot to me."
- "I was reviewing my [files, database, sphere] and realized it's been too long since . . ."
- "I found myself thinking about you today, so I thought I would write you a quick note."

The system for notes is very simple: Write notes that consist of three to five lines. Notes should be short and to the point. Use a broad-tipped pen; don't use a regular ballpoint. Use a medium roller ball or better. You want the note to be bold in its appearance. Use a unique close on the note or a call to action. Set yourself apart by sharing something you have that is a unique opportunity. Hit the minimum standard of ten per day, every day. Don't fail even one day to do this. This is one of the most effective marketing strategies you can use. It is easy to do and inexpensive. When you are a new agent, often your company will pay for note cards and postage, so it's free. Don't fail to embrace this personal way to market yourself.

7. **Mail announcement cards or letters to your sphere.** You need to announce to everyone you know that you are in business. They need to know that you are ready to serve them. You also want to ask for referrals from them. The referrals from your sphere can be the lifeblood of your business. You are going to have to contact either people you know or people you don't know: Which is easier to do?

8. **Spend at least an hour a day on personal development.** The keys to success for any agent are knowledge and control of time. Your ability to acquire the knowledge and skill now will dictate how quickly you become a success. The hour you invest daily into practicing scripts and dialogues or reading and studying success will be immeasurably more valuable than talking at the water cooler. Don't neglect to work to improve your skills daily.

You need to announce to everyone you know that you are in business. They need to know that you are ready to serve them. You also want to ask for referrals from them.

You want to repeat these steps each week for your first year or until you get eight listings. Then you can drop the preview property step from daily to weekly. There is one other activity you want to add starting in week two and continuing throughout the rest of your sales career.

9. **Prospect daily a set number of contacts.** As a new agent, you should start with a minimum of five contacts per day. Making a contact means actually talking to someone who could buy or sell or refer you to someone who could. Your job starting in week two is to call all the people in your sphere. By working to grow your sphere, you will be able to make more sphere calls and less cold calls. You can also call your sphere again every quarter. Gradually you will want and need to raise your contact total to ten per day. The most successful agents in the country prospect regularly. Start the habit of picking up the phone to generate revenue daily right now.

Create Financial Independence

If you apply the system we've outlined, you will be successful. The daily activities you do will create the success that you desire. Start each day with the focus to do these nine steps before the week is complete. One of the best things about being a real estate salesperson is the money you can earn. This profession, done well, can create your financial independence. It can give you the tools to achieve the American dream of homeownership, a large income, investments, and nice vehicles. It is all there for you.

MY FATHER'S ADVICE

Most people I know who decide to sell real estate do it because they think they can make a lot of money. They have a passion to earn a high income. They want to earn six figures and beyond. If I am describing you, let me give you some wise counsel. It is the same counsel I received many years ago from my father. He shared with me that his dental practice provided the cash flow that allowed him to make other investments. These other investments were the vehicles that created the wealth in the end. These other investments allowed him to retire at an early age. Dentistry provided the steady income and savings that allowed him to borrow for the real estate investments he made and the capital stocks he bought.

The most successful agents in the country prospect regularly. Start the habit of picking up the phone to generate revenue daily right now.

When I entered real estate I viewed my real estate sales business the same way he viewed his dental practice. It's the business that generates the cash flow that allows you to achieve your definition of financial independence. My real estate business allowed me to fund a retirement account annually, buy investment property, develop land into lots, build houses for resale, and make a number of other investments. Your career can do the same for you. You can create the life and wealth you have always desired. Apply a few simple rules and you can achieve the financial position you want in life.

CHOOSING AND ACHIEVING FINANCIAL INDEPENDENCE

Poor Preparation Brings Poor Results

Even when agents make more than a six-figure income, the vast majority have not dramatically improved their financial balance sheet. After looking at hundreds of agents' P&L (Profit and Loss) statements and personal spending habits, I've determined that real estate agents are poorly prepared for financial independence. Why should real estate agents be any different from the American population in general?

According to the Social Security Administration, of 1,000 randomly selected people from age twenty-five to age sixty-five, statistics indicate

- 190 are dead—19 percent
- 150 have incomes more than $30,000—15 percent
- 660 have incomes of less than $30,000—66 percent

Let's look at these numbers. There are more people deceased than earning something close to a decent quality of life. Of the people still alive, 66 percent of them exist on less than $30,000 per year. My question is: Which group do you want to be in? Which group are you heading for based on your financial plan, investment choices, and savings plan?

These are the top three reasons people fail in their finances:

- They never create a financial plan.
- They make poor investment choices.
- They put off starting a savings plan.

Getting on Track Financially

Let me share with you a few simple rules that will ensure that you don't join the 66 percent earning less than $30,000. I have used these rules with hundreds of agents to transform their financial picture in a short period of time.

Rule 1: Track Your Expenses, Both Business and Personal

You must know where the money is going. Separate your business from personal expenses. Establish a business checking account and pay all business bills through it. Too many agents mingle their business commission checks and business bills with personal and household expenses. It is more difficult to control your money when you can't track it. Enter all your expenses and revenue in an accounting software program. I think the easiest is Quicken. Quicken will allow you to accurately track your cost to run the business; then you can run a monthly P&L statement to see where you are spending your money. The money you earn in real estate can come in bunches. It can be very easy to spend that large commission check that's burning a hole in your pocket.

Separate your business from personal expenses. Establish a business checking account and pay all business bills through it.

When we have money, a want looks like a need because we have the ability to fulfill it. We begin to rationalize our wants into needs. For most of us a want that our neighbor already owns becomes a need.

Rule 2: Adjust Your Lifestyle

Spending less than you earn makes up 90 percent of financial planning. The premise involves saving money and making sacrifices. The ability to pay now in the form of adjusted lifestyle and saving the difference will allow you to play later. To play later you will need more than $30,000 per year. Thomas Stanley, who wrote the book *The Millionaire Next Door* (Longstreet Press, 1996), summed up how the vast majority of people accumulated their millions: "They lived well below their means." Roughly two-thirds of Americans who have credit cards do not pay off their monthly balance. We are clearly living beyond our means. Take a close look at your monthly obligations and evaluate where you are spending your money.

Rule 3: Aggressively Reduce Your Debt

There is an old proverb that speaks of a borrower being a servant to the lender. The weight and pressure of debt can be crippling. I have seen this happen to agents for years. I have even seen it manifested in my own life. I have not always made the wisest choices with my money. Fortunately, I have made more wise choices than foolish ones.

If you have credit card debts, make a decision to pay them off. Start with the credit card with the highest interest rate. Decide on a monthly amount that you can commit to reducing your debt. If you stretch, you will be able to find a few hundred dollars per month to pay toward your debt. Most credit card companies require you to pay 2 percent of the balance owed monthly. Let's look at that practice. Let's say you have a debt of $2,705 with an interest rate of 18.38 percent. If you paid 2 percent every month toward the outstanding balance it would take you twenty-seven years, two months to pay it off. You would pay $11,047 in total interest. How do you feel about eating out more often now? If you increased your payment to 8 percent or to $216.40 per month, it would take two years, one month to pay it off. You would pay $94 in interest. You need to accelerate your payments to reduce your debt. You must adopt a cash mentality. This cash mentality will allow you to charge only what you have funds to pay for.

Rule 4: Create a Savings Plan Now

The biggest enemy in financial planning is procrastination. People wait too long to start saving. The truth is, becoming a millionaire is not very difficult. The power of compounding interest will take care of your needs. According to *Investors Business Daily,* a twenty-year-old person needs to invest only $1,014 per year or $2.78 per day with an annual return of 11 percent to have $1 million saved by the age of sixty-five. Look at the daily number of $2.78. Who couldn't save that amount per day, even at the age of twenty? Even someone working for minimum wage could do that with ease. My mentor, Jim Rohn, used to say, "What is easy to do is also easy not to do." It's easy to save the $2.78, but it's also easy to buy a latte every day at Starbucks instead of saving. That's all we are talking about here—choosing financial independence planning rather than the latte.

Therefore, we need to create a system that automatically removes the money when we receive it. We need to transform ourselves into savers. We are not a nation of savers, although we really need to be. Savers pay themselves first. It's amazing how little you miss money that never comes into your possession. On average, Americans save less than 5 percent of their disposable income. Let's compare the United States to other countries with regard to income saved:

> Germans are saving 11.5 percent
> Japanese are saving 12.2 percent
> Belgians are saving 17.0 percent

You must adopt a cash mentality. This cash mentality will allow you to charge only what you have funds to pay for.

The secret to saving is writing checks to separate savings accounts first. Do it before paying other bills and obligations. Saving is a habit to be forged. Here is the formula I used on each of my commission checks for many years:

20 percent went to a tax account

10 percent went to a retirement savings account

10 percent went to a business savings account

These percentages ensured that my taxes were always current and my retirement account was always fully funded. There were also reserves for an investment opportunity or a slow closing month. The more you make your money disappear into protected accounts, the more you will have for later.

Pay Now or Pay Later

Creating financial wealth is the process of being diligent with your money. I remember some Fram oil filter commercials that were a lot like creating financial independence. The service station attendant, while looking under the hood of the car, was trying to convince the customer to use a Fram oil filter. The premise was that the quality of the Fram filter was better for his engine than the bargain brand. He said to the customer, "You can pay me now or pay me later." He was implying that the customer could spend a few more dollars now for the Fram oil filter or get the cheaper brand and have his engine rebuilt later. The same is true with your money. You will have to pay either way. The price you pay now is small compared to the price you will have to pay later if you are not diligent in managing your money and financial affairs. Which price do you want to pay?

FIGURE 1. Spheres of Your Life

FIGURE 2. Sphere of Influence

Name	Address	Phone	Relationship

FIGURE 3. Names Added to Sphere List

Name	Address	Phone	Circumstance	Note Sent

FIGURE 4. Statistics You Must Know

	The Board	Your Company
Total active residential listings	_____	_____
Compared to last year at this time	_____	_____
Average list price	_____	_____
Average market time	_____	_____
Compared to last year at this time	_____	_____
List price versus sales price ratio	_____	_____
Compared to last year	_____	_____
Number of sales YTD	_____	_____
Average sales price	_____	_____
Compared to last year	_____	_____
Current interest rate 30-year fixed	_____	_____

CHAPTER 14

TAKING YOUR CAREER TO THE NEXT LEVEL

Nobody wants to be a new agent forever. We want to learn, grow, and improve. This chapter will focus on some of the traps to avoid and the steps you must take to achieve your full potential in this business.

HOW TO AVOID SOME COMMON MISTAKES

Being successful as a real estate agent demands a wide variety of skills. All too often, the only way to develop these skills is to make mistakes. I was talking to an agent recently who had moved to a smaller town in a rural area after living and working in a big city. She told me how much she had had to learn the hard way about septic systems, wells, and water quality because prior to the move she had sold only homes on city sewer and city water. She described how she had just assumed that the water and sewer services were like her previous marketplace. Her new market was nothing like her old market. She had put one buyer through tremendous stress by the end of the transaction because of her lack of knowledge. She had exposed her buyer to a lower value for the property owing to her lack of diligence in checking out the facts regarding the property.

The Louisiana Pacific Fiasco

In Portland, Oregon, where I sold real estate in the nineties, Louisiana Pacific siding became a significant problem, as it did for real estate agents throughout the United States. A substantial number of homeowners faced the problem of swelling and deteriorating LP siding. Because new homes were selling as quickly as builders could put them up, hundreds of thousands of homes had been built in the nineties using LP siding. The rainy climate in Portland only made things worse. Added to that was the media frenzy that ensued, causing a panic among both buyers and sellers. As agents we had to be prepared to solve the problem for our clients; we had to be knowledgeable enough to help them evaluate their options and guide them to the best decision.

Never Assume

One of the first rules in real estate is to never assume. Take the time to verify the information if you have any doubt. For example, it was easier for that agent who had moved to the country to take the sellers' word that they were on a sewer line instead of having their own cesspool. Make sure you educate yourself on the different options of water supply and waste removal relative to a particular property. Be sure that you have a working knowledge of the types of roofs that are on homes in your marketplace and the longevity of the different types. Be able to recognize the different types of exterior siding applied to homes in your marketplace.

Acquiring knowledge is an essential step in taking your career to the next level. To take your career to the highest level you need to master your knowledge of real estate and real property. There are always areas of mastery that require our time and resources to learn.

CHECK THESE OUT!

When I entered real estate at age twenty-seven, I learned of a new arena of education—personal development. I had never heard of Earl Nightingale, Napoleon Hill, Zig Ziglar, Tom Hopkins, Les Brown, Jim Rohn, Brian Tracy, and many others. I was unaware that there were resources out there in the form of audiocassettes, seminars, and books that could help me to dramatically raise my thinking, skills, and income.

I remember attending my first Jim Rohn seminar where he dared all of us to spend as much time working on ourselves as we did on our jobs. Then he challenged us to buy and read two specific books. One was *Think and Grow Rich* (The Ralston Society, 1937) by Napoleon Hill. The other was *The Richest Man in Babylon* (Signet, 1926) by George Clason. Jim predicted that I needed to get both those books in the next twenty-four hours or I would never get them. He focused on causing action to happen right now. We often have good intentions, but those feelings will quickly fade. In life you have to act when the emotions are high. You must act when the intent is most passionate. I purchased both those books that very evening on the way home from the seminar. My total investment was around $12, but what a small amount it proved to be in relation to the benefits I received.

Don't Wait, Do It Now

I give you the same challenge today that Jim Rohn gave me more than twenty years ago: Go out and get those two books today! Don't wait until tomorrow; do it now. Those books will change your life. They will lead you as they have me down the path to other books, audiocassette tapes, CDs, and seminars. Their messages will expand your thoughts, beliefs, and actions.

In the final analysis, we don't get paid for the knowledge we possess; we get paid for the knowledge we *apply*. We are paid for action. Put the ideas in these two books into action. They will be the catalysts for you to walk the path of personal development. Your commitment to continually invest in yourself will bring you the greatest return on your investment and will bring returns far greater than the stock market or real estate investments. The objective is to invest in yourself.

THE FOUR PATHS TO "TOP GUN" STATUS

As a real estate agent, there are several paths you can take to get to the next level in your career. I have identified four paths that people take to reach the top level of success in the real estate field. You will use one of these trails to achieve "top gun" status, but you must expect to pay a price for whichever path you choose.

Become a Workaholic

The most common path is to become a workaholic. This path causes you to trade large amounts of time for the amount of income that is created. Workaholic agents toil six to seven days a week to achieve their goals. They never get off the treadmill of being controlled by their clients, not gaining the respect of their clients and prospects, being uncertain as to where their income will come from, and putting their career before their family. This path forces us to focus only on the result of earning a specific amount of money, regardless of the consequences. The process or journey along the way is of little value because the goal is income. On this journey the finish line of maximized income is all that matters. The vast majority of high-gross commission agents have taken this path to the top. They have paid the price in missed tee-ball games, piano recitals, and date nights with their spouse. Still, this is the most common route to financial success for agents.

Buy Your Way to the Top

This technique is the second most popular that agents use to reach the top. There are really two different ways agents buy their way to the top: They do it through reduction in commission or through massive expense in the marketing area. Either way, buying the business eventually catches up with you.

Commission Cutting

If you achieve "top gun" status through commission cutting, it is hard to reverse this trend. When that client comes back a handful of years later, she is going to want the same concessions as before. Most of the referrals of friends and family from this source are also going to expect a lowered commission. You will eventually turn your whole business into a discount operation. All your clients will expect the 5 percent charge that you gave to all the others. Don't be naïve in thinking that no one will know. The word will get around. Lowering your commission substantially reduces your gross revenue and your net profit. It may not seem like much when you look at one transaction, but when you look at the whole year or a whole career, it's a monstrous number.

The workaholic path causes you to trade large amounts time for the amount of income that is created.

Let me give you an example: You decide to list a home for 5 percent rather than 6 percent. It's a $200,000 home in a terrific neighborhood in your market—the kind of listing everyone wants. Instead of getting $6,000, you receive only $4,000. Your broker takes his 50 percent split and you are left with $2,000 for your effort. You are happy you did the deal because you made $2,000. If you did four more transactions this quarter under these exact circumstances, you would be short $10,000 in gross commission income (GCI). After the company split, you would have lost a total of $5,000 out of your own pocket. Repeat that process for a full year and you lose $40,000 in GCI and $20,000 in income to you after your company split. If you repeat this for your career of ten years, you have lost more than $400,000 in gross commissions. You have also lost at least $200,000 in real dollars of income for yourself.

Buying the business through reduction of commission is very expensive. I realize that it doesn't seem like much on one deal, but it adds up quickly. I was coaching an agent a year ago and had him add up all the commissions he gave away. He called me the next day and was physically sick because of the lost revenue. He had given away more than $50,000 that year in commissions. Reducing your commission causes future havoc for yourself, your company, and your clients.

Some of our clients and their properties are going to demand more of our time and energy and advertising dollars. If we reduce our commissions on the easy transactions, then all we have left are the difficult ones that require more time and energy to complete and close. Most clients at this time want a fixed price for your services. They want to know what you are going to charge. They are not willing to take the risk as to whether their home sells or not. Your objective is to fix your commission price and hold firm. Don't back down when someone asks, "Will you cut your commission?"

Buying the business through reduction of commission is very expensive.

Pay for Massive Marketing

The other way many agents buy the business is through massive advertising and marketing. This no-holds-barred, spend-money-to-make-money strategy always spells trouble. Anyone can attract more business by spending money in advertising, but we often get sucked into what I call the one-for-one trade: an ad or mailer that produces only one deal. Ads or mailers can cost us about what we would generate in one transaction. We feel good that we generated a deal, but we don't fully count the cost. We must avoid the one-for-one trade.

If I were going to advertise and market for additional business, my rule is a minimum tenfold return for the dollars and labor spent to produce the revenue. You need to either prepare the copy or hire someone else to prepare it, and there are real costs for labor associated with creating a marketing campaign. It's easy to get faked out by the one-for-one trade.

If I were going to advertise and market for additional business, my rule is a minimum tenfold return for the dollars and labor spent to produce the revenue.

Become Unethical

A third way to get to the next level is to become unethical. There are agents who don't treat their clients with the honor and integrity they deserve. They shade the truth in working with their clients and other agents. Some of these agents end up out of the business in a short period of time. Others manage to stay in business for years. These agents seem to be one step ahead of the ethics committee in their Board of Realtors or the state real estate agency. You will want to steer clear of this path. You could wake up one morning and be out of business.

Run Your Business as a Business

The last path is to create and operate a business that generates regular income and is repeatable in clients and net profit. This path gives you control of your income and your time. It replicates a high net profit because you know your business. You understand the sales ratios of your business. You know the costs associated with your business and how to generate more revenue.

   This path requires that you track your sales ratios and expenses. It requires that you prospect daily your past clients, sphere, expireds, FSBOs, or cold calls. The agents on this path create their income rather than react to the marketplace. They decide how much income they are going to earn monthly, quarterly, and yearly. They have the great feeling of satisfaction that they can repeat their performance at will.

"I'm the King of the World!"

I remember the exact time I realized I was on this path. It was the second week in January 1993. I was in the shower at 6:15 a.m. reviewing my day. I was going over my plan for the week and for the year. I remember thinking that I could make any amount of money I desired because I knew my sales ratios and how to create my business. It was one of the best feelings of accomplishment and satisfaction. You can have that same feeling of success of knowing where you are in your business and how you got there. There is truly no feeling in life that I can compare to it. The best analogy I can give you is in the movie *Titanic* when Leonardo DiCaprio was on the bow of the ship hanging over the rail shouting, "I'm the king of the world!" That is the feeling you have when you realize how to create and replicate your business at will.

THE INVESTMENTS THAT WILL GET YOU TO THE NEXT LEVEL

Your Financial Investment

The financial investment that needs to be made to get to the next level in real estate is minimal compared to in other businesses. If you compare the inventory of any retail operation that is selling a million dollars a year in products, our business investment as real estate agents is quite small. The initial investment for a retail operation is huge. And look at the investment in equipment that a dentist needs to make in order to earn $500,000 a year in gross revenue. A dentist has to have $500,000 to $1,000,000 in equipment just to open the doors of his practice.

As a real estate salesperson, you can earn what the doctor or dentist earns without this large overhead. Your overhead is merely your car, a cell phone, and a computer. You have the capacity to earn $100,000 your first year with equipment that you already own. How many businesses give you the same opportunity to earn such a high income with nothing down?

Your Investment in Knowledge

The real investment you need to make to take your business to the next level is knowledge and skill. You need to be knowledgeable in all facets of real estate sales. Your investment in yourself will bring you the greatest dividends. Because you are new in the business you should take advantage of every educational opportunity available to you.

Company Training

If your company provides training, take every class you can. The more you know about the products and services your company provides, the better able you will be to take advantage of them for yourself and your clients. Most agents do not take full advantage of the services the broker is providing. In most cases you are paying for these services whether you use them or not. You are paying for them with your commission split. Make sure you are getting value for your investment in your company. Be familiar with all the tools your company offers and use them.

The more you know about the products and services that your company provides, the better able you will be to take advantage of them for yourself and your clients.

Board Educational Opportunities

Most of the real estate boards or associations that you will need to join offer continuing education. They bring in expert speakers on technology, housing, investments, legal contracts, sales, time management, and many other subjects. The cost of most of these training classes are covered by your dues; others you can attend for a very small fee.

Annual Conventions

Most state boards also have annual conventions. These state conventions give you the opportunity to exchange ideas with other agents. You can learn from some of the best agents in your area and across the state, and the state boards often bring in nationally known figures as keynote speakers. Many conventions have break-out sessions—smaller, more intimate training events. This gives you a choice of a number of different seminars to attend and learn the skills for mastery.

An advantage of being with a larger nationally based company is that they have national conventions as well. These meetings allow you to rub elbows with agents across North America and, in some cases, from all over the world. These events are focused on the exchange of new ideas and techniques to expand your business. They also give you the opportunity to build a network of agents worldwide.

Networking

Developing a network of agents worldwide can increase your commission income and help generate more business for you now and in the future. Real estate agents often have the opportunity to earn income by referring clients. People in many other professions are not allowed to do this. When your dentist refers you to a specialist like an orthodontist, he cannot be paid for the referral. As real estate agents, however, we have that opportunity. We can refer a buyer or seller to an agent in another state or even another country and receive 20 to 30 percent of the total commission paid. Other agents can refer clients who are moving to or from your area of business to you. By developing a database of other agents you know around the world you can earn additional income. I know agents who make $100,000 a year or more just from inbound and outbound referrals. By attending national conventions you have the opportunity to exchange your business cards and create strategic alliances with agents worldwide.

Independent Training Companies

There are also educational opportunities that are not company- or board-based but are offered by independent training companies for real estate professionals. These companies hold seminars, sell CDs, and publish literature on all facets of real estate.

Some trainers focus on technology, such as Michael Russer, Stephen Canale, and Matthew Ferrera. Their seminars are designed to help you master the steps to become skilled in technology in order to expand your income and ease of business operation. There are other speakers and companies that are more marketing based. They will teach you how to increase your exposure in the marketplace. Some will teach you how to build your individual brand.

Other companies focus on sales skills. They teach you the skills of making the sale, keeping the client, and handling the objections in the selling process. An example of one of these training companies is my company, Real Estate Champions. This training category is often passed over by agents, who tend to gravitate toward events that offer the magic answer to success. The sales skills category is, however, indispensable. A dentist without good hands is not much of a dentist. A salesperson without the right words and delivery is not much of a salesperson. Don't neglect this category of sales training. It may not be as sexy as marketing, but it's more important.

Training in Business Skills

Lastly, you need training in business skills to take your career to the next level: skills to understand what your expenses are, what it costs you to acquire a client, what your time is worth and how to gain control of it, and how to spend more time in high-dollar activities and less time in low-dollar activities. Some of this necessary training is available in CRS (Certified Residential Specialist) classes sponsored by the Association of Realtors. The only independent company that really provides this type of training is my company, Real Estate Champions. If your desire is to be a multimillion-dollar producer, you have to learn how to create and control your business rather than just react to your business. Remember that you will need the skills of a good CEO to master your business. Resolve to get the training you need to hit the mark.

You have to learn how to create and control your business rather than just react to your business if your desire is to be a multimillion dollar producer.

KNOW YOUR BEHAVIORAL STYLE

Take your business to the next level by learning about your behavioral style. Your style of behavior will determine how you should build your business and how you will interact with your clients and prospects. Knowing your behavioral style allows you to adapt when necessary. It gives you the ability to read people and communicate with them in their own behavioral patterns.

A handful of behavioral assessments are available. I would recommend taking a DISC assessment. Dr. William Marston, a clinical psychologist, created the DISC model. In 1928 Marston published *Emotions of Normal People,* which describes the theory of DISC. (He was also the inventor of the polygraph.) DISC is an acronym for the four major assessment groups: Dominant, Influencing, Steady, and Compliant.

> Dominant: how you handle problems and challenges
> Influencing: how you interact with other people
> Steady: how you handle a steady pace and work environment
> Compliant: how you respond to rules and procedures set by others

DISC measures observable behavior and emotions. It is a language of watching people. Great salespeople are good observers. They have the ability to read others and adapt to their behavior.

DISC

DISC is the language of watching people and understanding how they do certain things such as

- how they buy
- how they act
- how they walk
- how they dress
- how they communicate

If you knew how your clients or prospects were going to react before they reacted, you would be able to help them more. You would be able to sell them more solutions to their problems.

DISC Behavior Types

High "Dominants": Their natural tendency is to be active and aggressive at achieving a result. They are highly competitive and will face a problem with little or no fear. These people can cold call for business and it doesn't bother them. To them it's a means to an end. It's something they must do to reach the level of success they desire.

High "Influencers": They have a tendency to want a high degree of contact with people. They are outgoing, social, and verbally persuasive. These people need to build their business around their social relationships. They gain energy from people contacts.

High "Steadies": These people are structured and predictable in their work environment. They prefer a secure situation. Their business has to be built through systems and structures that create results. They could create a mailing or advertising campaign. They could also create a prospecting process as long as it doesn't involve cold calling.

High "Compliants": They follow the rules set by others. They are also aware of the problems that arise when one doesn't follow the rules and procedures. These people struggle in real estate sales. It takes them a long time to make any money. They are so busy building the rules and procedures they make very few sales, but their paperwork is always impeccable.

We all have low or high scores in each area. These scores determine how we respond in a given situation or environment. All individuals have some or all of these factors in them. It is rare that we will exhibit only one behavioral factor. Four percent of the population exhibit behavior primarily from one factor. Fifty percent exhibit behavior combining two of the factors. Forty-six percent of the population exhibit behavior combining three of the factors.

By knowing your own DISC behavioral style, you can also recognize the styles of others. You will face these styles daily in prospects and clients. Some of these people are going to be quick to make a decision, such as the Dominants and Influencers. Others are going to be slow, like the Steadies. Some are going to wait for the next millennium, like the Compliants. You have to be able to recognize with whom you are dealing. This will enable you to take your sales career to the next level. The first step is to know yourself. Lao-tzu, the famous Chinese philosopher said, "He who knows others is learned. He who knows himself is wise."

> ## *Lao-tzu, the famous Chinese philosopher said, "He who knows others is learned. He who knows himself is wise."*

If you need help with a DISC assessment, ask your broker. She may provide the assessment. Some of the large national companies are using DISC assessments. You could also contact our office at Real Estate Champions. We have an incredibly in-depth assessment that will provide you with the tools you need. You can reach us at 541-383-8833, or you can visit our Web site at www.realestatechampions.com. We have a number of assessments that will aid you in your career.

CHAPTER 15

SOLVING PROBLEMS

A career in real estate sales can provide incredible income, incredible frustration, or both. The most exciting part of your new career is that you will receive what you put in. Your ability to learn and to continue to take calculated risks will eventually lead you to top honors in your company.

These chapters have covered what you need to know about relationships in your real estate career and the skills that will help you through your first year. Here are some frequently asked questions that we hear from new agents, and a final bit of advice.

The most exciting part of your new career is that you will receive what you put in.

WHAT IS THE FIRST THING I NEED TO DO ONCE I FIND A BROKER TO WORK WITH?

Ask your broker for scripts, dialogues, and objection-handling techniques and then practice, practice, practice! Suppose your broker plans to teach you how to write contracts and listing agreements—what I call "Real Estate 101." Although this is very important, I would rather you begin by practicing your sales skills. We are all going to be successful in our real estate career based on our ability to sell. Therefore, it is vital for your success to study and practice the art of salesmanship.

Your ability to become a sales master will do more for your sales career than anything else you can do at this stage. Partner with another new agent and role-play every day your scripts and dialogues for the listing presentation, buyer interview, follow-up calls, and objection-handling. We play at the level we practice. If we rarely practice, as most agents don't, our performance will reflect that fact.

WHAT IS THE BEST WAY FOR ME TO HANDLE PROBLEMS?

Most solutions to the problems we experience in real estate are based on common sense. Fine-tune and use your common sense regularly. When something doesn't feel right there is usually a good reason. For example, when a buyer is evasive about disclosing the source of his down payment, it is quite often because he doesn't have the money and is hoping to raise it before closing. When buyers disappear every time you ask them to redeem their earnest money note for a check, this again means that they are short on funds or they are having second thoughts about their commitment to purchase this home.

Handle Problems Promptly

As real estate professionals, we are faced daily with these challenges. One element of being a professional is getting the situation handled right away. Too often we use the ostrich technique of problem solving—sticking your head in the sand and hoping the problem will go away. The best technique for resolving a problem is to face it head-on as soon as possible so you can either hold the transaction together or release the seller and buyer to go in another direction. The longer the problem is left in limbo, the greater the agony when you finally release the deal.

Operate with Full Disclosure

Be sure to steer clear of all the gray areas in a real estate transaction. When you are working with clients or prospects and what they are telling you doesn't pass the litmus test, either confront them or disengage from them. Many people will prey on a new agent because that agent lacks the experience to see the challenges with clarity. For example, a buyer may ask you not to disclose to the lender that there is a second mortgage by another party, either the seller or another person.

It's easy to sidestep the truth when you need the money. We as professionals have an obligation to our clients because of the size of the investment and the emotions involved in buying or selling a home. But through it all you must avoid gray areas and keep to the straight and narrow path. The truth is seldom a superhighway. It's a narrow path with narrow gates at both ends. Therefore, we must operate with full disclosure at all times.

HOW DO I GET MORE LISTINGS?

That question can be answered in a single word: prospect! If you are entering real estate sales, as most people do, without money to burn, start by prospecting. Learn the fundamentals of prospecting and generate business from the regular application of that discipline. Set up a specific time and place to prospect and then do it. In the end, we are paid for action and for what we do. Become a person of action.

Your journey to becoming a "top gun" agent is just beginning. There will be many turns in the road ahead. If you get up each morning with a strong conviction that you are going to improve your skills and abilities each day, you will. If you make the commitment right now that you will prospect each day no matter what, you will win.

Sow New Seeds Every Day

Success is built by the application of daily discipline. This law of success is illustrated by a biblical parable: A farmer went out to sow seed. Some of that seed fell on the path and was eaten by birds. Still other seed fell on rocky places; it sprang up, but without enough soil it soon withered. Other seed fell among the thorns and was eventually choked out. Some seed fell on good soil and it produced a crop thirty, sixty, or even one hundred times what was sown.

Success is built by the application of daily discipline.

The moral is: Keep sowing! Your job is to be like the farmer: Keep sowing new seeds every day. You will encounter all types of people when you sow—people on the path who aren't moving, people on rocky soil who are easily excited but won't take a deal to completion, and people who are thorny and negative all the time. The good part is you will find people who are fertile soil. These people will help build your real estate career. They will enable you to earn a high income and build the business we have described in this book. But remember that you must keep sowing.

Many agents expect every seed they sow to bring forth fruit. They get discouraged when each seed planted with a prospect doesn't germinate. Don't worry so much about getting each seed to germinate; instead, just keep planting. Never stop planting new seeds. The farmer will always receive a crop if he plants long enough and consistently. Flood or drought may wipe out this year's crop, but eventually the crop will come in thirty-, sixty-, or even a hundredfold.

So it will be with your real estate career. Resolve today to be great at sowing. Become a great prospector and your business and income will multiply. You have the gifts and ability to become great. The seeds of greatness have been sown inside of you by the Master Sower. You have begun the watering process with this book. You can become that "top gun" agent you desire to become.

God's gift to you is more talent and ability than you could possibly use in a lifetime. Your gift to God is to develop as much of that talent and ability as you can in this lifetime. —Steve Bow, quoted in *The Science of Getting Rich* by Wallace Wattles

APPENDIX I: State Realtor Associations

Alabama
www.alabamarealtors.com/
Alaska
www.realtorsofalaska.com/
Arizona
www.aaronline.com/
Arkansas
www.arkansasrealtors.com/
California
www.car.org/
Colorado
www.colorealtor.org/
Connecticut
www.ctrealtor.com/
Delaware
www.delawarerealtor.com/
District of Columbia
www.gwcar.org/
Florida
http://planetrealtor.com/default.asp

Georgia
www.garealtor.com/
Hawaii
www.hawaiirealtors.com/
Idaho
www.idahorealtors.com/
Illinois
www.illinoisrealtor.org/
Indiana
http://indianarealtors.com/
Iowa
http://ia.living.net/
Kansas
www.kansasrealtor.com/
Kentucky
www.kar.com/
Louisiana
www.larealtors.org/members/default.asp
Maine
www.mainerealtors.com/

Maryland
www.mdrealtor.org/
Massachusetts
http://ma.living.net/
Michigan
www.mirealtors.com/
Minnesota
http://mn.living.net/
Mississippi
http://ms.living.net/
Missouri
http://mo.living.net/
Montana
www.mtmar.com/public_html/index_html/
Nebraska
http://nebraskarealtors.com/
Nevada
www.nvrealtors.org/
New Hampshire
www.nhar.com/
New Jersey
www.njar.com/
New Mexico
http://nm.living.net/
New York
www.nysar.com/
North Carolina
www.ncrealtors.org/
North Dakota
http://nd.living.net/
Ohio
www.ohiorealtors.com/

Oklahoma
www.oklahomaassociationofrealtors.com/
Oregon
http://or.realtorplace.com/
Pennsylvania
www.parealtor.org/
Rhode Island
www.riliving.com/
South Carolina
http://screaltors.com/
South Dakota
www.sdrealtor.org/
Tennessee
www.tarnet.com/
Texas
www.tar.org/
Utah
www.utahrealtors.com/
Vermont
www.vtrealtor.com/
Virginia
www.varealtor.com/index.asp
Washington
www.warealtor.com/
West Virginia
www.wvrealtors.com/
Wisconsin
www.wra.org/
Wyoming
http://wy.living.net/

APPENDIX II: ADDITIONAL READING

Clason, George. *The Richest Man in Babylon.* New American Library.
Clason describes in parable form the steps to achieve wealth in life.
Hill, Napoleon. *Think and Grow Rich.* Fawcett Books.
This is the original self-help book for successful professionals. As a young man, Napoleon Hill was commissioned by Andrew Carnegie to write the secret to success. Carnegie introduced Hill to all the movers and shakers of his era, like John D. Rockefeller, Henry Ford, and Thomas Edison. He distilled their secrets into this book.
Hopkins, Tom. *How to Master the Art of Listing and Selling Real Estate.* Prentice Hall.
This is a timeless classic on how to be successful in the real estate business. A must-read for any agent.
Rohn, Jim. *Seven Strategies for Wealth and Happiness.* Prima Publishing.
Jim shares how to achieve everything you want in life and how to craft the grand life you desire. Jim is America's foremost business philosopher.
Tracy, Brian. *Advanced Selling Strategies.* Fireside.
Brian shares the steps to being a master salesperson. You will learn the techniques to more effectively prospect, present, and close.
Tuccillo, John. *The Eight New Rules of Real Estate.* Real Estate Education Company.
This is a recent look at the changing face of real estate in the new millennium.

Zeller, Dirk. *The Champion Real Estate Agent.* McGraw-Hill.

———. *The Champion Real Estate Team.* McGraw-Hill.

———. *Success as a Real Estate Agent for Dummies.* Wiley.

———. *Successful Time Management for Dummies.* Wiley.

———. *Telephone Sales for Dummies.* Wiley.

Audio CDs

Nightingale, Earl. *Lead the Field.* Nightingale-Conant Corporation.

———. *The Strangest Secret.* Nightingale-Conant Corporation.

Rohn, Jim. *The Art of Exceptional Living.* Simon & Schuster.

Tracy, Brian. *The Psychology of Achievement.* Simon & Schuster.

———. *The Psychology of Selling.* Simon & Schuster.

Zeller, Dirk. *The Champion's Guide to Tough Market Dominance.* Real Estate Champions.

———. *Convert and Commit the Buyer . . . Every Time.* Real Estate Champions.

———. *Creating Market Dominance.* Real Estate Champions.

———. *The Five Steps to Having Your Best Year Ever.* Real Estate Champions.

———. *Foreclosure Mastery.* Real Estate Champions.

———. *How to Become a Champion Objection Handler.* Real Estate Champions.

———. *How to Create and Deliver a Dynamic Listing Presentation.* Real Estate Champions.

———. *How to Protect Your Commission.* Real Estate Champions.

———. *Instant Listings from Expireds.* Real Estate Champions.

———. *Lead Mastery.* Real Estate Champions.

———. *Mastering Powerful Scripts and Dialogues in a Changing Marketplace.* Real Estate Champions.

———. *Objection Handling.* Real Estate Champions.

———. *REALTOR's Ultimate Business Planning Kit.* Real Estate Champions.

———. *REALTOR's Ultimate Car Companion.* Real Estate Champions.

———. *Survivor Sales Skills.* Real Estate Champions.

———. *The Top Secret Tough Times Survival Bootcamp.* Real Estate Champions.

———. *The Champion Agent's Ultimate Buyer Presentation Manual.* Real Estate Champions.

Zeller, Dirk, and Gualtieri, John. *The Champion Agent's Ultimate Listing Presentation Manual.* Real Estate Champions.

Ziglar, Zig. *Goals.* Simon & Schuster.

Audio Books

Zeller, Dirk. *The Champion Real Estate Agent.* Real Estate Champions.

Ziglar, Zig. *See You at the Top.* Pelican Publishing.

Zig teaches us to climb the mountain of success one step at a time. Zig is recognized as one of the greatest sales trainers and motivators in the world.

Relevant Magazines

Broker Agent

Broker Insider

Real Estate Champions Coaches Corner E-Zine

Real Estate Professional, The

Realtor Today

Selling Power

Web Sites

International Real Estate Digest: www.ired.com

National Association of Realtors: http://nar.realtor.com/

Real Estate Champions: www.realestatechampions.com

Realty Times: www.realtytimes.com

GLOSSARY

Abstract of title A complete summary of the public records of a piece of property that relates to the title. An attorney or title company reviews this and determines the defects in the title before the property transfer.

Agreement of sales A contract in which a seller agrees to sell and a buyer agrees to buy under specific terms and conditions. These terms and conditions are clearly spelled out in writing. Also known as purchase agreement, sales agreement, contract of purchase, or earnest money agreement.

Appraisal An estimate of value of real property on a given date. A mortgage company usually requires one before a loan is granted.

Closing costs The expense in addition to the sale price that buyers and sellers incur to complete the transfer of ownership from the seller to the buyer.

> **Buyer's Expenses**
> Recording fee for deed and mortgage
> Escrow fees
> Attorney fees
> Mortgage fees
> Points
> Document prep fee
> Origination fees

Appraisal
Home inspection
Title insurance

Seller's Expenses
Abstract of title
Real estate commission
Escrow fees
Attorney fees
Recording of the deed
Release of deed of trust

Closing day The day when transfer of title is concluded. The buyer and seller sign the final papers and recording of the deed takes place at the county. All final documents are signed—that is, the deed of trust.

Cloud on the title An encumbrance that negatively affects the marketability of the title. This cloud needs to be removed before transfer can take place.

Commission What is paid to the real estate broker by the seller for the completion of the sale between the buyer and the seller.

Cooperative broker A real estate broker who brings an offer or a sales agreement to the listing broker on behalf of a buyer.

Deed The legal instrument used to transfer ownership of a property from the current owner to the buyer. There are two parties in a deed: grantor and grantee.

Deed of trust A security instrument used in many areas by a mortgage company to secure its position on real property. This deed of trust allows the trustee to sell the property at a public sale if there is a default by the purchasers.

Default Failure by the purchaser to make mortgage payments as agreed to based on the terms agreed upon.

Down payment The amount of money to be paid by the purchaser at the time of closing that goes toward the purchase price of real property. This down payment, plus closing costs, plus mortgage are the costs needed to close a transaction.

Earnest money The deposit money given to the seller by the buyer upon initial offer of the agreement of sale. If all parties agree to the agreement of sale, the earnest money becomes part of the down payment.

Encumbrance A legal interest in real property that affects clear title and can diminish the value of the property. Encumbrances can be easement rights, mortgages, liens, unpaid taxes, zoning ordinances, conditions, covenants, and restrictions of a subdivision.

Equity The encumbrance value of a property owner's real property. Usually computed by subtracting the mortgage balance and encumbrances and fees for selling from the property's fair market value.

Escrow An independent third party that holds the funds and prepares the documents in a real estate transaction. This party cannot act without written instructions from both parties (the buyer and seller).

Expireds Properties that have been listed by a real estate broker and remain unsold. The exclusive right-to-sell listing contract between the broker and seller has reached its term and is no longer in force.

Foreclosure The enforcement of payment of the secured debt by a deed of trust or mortgage holder. Often enforced by selling mortgaged property at a sheriff's sale.

FSBOs (For Sale By Owners) People who are trying to sell their home on their own without the aid of a real estate broker.

General warranty deed or statutory warranty deed Conveys all interests of the grantor of title of property to the grantee. It also warrants the property is clear of all encumbrances except what goes with the property, for example, zoning ordinances, and CC & Rs (conditions, covenants and restrictions). This also allows the grantee to hold the grantor liable if encumbrances appear later.

Grantee The buyer on the deed.

Grantor The seller on the deed.

Hazard insurance Property insurance against fire required by most mortgage companies before closing.

Lien A claim on a property by another who is owed money. This is a security instrument. A lien could include unpaid property taxes, judgments, homeowners' dues, or construction or contractor bills that are unpaid.

Marketable title A title to the property that is free and clear of all liens and encumbrances that don't go with the property permanently. It allows the seller to sell and the buyer to buy.

Mortgage A lien against real property given by the buyer to the lender. The mortgage is security against the money borrowed by the buyer.

Mortgage commitment A document from a lending institution that guarantees that it will provide a certain amount of funds for the buyer to use to purchase real property.

Mortgagor The lender in a mortgage agreement.

Mortgagee The borrower in a mortgage agreement.

Points Often called discount points. A point is paid to lower interest rates. It is prepaid interest in advance at the time of closing. A single point is 1 percent of the amount of the mortgage loan.

Quitclaim deed A deed that transfers the interest one has in a piece of real property. There is no warranty element of a quitclaim deed. The buyer assumes all the risk by accepting a quitclaim deed.

Real estate agency The state's governing body that controls and regulates the activities of real estate brokers and agents, and, in many states, title and escrow companies as well.

Real estate agent Helps people buy and sell homes, office buildings, industrial property, and corporation farmland and handles property management and land development. Licensing is required and can vary across the nation, but all states require prospective salespeople to pass a written exam.

Real estate broker With more experience and upon passing an additional exam, the next step beyond being a real estate agent. Brokers can own their own businesses and employ other real estate agents.

Survey A map or plan of the dimensions of the land based on its relationship to the surrounding parcels, created by a licensed surveyor. Can often be required by a lender to assure them of the value of property and that buildings are sited on the right parcel.

Title Ownership interest one has in real property; may also refer to the document by which ownership interest is established.

Title insurance Protects the buyer and lender against a loss against their interest if later legal defects or clouds are found on the title.

Title search A check of the title records by either an attorney or a title company at the courthouse. This ensures that no unforeseen encumbrances or liens appear later that would adversely affect the value of the property.

INDEX

ABOUT THE AUTHOR

DIRK ZELLER started his real estate career in 1989. Working for a major national real estate company, he quickly distanced himself from the crowd by becoming a top-ten producer in units sold and commission earned in a four-state, 1,400-agent region. Dirk has been described by industry experts as "the Realtor who created the ideal real estate business" because of his ability to sell 150 homes annually while working a Monday through Thursday workweek and taking Friday, Saturday, and Sunday off to be with his family.

Dirk is a highly accomplished author with over 500 different articles published on real estate sales and life success. His articles have appeared in such national publications as *The Real Estate Professional, Broker Agent Magazine, Broker Insider, Realty Times,* and *International Real Estate Digest,* as well as countless regional, state, and local publications. He is a regular columnist for the National Association of Realtors.

He is also one of the most sought after professional speakers in the real estate industry, addressing such topics as sales strategies, time management, motivation, and life balance. Dirk has been a keynote speaker at large sales conferences on five continents. His training materials are used in more than ninety-seven different countries.

Dirk is the founder and CEO of Real Estate Champions, which provides business consulting, coaching, and development training for real estate companies, managers, and agents worldwide. He and his wife, Joan, and their two children live in Bend, Oregon.